Iowa and the Midwest Experience

SERIES EDITOR
William B. Friedricks,
Iowa History Center
at Simpson College

Main Street Public Library

COMMUNITY PLACES AND READING SPACES
IN THE RURAL HEARTLAND, 1876–1956

Wayne A. Wiegand

UNIVERSITY OF IOWA PRESS | IOWA CITY

University of Iowa Press, Iowa City 52242
Copyright © 2011 by the University of Iowa Press
www.uiowapress.org
Printed in the United States of America
Design by April Leidig-Higgins

The University of Iowa Press is a member of Green Press
Initiative and is committed to preserving natural resources.

Printed on acid-free paper

Library of Congress Cataloging-in-Publication Data
Wiegand, Wayne A., 1946 –
Main Street public library: community places and
reading spaces in the rural heartland, 1876–1956 /
by Wayne A. Wiegand.
p.   cm.—(Iowa and the Midwest experience)
Includes bibliographical references and index.
ISBN-13: 978-1-60938-067-0 (pbk.)
ISBN-10: 1-60938-067-3 (pbk.)
ISBN-13: 978-1-60938-068-7 (e-book)
ISBN-10: 1-60938-068-1 (e-book)
    1. Public libraries—Middle West—History.   2. Rural
libraries—Middle West—History.   3. Libraries and
community—Middle West—History.   I. Title.
Z732.M69W54   2011
027.4'77—dc22   2011013862

To Alysha
Patrick and Ryan
Teague and Reese

(It's fun being "Grandpa Wayne")

Contents

Acknowledgments and Permissions

This project has been a long time coming, and I owe great debts of gratitude to scores of people and libraries over the years. My thanks to Jane Robbins, Louise Robbins, and Doug Zweizig (the first two are former directors of the University of Wisconsin–Madison School of Library and Information Studies), who supported me in numerous ways while I taught there, and Jane Robbins (again) and Larry Dennis, deans of the School of Information Studies and now the College of Communications and Information Studies at Florida State University, who did the same after I moved to Tallahassee in 2003. That I list Jane twice should give readers some idea of how I came to the South. I especially want to thank librarians at the University of Wisconsin–Madison (where Michelle Besant of the School of Library and Information Studies Library helped me find essential details to this story in the collections she manages), and archivists at the Wisconsin Historical Society and the University of Wisconsin–Madison Archives. At Florida State University I owe thanks to librarians at Strozier Library and at the School of Library and Information Studies Goldstein Library, to Director Pamala Doffek and her staff, many of whom in the three years before completing this study chased down that "last" elusive footnote. I also want to thank librarians and archivists at the Library of Congress and Yale University's Beinecke Library.

A fellowship at the Institute for Research in the Humanities (IRH) at the University of Wisconsin–Madison in the spring semester of 1998 allowed me to complete conventional historical research on *Main Street Public Library*. My thanks to other fellows at the IRH during that delightful semester for their commentary on my research, and especially to its then director, Paul S. Boyer, who suggested I apply for the fellowship.

Visits to each of the four libraries described in this book brought me into contact with people who care much about what their public libraries can do for their communities. Each helped me find my way around, each made special efforts to make sure I was comfortable and my needs addressed. Often that involved giving me a door key so I could use collections and archives during times a library was not open. For helping me at the Bryant Library I owe thanks to Phyllis Lahti, Nancy Kazlauckas, and Dawn Shay, and especially to John Christenson, who in the early 1990s suggested the Bryant Library as a suitable site as I was contemplating this study. Thanks also to Richard Hedin, who spent an hour with me in a telephone conversation in 2008, telling me about his Bryant Library experiences as an adolescent in the 1930s. For helping me at the Sage Library, many thanks to Cindi Youngblut, recently retired, who was director during the entire time of this study. At Rhinelander, I owe thanks to Lisa Cochenet, Robert Toth, Ed Hughes, and Kris Wendt. Finally, at the Moore Public Library, I want to thank Beth Schumacher, and especially I want to remember the late Philomena M. Falls, president of the board of trustees of the Moore Library, who worked very hard in the 1990s to make sure her library was among those in my study. I am glad she was so persistent, and I hope this study is a fitting memorial to her efforts.

For six years I employed scores of college work-study students, paying them with money from rent I charged residents of an apartment attached to my home. By 1998 these students had transferred all the information in the accessions books of the four libraries covered in this book into one database. The database also contains the records of a fifth library—the Morris Public Library of Morris, Illinois—not described in this book. Readers will find a discussion of the Morris Public Library (including a discussion of its collections) in the Winter, 2010, issue of the *Journal of Illinois History*. For help with this database I especially want to thank Bria Rewey, Toni Samek, and particularly Kendall Larson (who prepared a set of instructions so others could use the database and traveled with me to several conferences to demonstrate its potential to others). The entire database is now available at http://cms.bsu.edu/Academics/CentersandInstitutes/Middletown/Research/MiddletownRead/MainStreetPublicLibraryDatabase.aspx.

Because I am pairing this book with another project consisting of a series of essays by subject experts who analyze my database from perspectives I could not cover, I want to thank Rima Apple, Joanne Passett, Sarah Wadsworth, Kate McDowell, Charles Johanningsmeier, Melanie Kimball, Christine Jenkins, Emily Honey, Michael Chasar, Michael Hedstrom, and Sarah Wadsworth for comments on the manuscript they read as background information for their own essays. I especially want to thank Christine Pawley, who read the manuscript in its entirety, and the University of Iowa Press anonymous readers, who suggested major revisions that made this a much better book. Errors of fact, of course, are my responsibility alone.

Working with University of Iowa Press editors has been a delight. To Holly Carver (for whom this was the last book she approved before she retired), Jim McCoy, Charlotte Wright, and Karen Copp, many thanks for patience and diplomacy. Thanks to Chris Dodge for a marvelous job of copyediting and to Amanda Hopkins for preparing the index. Amanda did it gratis in large part because all royalties for this book go to an endowed fund at Florida State University, and as an alumna of FSU's School of Library and Information Studies, she chose to share in that gift.

Thanks also to David Rottinghaus, who so graciously granted permission to reproduce his painting for the cover.

Finally I want to thank members of my family. To my wife, Shirl, who has stood with me through many historical research projects for forty-five years, to our children and their partners (Cori and Jeff McDermott, Scott and Erin Wiegand, and Andy Wiegand and Jenelle Welling), all of whom tolerated me for my anecdotes about small-town America, and my grandchildren, Alysha Sheets, Patrick and Ryan Wiegand, and Teague and Reese Wiegand, none of whom were born at the time I started this study, but all of whom have greatly enriched my life ever since. It is to the latter—all current and future readers—that I dedicate this book.

Some of the material in this book has appeared in different form in the following publications: "Collecting Contested Titles: The Experience of Five Small Public Libraries in the Rural Midwest, 1893–1956," *Libraries & Culture* 40 (July 2005): 368–84; "Library as Place," *North Carolina Libraries* 63 (Fall/Winter, 2005): 76–81; "The American Public Library: Construction of a Community Reading Institution, 1876–1924," in *History of the Book in America, Vol. IV*, ed. Carl Kaestle and Janice Radway (Chapel Hill, NC: University of North Carolina Press, 2009), 431–51; "Tourist Attraction: The Moore Library of Lexington, Michigan, 1903–1953," *Library Quarterly* 81 (July 2011): 1–27. I thank the publishers for permission to incorporate this material into a larger historical narrative.

The University of Iowa Press gratefully acknowledges Humanities Iowa for their generous support of the Iowa and the Midwest Experience series.

Information, Reading, Place

As of this writing, the United States has more public libraries than McDonald's restaurants. In the first decade of the twenty-first century, two-thirds of Americans annually visited a public library at least once, and two of three were registered borrowers. These statistics state the obvious. The American public library is a heavily used and ubiquitous institution, and because 80 percent of public library systems serve towns with populations less than twenty-five thousand, this is especially true in small-town America. Rare is the small town without a public library, an institution that since the late nineteenth century has become the model other countries seek to emulate. In the twentieth century alone, thousands of small public libraries served as particular destinations, and have circulated billions of books to citizens young and old, rich and poor, male and female, black, red, white, yellow, and brown. With few exceptions,[1] however, we know little about the overall history of the small-town public library.

Main Street Public Library attempts to address this deficiency. Chronologically, the study covers from 1876, when the federal government published its first report on U.S. public libraries, to 1956, with the enactment of the Library Services Act, which for the first time provided federal funds for public library services through state library agencies. Geographically, it focuses on public libraries in four small Midwest communities: the Bryant Library in Sauk Centre, located in central Minnesota amid rolling prairies, diversified groves of hardwoods, and hundreds of lakes; the Sage Public Library in Osage, situated in northeast Iowa amid agriculturally productive and predominantly rural prairie land; the Charles H. Moore Library in Lexington, Michigan, nestled on the shores of Lake Huron seventy miles north of Detroit, where, like so many of the state's communities, its character was shaped by water; and the Rhinelander Public Library in Rhinelander, Wisconsin, located in Wisconsin's Northern Highland region where tourism and the wood product industry sustained the local economy—and where, unlike the other three, the community supported labor unions and fostered a strong distrust of state control. All four communities owe their origins to emigrant largely Republican Protestant Yankees who crafted commercial, social, educational, religious, and cultural institutions in the mid-nineteenth century. During the eighty years covered in this book, none of the four communities possessed great wealth or great poverty; instead they were home to tidy, stable, and largely homogeneous populations that shared cultural values and an ethic of hard work. Their public libraries reflected these values.[2]

Readers may recognize the name Sauk Centre; Sinclair Lewis was born and raised there, and many have argued that it is the model for Gopher Prairie, whose small-town values he excoriated in *Main Street* (1920). Lewis's novel follows the experiences of Carol Kennikott, a college-educated librarian from St. Paul who had recently moved to Gopher Prairie after marrying the town doctor. Because of *his* position, she joined the town's leading families. But her attempts to bring big-city ideas to small-town people always ended in disaster. Lewis does give Gopher Prairie a public library, "housed in an old dwelling, sufficient but unattractive." When she visited the library "Carol caught herself picturing pleasanter reading-rooms, chairs for children, an art collection, a librarian young enough to experiment." Lewis makes his *Main Street* librarian an unhappy female disgruntled at not being accepted by the leading women's club (to which Carol, of course, belonged): "If they prefer to have papers on literature by other ladies who have no literary training—after all, why should I complain," the librarian tells Carol. As the librarian talks, Carol notices that she has "emphatically stamped a date in the front of 'Frank on the Lower Mississippi' for a small flaxen boy" and "glowered at him as though she were stamping a warning on his brain."[3]

To what extent did the Main Street public library Lewis described accurately represent the people who supported and used this civic institution in the first half of the twentieth century? Published local histories of these four communities show that each was proud and very loyal to its public library, but none offer obviously unusual or colorful stories. All the libraries, in fact, seemed typical, two situated on Main Street, two just off Main

Street. Three of them were housed in early-twentieth-century buildings whose construction was funded by Andrew Carnegie.

To more accurately locate their roles in host communities and discern differences and commonalities among these "typical" libraries, this book approaches its subject from a different perspective than conventional histories of American public libraries. Most of the latter assume not only that the public library has played an essentially positive role in the community, but also that it has functioned in similar ways for most of its users. In the professional rhetoric, the public library is seen as a neutral agency whose primary responsibility is to make accessible the kinds of information thought essential to democracy—itself a legacy of the Enlightenment's faith in the power of knowledge. Literature on the history of public libraries in the United States builds on these assumptions and largely chronicles their evolution with a top-down focus that concentrates on biographies of library organizers, managers, and trustees, the growth and development of collections over time, shifting circulation rates, numbers of visitors, and professionalized activities like reference, cataloging and classification, and service to children. *Main Street Public Library* will address these issues, but it will also question the conventional rhetoric and the "library faith" that assumes that without an informed and educated citizenry democracy cannot exist, and then extends this Jeffersonian principle by arguing that without libraries available to all citizens Americans cannot be fully educated or informed.[4]

At a particular moment in the late nineteenth century the library profession defined a jurisdiction creating a set of professional boundaries that have governed its options ever since. When in 1879 the American Library Association (ALA) adopted its motto, "The best reading for the greatest number at the least cost," it identified a set of goals that library leaders used to distinguish librarianship from other emerging professions. On the one hand, it was built on an ideology of reading shared with fellow middle-class professionals who believed that good reading led to good social behavior, bad reading to bad social behavior. On the other hand, it relinquished to other professionals—especially those in the academic and literary establishments—the authority to identify "good reading." The only exception was the authority to evaluate children's literature, which children's librarians seized as their arena of professional responsibility at the beginning of the twentieth century.[5]

Librarians chose not to compete for this authority, partly to streamline efficiency among professional responsibilities and partly to avoid confrontation. Librarians' connections to other professionals made it easier to abdicate responsibility for defining canonical literature. Like most university professors and members of the nation's literary establishment, late-nineteenth-century library leaders tended to be middle-aged, white, Protestant male alumni of northeastern colleges, born to families that had emigrated from northwestern Europe three or more generations earlier. By the turn of the twentieth century the library profession had settled into a familiar if sometimes uncomfortable niche in a growing fraternity of professions, a niche it has occupied ever since.[6]

As the literary establishment and academy identified the best books in the first half of the twentieth century, the library profession capitalized on their authority and legitimated their recommendations in a series of selection guides, including *Booklist* magazine, American Library Association catalogs, and H. W. Wilson Company publications like *Fiction Catalog* and *Standard Catalog for Public Libraries*.[7] Librarians were pressed to follow these recommendations, which by mid-century had evolved into a professional practice that not only seemed "neutral" and "objective," but found expression in the phrase "not censorship, but selection" made famous by Lester Asheim in 1953.[8] *Main Street Public Library* challenges the validity of that phrase.

Finally, this book argues that public libraries have been shaped both by the people who have run them (trustees and managers) and by the people who have used them. Unlike most other civic institutions (courts and schools, for example), the American public library is not compulsory—people use libraries because they want to, not because they have to. Because of this fundamental difference, users have influenced the library institution in multiple ways over the generations. But how have they done so?

Searching for ways to answer that question led me to two new areas of scholarship with theoretical principles that offer alternate ways of thinking about the "library in the life of the user" (which gives the latter agency and power) rather than the "user in the life of the library" (which encourages top-down thinking, and mimes the current management-oriented discourse in professional librarianship).[9] The first area is the history of reading. Part of that literature follows the influential "communications circuit" theory of Robert Darnton, who envisioned a relatively passive

group of readers as the final link in a chain of production that began with the producers of print (writers and publishers). Other histories of reading follow scholars like Michel de Certeau, who focus on the "resistance" that readers evidence when they "poach" texts for purposes unique to their reading experiences. For this study, however, Darnton's theory gives too much authority to structure, while de Certeau's is too focused on opposition that individual readers build into their reading practices. Instead, *Main Street Public Library* requires an intellectually comfortable middle ground—one in which theoretical principles will illuminate the complexities of how spatially bound, gender-, race-, class-, and creed-based information cultures interacted with the services and traditions of the local cultural institutions they created to connect readers—specifically readers in local public libraries.[10] Several texts were particularly helpful.

Janice Radway's *Reading the Romance: Women, Patriarchy, and Popular Literature* is an ethnographic case study describing how romance novels have functioned as agents in the everyday lives of suburban women. Radway demonstrates the multiple ways women used their reading to claim mental space and to escape—if only temporarily—the practical demands of being wives and mothers.[11] Benedict Anderson's *Imagined Communities: Reflections on the Origin and Spread of Nationalism* has been equally influential. People organize themselves into large and small "imagined communities," Anderson argues, to orient and affiliate with each other. Cultural texts of all kinds function as agents to help construct these imagined communities by providing common sets of experiences, including the reading of shared printed texts. Anderson adds another dimension to the social nature of reading—sometimes this reading takes place in groups, on public property, and in cultural spaces.[12]

In *Book Clubs: Women and the Uses of Reading in Everyday Life*, Elizabeth Long analyzes the capacity of reading to stimulate imagination and construct community through shared meaning. "Familial reading," she notes, "is both a form of cultural capital and one of the most important determinants of adherence to reading in later life." Reading also functions as proof of moral achievement. As a cultural practice, reading is socially framed. Groups of authorities (like literary critics and teachers) and cultural institutions (like schools and universities) "shape reading practices by authoritatively defining what is worth reading and how to read it."[13]

Laced throughout the act of reading are issues of power, privilege, exclusion, and social distinctions, all combining in multiple ways so that reading is never "disembodied," never "unsituated." In the free act of social reading, Long argues, readers "move into and out of the text," and thus "appropriate" meaning relevant to their own lives. Because readers can control it, the act of reading becomes dependably pleasurable, empowering, intellectually stimulating, and socially bonding. And it is in the act of reading that social and cultural acts of defiance—whether overt, covert, conscious, or subconscious—take place. If authorities at whatever level lack the power to check voluntary reading for an interpretation made legitimate by dominant cultures, ordinary readers can and do construct their own meanings, sometimes as groups, sometimes as individuals. Elsewhere Stephen Greenblatt calls this process "self-fashioning"; Barbara Sicherman calls it "self-authorization"; Gordon Hutner notes "how the talk about books becomes the sound of culture conversing with itself."[14]

"Imagined communities," "civic texts," "appropriate," "self-fashion," "self-authorize," "the sound of culture conversing with itself." These words and phrases now function as part of a new vocabulary to explain how reading constructs community, even if the act of reading is done in solitude. Where some see reading primarily as a solitary behavior, a growing number of scholars examining the act of reading see it primarily as an associational behavior.

The second body of scholarship that helps illuminate "the library in the life of the user" focuses on place, and specifically on the use people make of public spaces. In *The Structural Transformation of the Public Sphere: An Inquiry into a Category of Bourgeois Society,* Jurgen Habermas argues that during the eighteenth century the growing middle classes sought to influence government actions by assuming control of an emerging "public sphere" of deliberation that eventually found an influential niche between forces exercised by governments and marketplaces. Within this public sphere members of the middle classes developed their own brands of reason, and over time created their own network of institutions and sites (for example, newspapers and periodicals, political parties, and academic societies). In and through these institutions and sites they refined a middle-class-based rationalized discourse into an expression of the "public interest" that governments and markets dared not ignore.[15]

Once Habermas's theory established an understanding of how social and cultural preconditions shaped the public sphere, other scholars began to analyze the institutions and sites where this rationalized discourse was practiced by communities and groups not primarily concerned with political ideologies or marketplace activities. Out of these analyses a refined concept of the role of "place" as cultural space has emerged. Over the generations, millions of patrons have demonstrated their support of the public library as a place by visiting it again and again, in part to "exchange social capital"—a phrase integral to "public sphere" thinking and yet another dimension to the social nature of reading. Only recently have library researchers begun to explore the role libraries play as "place" in their communities.[16] Although *Main Street Public Library* will address "library as place" in ways that library historians have overlooked, this focus will not occupy as much attention as the social nature of reading that the public library facilitates, which nonetheless requires library space in order to function.

Jeffrey Alexander provides a useful bridge between the theory of place and the social nature of reading. In *The Civil Sphere*, he argues that a set of "communicative institutions" in civil society functions to "regulate" public discourse. Communicative institutions can exert influence on political questions by what information they make available. They can also function as sites where political and social dissent are organized and articulated, or where dominant cultures reinforce themselves. These communicative institutions function through a variety of agencies, including "factual media" and "fictional media." The latter "weave the binary codes of civil society into broad narratives and popular genres," Alexander argues, and create "long-lasting frames for democratizing and anticivil processes alike. They constrain action by constituting a teleology for future events, even as they seem merely to be telling stories about people and life in an ahistorical and fictional way." The folklore and folk dramas contained in popular fiction "have always performed similar kinds of sentimental education," he says, and provided representations that allow Americans "to express their civil judgments in figurative rather than intellectual language, which made it easier, in turn, to identify with one or another solidary group."[17] For an analysis of the public library, Alexander's conclusions create a platform from which one can observe a marriage of place and reading—and especially the reading of popular fiction—that still allows both a multiplicity of roles, all the while retaining agency for library users.

Armed with these perspectives on the social nature of reading and on the role public spaces play in the construction of community, this book attempts to look at the local public library in the life of the local public library user, and particularly public library users in midwestern small towns—often symbolically referred to even today as Main Street.[18] By focusing on Main Street, which has been heavily invested with civic meaning and perceived as a reflection of the democratic ideal and as a community melting pot, this book deliberately avoids using a national story of library development as a point of departure, and instead allows local libraries, their managers, and as much as possible their users to identify their particularities and speak memory to history. I hope that this approach will create greater understanding of the multiple roles public libraries have played in their communities over the generations.

Now a word of warning. Readers should perhaps read no further if they cannot accept that fictional media—stories packaged in cultural forms like novels, songs, films, and plays that even today account for most use of American public libraries—can inform, inspire, bond, entertain, socialize, authorize, validate, empower, and educate.[19] Conclusions reached at the end of this book will not be convincing unless one is prepared to accept that people use the fictional media their public libraries make available to them to deepen their understanding of the world around them, minimize confusion in their everyday lives, and reinforce existing value systems.

All four public libraries covered in this book were part of the public library movement that took place in the last half of the nineteenth century. The movement emerged from a mixture of social concerns, most occasioned to some degree by the nation's rapid industrialization, urbanization, and immigration. The latter, immigration, was especially bothersome to community founders, for without an educated and enlightened citizenry, they reasoned, the republic could not survive. One answer to this problem was compulsory education, which maximized chances that forthcoming generations of citizens would at least be literate. By that time, antebellum community leaders—especially in New England and the mid-Atlantic states—had for generations already experienced social libraries, generally joint-stock companies in which locals pooled resources to purchase book collections accessible to all stock owners. It was a short leap for many to become advocates for public libraries supported by tax dollars, and by mid-century many state legislators who agreed proposed enabling legislation to facilitate this.

In justifying legislation to support Massachusetts public libraries in 1851, state legislator Rev. John Burt Wight outlined four advantages the libraries would bring. First, they would become "needful and valuable" extensions to public schools. Second, they would "supply the whole people with ample sources of important practical information." Third, they would serve as depositories for federal, state, and local government documents. Finally, because they would "contain many instructive and excellent books" that would "be greatly increased . . . by continual additions in subsequent years," they would help effect their community's intellectual and moral advancement. Wight was especially excited about the last. Public libraries, he confidently predicted, "will be favorable to all the moral reforms of the day, by leading to more domestic habits of life, by diminishing the circulation of low and immoral publications, and by producing higher and more worthy views of the capabilities of human nature."[20]

These convictions were shared. "Reading ought to be furnished to all, as a matter of public policy and duty, on the same principle that we furnish free education," Edward Everett and George Ticknor wrote a year later in their now famous *City Document No. 37—Report of the Trustees of the Public Library of the City of Boston, July, 1852.* "Under political, social and religious institutions like ours it is of paramount importance that the means of general information should be so diffused that the largest possible number of persons should be induced to read and understand questions going down to the very foundations of social order." With these convictions fixed in print, the Boston Public Library (BPL) opened on March 20, 1854. By mid-October the 6,590 people who had registered for borrowing privileges had withdrawn 35,389 books.

By most accounts the BPL was a civic success, and for the remainder of the nineteenth century it and the legislation Massachusetts passed to enable support for that library became blueprints for establishing hundreds of other public libraries across the nation. Initially their numbers grew rapidly in New England and the mid-Atlantic states as numerous social libraries converted to public libraries. Then, when many from these states emigrated to the Midwest, they sought to replicate the familiar civic and cultural institutions they had known back home. As the following history of four small midwestern public libraries demonstrates, however, the civic institutions they created did not evolve quite as Wight, Everett, and Ticknor desired or predicted.[21]

The first four chapters of this book cover the histories of these Main Street public libraries, and demonstrate the commonalities and differences that evolved as they responded to pressures exercised by forces inside and outside their communities. A subsequent chapter analyzes in greater detail the contents of their collections for the presence (and absence) of books on controversial subjects. An epilogue summarizes research findings and brings the reader up to date on services these libraries have provided in the first decade of the twenty-first century.

CHAPTER ONE

Pride of a Century

The Bryant Library of Sauk Centre, Minnesota

In 1856—two years before Minnesota became a state—New England settlers founded a town ninety miles west of Minneapolis. They named it Sauk Centre after the nearby Sauk River and Sauk Lake. As in hundreds of other mid-nineteenth-century Midwest towns, settlers quickly set up businesses and attempted to replicate social institutions they had left behind. Ten years later the staunchly Republican weekly *Sauk Centre Herald* began informing the good citizens of Sauk Centre about what was happening in their community.[1]

The village of Sauk Centre incorporated on March 28, 1876. After the Great Northern Railway reached it in 1878, the local economy evolved into a farmers' trading center. Founders from the northeastern states made it a Republican bastion, but the German and Scandinavian immigrants who farmed the fertile prairies in surrounding Stearns County consistently voted Democratic. They brought their grain to Sauk Centre for milling, and while there patronized general stores for essential goods, local professionals for essential financial, legal, and medical services, and local saloons for entertainment. The tensions between farmers and townies that characterized most of late-nineteenth-century Minnesota were obvious in Sauk Centre. Swedish immigrant Henrik Jönson remembers being called "Norske" by town toughs, and told by his teachers to spell his name "Henry Johnson" because he was now "in America."[2]

BEGINNINGS OF A LIBRARY

On November 19, 1868, the *Herald* reported that a women's reading club had established a library association "to raise funds for the purpose of purchasing books for a library." Officers included President Solomon Pendergast, who had arrived in Sauk Centre from New Hampshire in 1861

to open a hardware store. He was a Republican and a Congregationalist. Treasurer was Pendergast's business partner, Edward Oakford, who
had been a Union Army captain. Vice president was Mrs. Philoman Lamb,
born in Vermont, a Congregationalist, and a charter member of both the
local chapter of the Order of the Eastern Star and the local Ladies Musical
Club. Other officers had similar biographies. "Meetings are conducted on
the sociable plan," the *Herald* noted of the Library Association. Admission
was one dollar for "gentlemen," fifty cents for "a lady." "Norskes" were not
invited to become members.[3] In its first decade the Library Association
survived poorly, supported indifferently by irregularly scheduled benefits
like lectures, musical events, and buffets.

In hopes of reinvigorating their enterprise, Library Association members hosted a public meeting on December 13, 1878, to transfer their four
hundred volumes to a new association and incorporate it under Minnesota laws. Prior to the meeting, members solicited New England poet William Cullen Bryant for a donation. While they may have hoped for something akin to the $12,500 Bryant had recently donated to Cummington,
Massachusetts, for a new public library there, Bryant instead sent Sauk
Centre an autographed book of poems. Likely disappointed, organizers
of the new endeavor still named their association after him.[4] As with the
original association, Bryant Library Association charter members and officers represented the town's leading families.

"The general purpose of this corporation is the establishment and
maintenance of a public library . . . and to provide public lectures, readings
and other similar means of literary entertainment, and mutual improvement for the use of its members," noted the first article of incorporation.
Funding came from membership fees and contributions, most of which
purchased books. That the new institution was a source of local pride was
immediately evident. "A public library furnishes first class literature to
all who will avail themselves of its privileges," noted a real estate agent's
advertising pamphlet.[5] On February 14, 1879, the association adopted a
set of bylaws that recompensed the librarian fifty cents weekly to open
the library on Saturday afternoons, keep a catalog of books, and register
borrowers. Although only members had borrowing privileges, "the librarian may loan books," it was said, "to any person at a rental of 10 cents
per week payable in advance." Before convening, the association board
approved a schedule of lectures and entertainments to raise funds. In its

1. Bryant Public Library, Sauk Centre, Minnesota, ca. 1935.

first year, dues accounted for 40 percent of revenue; book rentals and fines accounted for 30 percent; and the "Ladies Leap Year Benefit"—an obvious manifestation of community support—took in the remaining 30 percent.[6]

Although the Bryant Library Association was successful, some board members wanted to take advantage of a recently passed state law permitting Minnesota communities "to authorize the establishment of Village Libraries, and provide for their maintenance." In April 1879, the village council voted to organize a tax-supported "public library." When the newly appointed directors of this public library met on April 26, they appointed a committee to solicit the Bryant Library Association for its books and property, and the school board to locate the library in the school building. On May 7, Bryant Library Association board members voted unanimously to cede their collection to the village library, provided that the village would assume its eight-dollar debt. Five days later (and two days after the school board joined the project), the Bryant Library Association turned over to the new library all its property, "consisting of a library cabinet and desk and library books . . . and catalogue of the books of said Association numbers from one to 390 inclusive." As a result, Sauk Centre became the third Minnesota town with a "public library," the second to organize one under a law permitting a combined public and school library.[7]

On May 25, public library trustees acknowledged William Cullen Bryant's role in the original association by naming their institution the Bryant Library of Sauk Centre. It is not known if they contacted Bryant seeking a gift or another autographed book. The original book from Bryant had already disappeared. Trustees then adopted a constitution and bylaws. The librarian was required to report to the board annually, including such information as "the number of books loaned out and the general character and kind of such books." Located in the high school within the village's one school building, the library was open Saturdays, 2:00–6:00 P.M. "None but the inhabitants of the village of Sauk Centre shall be entitled" to borrow up to one book one week at a time, it was stated, although the librarian might "loan books to any person not a resident" for two cents per week advance payment. The high school principal was responsible for the library during school days, and any teacher could use books from the collection in classrooms. All, however, had to return borrowed books by Friday afternoon each week.[8]

In his first annual report, the Bryant board secretary noted that in the nine months since opening, 1,824 persons had come to the library, and that the library had circulated 477 books in its first three months, 618 in the second three, and 729 in the third. Only three books had gone missing, and each had been replaced by the person responsible. "The success of the library under the new arrangement has been beyond our expectation and fully vindicates your judgment and wisdom in establishing an apartment of such convenience and worth to the public," the secretary told his board, "and particularly the poorer classes by whom it is largely patronized." In April 1881, trustees appointed a committee to prepare "a list of books from which to make purchases." In February 1883, the librarian reported that titles by popular authors like Mary J. Holmes, Allen Pinkerton, Louisa May Alcott, James Fenimore Cooper, William Thackeray, and May Agnes Fleming were "in great demand." In May the board purchased Charles Dudley Warner's eight-volume *Library of the World's Best Literature*, and ordered the *American Cyclopaedia*. On May 20, the librarian reported that circulation had nearly doubled the previous year.[9]

While library trustees were grateful for space in the high school, they longed for separate quarters. In February the board bought an office building on Third Street. "The library is no longer dependent for a room, but is now settled in a neat commodious home of its own," wrote the secretary. "Our village library is a perfect success," the *Herald* reported. "Parties having a list of books they desire to have in the library will please leave the same with the librarian." More often than not, recommendations called for the genteel popular fiction people were reading elsewhere in the United States. The Bryant Library gladly supplied it.[10]

In 1885 Sauk Centre boasted a combined village and township population of 2,807. All were white. "A colored man passed through town on Friday," the *Herald* reported in 1886, "and was almost as much of a curiosity as a dime museum freak." It was an orderly town, with only a few drunks to disturb quiet evenings. Besides frequenting saloons, many residents obtained alcohol, via prescriptions, from J. B. Perkins's drugstore. "This store was the chosen guardian of secrets which suggested that life in Sauk Centre was not so pure as I had previously supposed it to be," Henry Johnson recalled. At that time Sauk Centre residents could still feed their hogs and milk their cows on Main Street, which had no streetlights and only a few blocks of wooden sidewalks. Ten organized church societies and seven churches addressed the spiritual needs of citizens, who were also served by lodge halls, two newspapers (the *Avalanche* was Sauk Centre's Democratic paper), an opera house, and a railroad station that connected people to the outside world. Citizens endured temperature extremes—from as cold as –40 Fahrenheit in the winter to 110 in the summer—but enjoyed Sauk Lake and its environs in all seasons. Occasions like the annual firemen's dance and an "Easter Monday Ball" dotted their social calendars; county fairs, circus visits, local athletic events, socials put on by the Ladies Reading Club, and public lectures supplemented. The Bryant Library–sponsored lyceum course was well attended, if not particularly profitable. Because the library trustees heavily represented leaders of local lodges, churches, and civic organizations, casual conversation around town about the library was easy and probably frequent.[11]

Sauk Centre's culture of print extended far beyond the Bryant Library collection. Churches supplied parishioners with devotional aids, Sunday school books, and denominational periodicals. Traveling salesmen canvassed the town regularly, selling books. In 1888 the *Herald* reported someone selling copies of Mary Livermore's *My Story of the War* (1888) that a Bryant trustee had publicly endorsed. Printed materials less highly regarded (and not in the public library) were also available. Barbershop patrons regularly read *Police Gazette*. At home, many families subscribed to *Youth's Companion*. "How we looked forward to the day of its appearance!," Henry Johnson recalled. "We also read with avidity . . . numerous dime novels." He clearly remembered reading *Peck's Bad Boy* in the parlor when his Methodist minister visited. "The nature of my offense was made so clear that I finished [reading the book] in the haymow. It was something of a comment on the literary standards of Sauk Centre that most of such reading was surreptitious." For the Bryant Library, however, genteel popular fiction was acceptable and desired. It was into this community and culture of print that Harry Sinclair Lewis was born on February 7, 1885.[12]

After the Bryant Library paid off its building debt in 1888, trustees hoped to annually add four hundred new books to its collection. About that time politicians representing Sauk Centre in Washington began sending free government publications.[13] The *Herald* rejoiced at the Bryant's 1889 annual report, which showed that the library was "growing much more rapidly in public favor than in extent." Every member of Henry Johnson's family visited the library once a week, and each brought home a book. "To the Bryant Library I owed many escapes from things that were sordid and disheartening and my gratitude can never cease," he later wrote. Johnson probably obtained direct access in 1891, when the library board allowed all Sauk Centre high school students to check out books provided they had "a voucher" from their principal. Thereafter, trustees increased juvenile collections.[14]

In September 1891, community leaders formed the Bryant Literary and Historical Association (BLHA) to discuss relevant matters of the day. Not coincidentally, many involved in the BLHA were also Bryant Library trustees. The BLHA met Monday evenings, and at the first meeting "the question under discussion was limited and restricted suffrage." That *Sauk Centre Herald* editor (and former Bryant Library trustee) Charles F. Hendryx was a founder guaranteed BLHA generous press coverage. Within a year, meetings averaged one hundred attendees. Helping the BLHA obtain information for its discussions was the Bryant Library, which in May 1892 began subscribing to *American Book Seller* and *Current Literature*. Henceforth all BLHA members would know what books literary authorities in the East were recommending. That summer the Bryant Library added five hundred volumes to bring its collection to twenty-two hundred but growth also brought problems. "The building is so crowded as to be thoroughly inconvenient both for the librarian and the public," the *Herald* noted. "Here is an opportunity for some wealthy, public spirited citizen to erect a lasting monument to his memory.... Don't speak all at once."[15]

On December 29, 1892, board members circulated a clipping about an American Library Association (ALA) "Model Catalog" to be published by the U.S. government. The catalog was a bibliography of a model library that the ALA had put together for an exhibit at the 1893 World's Columbian Exposition in Chicago, and carried the association's imprimatur—all titles cited were recommended for any public library. The ALA catalog soon became a collection guide for hundreds of small public libraries; many were then being established around the country, especially in the Midwest. In red ink, the Bryant Library board secretary noted in his book of minutes on April 12, 1894: "Wrote to Hon. R. Baldwin, Feb. 20/94 requesting him to kindly see that a copy of above catalogue was sent to our library as soon as issued.... Rec'd catalogue April 2nd."[16] One major reason the ALA put its catalog together was to discourage the reading of popular fiction; only 15 percent of titles it cited were fiction. Bryant Library trustees, on the other hand, continued to select the popular fiction titles their patrons expected, and these circulated heavily.[17]

The Bryant Library finally found relief from its space problems by trading places with the municipal court room in City Hall in June 1894. "Patrons cannot fail to be pleased," the *Herald* wrote. While users could not access the books directly—"the library is separated from the corridor by a light and neat screen"—they could see through the screen that aisles between stacks were large and well-lit. A "suitable number" of chairs were available for patrons waiting for their books, and a writing table was "provided for patrons where their cards may be inspected by them and corrected, if desired." The *Herald* also noted a new rule—patrons could now check a book out for two weeks rather than one. Among those visiting the Bryant Library in its new location was the family of Dr. E. J. Lewis, including nine-year-old Harry.[18]

Shortly thereafter the women of Sauk Centre's leading families organized the Gradatim Club. "This organization is for the study of literature, science, art and current topics," said its constitution. But the club, which also was a charter member of the Minnesota Federation of Women's Clubs, participated in civic matters in other ways. Its members lobbied for curfew and anti-spitting ordinances, and gave flower seeds to schoolchildren for planting in the community. Not surprisingly, many of the Gradatim's members were married to Bryant Library trustees. In subsequent years the Gradatim took an active interest in the Bryant, in part because the national General Federation of Women's Clubs had targeted the establishment of public libraries as a major initiative.[19]

In January 1897, the Gradatim passed a resolution approving endorsing a bill then pending in the Minnesota legislature to establish a state library commission and a system of traveling libraries. Two months later, the newly formed Gradatim Library Committee, chaired by Harry Lewis's stepmother, solicited the Bryant Library for help in "establishing and maintaining a Reading Room." After considerable discussion, the Bryant Library board agreed to allow the Gradatim use of the public library "for said reading room every night in the week excepting Thursday, Saturday, and Sunday."[20] The Sauk Centre Reading Room opened that December in the Bryant Library. For the reading room the Gradatim asked Sauk Centre citizens to donate their back issues of magazines; the club also subscribed to "all the leading magazines and a number of solid weeklies and several dailies." The word "solid" told *Herald* readers that they would not find copies of *Police Gazette* there. While Bryant Library books were accessible, none could be withdrawn unless visitors registered.

At the time, the Bryant contained 3,731 volumes, boasted an annual circulation of 10,700, and served 918 patrons. Twelve-year-old Harry Lewis accounted for many transactions. Although he had access to his father's limited library, Harry found the Bryant Library particularly attractive, and according to one of his biographers "through that collection he read his way voraciously." Lewis's brother recalled, "We used to feel sorry for Harry. He never hunted or fished. He'd go out and mow the lawn, cut a couple of strips and then read under a shade tree for half an hour."[21] The Gradatim's reading room experiment, monitored by his stepmother, proved a success. Two months after its opening, the *Herald* announced that it "has been fairly well attended nearly every evening—from a dozen to twenty-five young men availing themselves of its benefits habitually." Better than having them frequent saloons, the *Herald* surmised.

But success had a price. In August, Gradatim Club leaders told the library board that "the ladies do not feel equal to the burden of operating it another year." When the board responded that it had "all it felt able to do, with the very limited resources at its disposal," the city council agreed to give the Bryant Library an additional five dollars per week to keep the reading room open. Then, on November 2, 1899, the *Herald* reported that Duluth had just been promised $50,000 from Andrew Carnegie to erect a public library building "as soon as a suitable site is secured." To that note the *Herald* added: "A gentleman of this city offers a suitable site for a Sauk Centre library providing a Carnegie can be found to erect a building. Here is a chance for someone to erect a monument more lasting than brass."[22]

That year the newly formed Minnesota Public Library Commission (MPLC) created a system of traveling libraries for rural residents. Like commissions in other states, the MPLC selected twenty-five to fifty books, then sent them in boxes to sites across the state where rural citizens could check them out for several weeks. "Each box contains a large proportion of good fiction," the *Herald* reported. While the commission set up several sites in rural Stearns County, the Bryant Library took no responsibility for these collections and did not participate in their dissemination.[23] To its board members, the Bryant was a Sauk Centre institution supported by local taxes and run by community leaders seeking ways to identify and mediate the community's literary values.

As the Bryant Library collection grew, space continued to be a problem. In December 1900, the school board gave the Bryant $500 to make it "the auxiliary to the public school system," and matched the town's monthly $5.00 to keep the reading room open evenings for high school students. The city council also gave the fire department permission to meet at the library—the first time the Bryant Library's public space was used for a community nonlibrary purpose. Both agreements put more people and more books into the library, and exacerbated space problems.[24]

In 1901 the state legislature passed a law mandating that public library board members throughout Minnesota be elected by local citizens; they could no longer be appointed by mayors and city councils. The *Herald* bristled. Bryant trustees, said the *Herald*, "not only know books, but they know the public demands of the patrons of the library." Although the *Herald* worried about injecting politics into the Bryant's management, a July election returned to the board the same people previously appointed. They were less connected to the merchant class that had organized the library a generation earlier, but they included more professionals—most were lawyers, doctors, and store and bank managers. In his diaries, Harry

Lewis noted on January 24, 1900, that he had checked out two books; on the evening of March 30, 1901, he visited the library's reading room "to write."[25]

CARNEGIE BUILDING

On December 17, 1902, the day before the Bryant Library board voted to put Mrs. Hugh Fraser's controversial novel *A Little Grey Sheep* (1901) on library shelves, City Clerk J. F. Cooper wrote to James Bertram, Andrew Carnegie's personal secretary. "Our people are largely Americans of the intelligent and appreciative class and our town one of the best in the state. If we could get a donation of $15,000 our citizens would gladly donate a fine site and pay $1,500 per annum for the maintenance of a public library." Quarters for the current collection were too small, he noted, and the library was "too remotely situated for convenience. Sauk Centre is looking for a Christmas present—a new public library building, the gift of Andrew Carnegie, would just about fit the size of stocking she means to hang by her fireplace."[26]

Cooper's letter preceded a flurry of activity. On January 13, 1903, Mayor Michael Hogan told Minnesota Congressman Page Morris that he had written to Carnegie in early 1902 about a grant, but had been told that Carnegie "was not putting buildings in the small cities." Thereafter, however, Hogan had noticed that Carnegie had given grants to Valley City, North Dakota, Redfield, South Dakota, and St. Peter, Minnesota, all of which, he argued, "are not better towns than ours." He asked Morris to support Sauk Centre's bid, which Morris did days later. On February 12 Hogan received a letter promising $10,000 for a building if Sauk Centre agreed to provide a site and $1,000 annually for maintenance. The council accepted those conditions in secret session on February 18. On February 26 Hogan wrote that a site had been secured, and on March 5 Bertram told the mayor that payment had been authorized. Until Hogan received Carnegie's authorization, most of Sauk Centre knew nothing about this initiative.[27]

On February 19 both the *Herald* and *Avalanche* splashed the news across their front pages. "Let no mistake be made," the *Herald* announced, "the building will be a beautiful one—an ornament and a source of personal pride to every citizen. It is not for a day, a month or a year—but a century perhaps." (The *Herald*'s prediction proved true; as of this writing the building continues to serve Sauk Centre.) "A credit to the city for many years to come," the *Avalanche* chimed in.[28] Efforts to select a location moved rapidly. On February 22 the council offered $1,000 for a site; two days later the school board offered to match that sum "provided that all residents of the school district be given free use of the library, and also that all teachers in the public schools be given free use of the library at all times subject to the direction of the Superintendent." On February 25 trustees of the Congregational church (several were Bryant Library board members) agreed to sell a plot on Main Street for $2,500, but also subtracted $500 from that sum in exchange for other property the city already owned. Three days later Hogan informed Bertram, Carnegie's secretary, that a site had been secured and that the council had resolved to support the library at $1,000 per year. "It is central to the population, only one or two blocks from the center of the business part of the city," the *Herald* reported.[29]

In June the library board approved plans offered by a Minnesota architect and instructed its secretary to advertise for bids to complete construction by November 1903. At best, projections were optimistic. In August MPLC Director Clara F. Baldwin conferred with the board about reorganizing the collection according to Dewey Decimal Classification (DDC), recataloging it by ALA rules, and purchasing Library of Congress catalog cards for a new public card catalog to be ready when the new building opened. In September the foundation was laid, and in October the reclassification project (for which the MPLC hired a trained professional) was well underway.[30]

Construction did not go smoothly. In January Mayor Hogan asked Carnegie for an additional $2,000 "to complete the building as we would wish. The high price of labor and materials during the past building season are some of the factors that make it necessary for us to appeal to you again." In responding for Carnegie, Bertram was characteristically curt. "Sauk Centre is a very small place and Ten Thousand Dollars might well have been ample to erect a building with adequate library facilities. Should also like . . . an itemized list of how the ten thousand has been spent and how the other two thousand dollars is to be spent." Although Hogan provided the list, Carnegie refused Sauk Centre's request.[31]

The new building that opened to much fanfare on November 12, 1904, was a typical Carnegie edifice. Board member E. J. Lewis attended; so did his wife Grace. Their son Harry, frequent Bryant Library patron while in high school, was then in his freshman year at Yale. From Main Street patrons walked across a sidewalk splitting a well-manicured lawn, and as they approached the building they mounted ten steps to front double doors located between two heavy, classical Greek columns. Once inside they found themselves in front of the circulation desk "commanding a clear view of the whole floor." Behind the desk stood the stacks, which not only contained most of the books that the library owned, but also provided open access. For the first time in their lives, borrowers could experience the empowering sensation that browsing the collection brought. To the right was a reading room, complete with fireplace and "handsome tables," including "two of kindergarten size" built by high school shop students. The school board donated matching chairs. "Owing to a lack of funds," the *Herald* reported, "the children's room will not be opened at present, a fact very much regretted."

Opposite the reading room was the reference room. "Here there are 232 volumes of bound magazines and many of temporary binding," it was said, "Poole's Index, Readers' Guide, Warner's Library, encyclopedias, dictionaries, etc. This room is to be reserved exclusively for quiet reading and study." Woodwork in naturally finished birch adorned the entire first floor, which was covered with linoleum "to soften the footsteps." A large "well lighted" basement housed the heating plant, storage rooms, toilets, and "a large lecture room," the *Herald* announced, available for community meetings. Thus, less than two years after writing Carnegie, the Bryant Library occupied a new Main Street building ready to serve its local citizens.[32]

When the building opened, the library board consisted of President James A. Norris (Republican, Mason, local agent for the Great Northern Railway, clerk of the local Congregational church, Grand Army of the Republic member), Dr. Julian DuBois (Democrat, Sauk Centre health officer, Merchant's National Bank director), Menzo C. Kelsey (city attorney, Episcopalian, Odd Fellow), Dr. E. J. Lewis (Mason, Congregationalist, Odd Fellow), Rev. F. M. Garland (Episcopalian, Mason), Fayette W. Sprague (Episcopalian, Republican, First National Bank director), Mrs. Charlotte Barto (Congregationalist, widow of a Bryant Library founder), and Mrs. Lyman Barto (daughter-in-law to Charlotte Barto, Congregationalist, married to prominent attorney who became mayor in 1904). Both women on the library board were charter members of the Gradatim Club; so were the wives of all the male trustees. Lives of these community leaders threaded tightly through the fabric of Sauk Centre's social and civic life.

In the summer of 1905, Harry Lewis returned home from Yale. By that time he had decided to become a writer under the name of Sinclair Lewis. After observing the Sauk Centre society he had left behind for Yale, he wrote in his diary: "'The village virus,'—I shall have to write a book of how it getteth into the veins of a good man & true. . . . In Sauk Centre there is nothing to do save drink or play poker (for those who do not read much)." The Bryant Library continued to occupy a warm place in his heart.[33]

In April 1906 the library board again wrote to Carnegie. Unlike most receiving Carnegie donations, its secretary noted, Sauk Centre had used all its grant money to erect the building, none for "decorations or ornamentation." Given the fact that Sauk Centre was annually allocating up to $1,300 for maintenance, would Carnegie consider an additional $1,000 "for beautifying the entrance and decorating the walls and ceilings"? Although "your explanation of the amount being exceeded seems somewhat farfetched," Bertram responded, he said that Carnegie was willing to give another $1,000 "if the city will correspondingly increase its guarantee for maintenance." Sauk Centre agreed. In September the local Ladies Musical Club donated a bookcase to make the club's music and literature accessible; the club met regularly in the lecture room. The Bryant Library closed in October while walls were decorated, and electric chandeliers, steel book stacks, and a circulation desk (still in use today) were purchased and installed with the additional Carnegie money.[34]

Beginning August 1, 1906, the Bryant Library was open between 2:00 and 5:00 P.M. and again from 7:30 to 9:00 P.M. every day of the week except Sunday. To pay for the additional hours, the board eliminated an assistant librarian position and made the librarian full-time at $25 per month. She was expected to serve the public during open hours and accomplish her administrative work when the library was closed. In addition to the Ladies Musical Club and a needlework club run by Mrs. E. J. Lewis, more civic groups were given permission to use the library's assembly room, including the Young Men's Athletic Association (YMAA), and local chapters of the YMCA, Grand Army of the Republic (GAR), and the Women's Relief Corps (WRC). The YMAA used the room for exercises (they supplied the equipment), the other three for monthly meetings. The GAR and WRC donated furniture.[35]

WORLD WAR I–ERA CHANGES

The year 1913 brought significant changes in Bryant Library services. First, borrowing privileges were extended to residents of the local Home School for Girls, a state institution for delinquent juveniles. To show their "appreciation," the girls hemstitched a set of curtains for use in the reading room, which also contained two library tables donated by the Gradatim Club. More important, however, in February the library implemented a Saturday afternoon "story hour" in the Southeast Room, intended for all Sauk Centre children. Local public school teachers and high school students (not the librarian) read to "the little ones"; fifty showed up for the first story hour. "The new departure of the Library Board is regarded with much favor by the public," noted the *Herald*.[36] Institution of story hour was a prelude for a more complex move that occurred several months later.

A 1912 law typical of the big-government traditions evolving in Progressive Era Minnesota required all public schools to have a "separate room for a library." As long as the school superintendent was a member of the public library board, however, schools having cooperative agreements with a library did not need to establish a school library. When Sauk Centre's superintendent told officials it would cost taxpayers two thousand dollars to set up and maintain a school library, the council quickly agreed to a cooperative arrangement. On October 29, 1913, school officials offered to cover the cost of opening the library every weekday morning, with money given them by the state to select books for schoolchildren from lists furnished by the Minnesota Library Association (MLA). In turn, the Bryant Library trustees promised to catalog, classify, and manage the collections acquired, and agreed to furnish classroom collections if requested. "The Sauk Centre school is the pioneer in consolidating under the new law," the *Herald* noted, "and if it works out well here it will, no doubt, be followed generally by the schools of the state . . . where there are public libraries." Within one year Bryant Library collections grew from 7,693 to 9,670, its annual circulation rose from 16,356 to 17,323, and increasingly more teachers participated in Saturday story hours. One problem, however, that the *Herald* noted later: "How to get the kids to read books they ought to read instead of the ones they want to read."[37]

In the spring of 1914 citizens of Sauk Centre voted against the prohibition of alcohol by 290 to 150. Behind this vote was a shifting economy. At the end of the nineteenth century most Stearns County farmers grew wheat and prospered. Without fertilizers and crop rotation, however, yields diminished, and regional agriculture diversified into dairying. In 1880 the county had just over one thousand milk cows; in 1910 there were thirty-five thousand and much of their milk was processed into butter. By the century's second decade, the county had a reputation as "the butter capital of the world"; some nicknamed Sauk Centre "the Sweet Cream Town." But politics were never far from view. When a European war broke out in August 1914, German-Americans residing in Stearns County made no secret of their loyalties, and found their voice in Father F. Anthony Arzt, a German-born Catholic priest who routinely picked up mail at the post office and, upon reviewing battle reports in newspapers, became "furious if there were German reverses, crowing at successes, and emphasizing both reactions by banging on the floor with a heavy cane." On the other hand, Sauk Centre's first families (and not coincidentally the Bryant Library they controlled) generally followed President Woodrow Wilson's advice to "remain neutral in thought as well as deed." In the summer of 1916 Sinclair Lewis returned for a visit, and delivered lectures to benefit the Bryant Library. Before the Commercial Club and the Citizens' Club he gave "the real 'inside' of how the modern literature of today is made"; to high school students he spoke on "Modern Literature." For each appearance attendees paid twenty-five cents; proceeds went "to the Library fund."[38]

The war in Europe had no obvious effect on Bryant Library services, even after the United States joined the Allies in April 1917. But local cultural developments did follow nationwide trends somewhat. In June the *Herald* ran an ad for a local store. "ATTENTION! BOOKLOVERS!," it read. "We have been fortunate in procuring from the New York Book Co. a large assortment of popular and first class story books," including "Horatio Alger, Oliver Optic, the Girls, Young Folks, Camp Fire and Trail Series, the Ridge Boy Scouts, Meade Books, and Economical Cooking." The Bryant Library had none of the series books mentioned, but it did show independence by acquiring twelve Horatio Alger books and twenty-one Oliver Optic titles that ALA catalogs had not recommended. Popular books in local stores and the new availability of movies—in September a theater opened in Sauk Centre—did not lead to a decrease in use of the Bryant Library collection; borrowing statistics continued to increase.[39]

The Bryant Library could not entirely avoid literary disputes occurring elsewhere in the nation. On March 21, 1918, its trustees considered a petition that John Galsworthy's *Beyond*, published in 1917 by Scribner's, "not be placed on the shelves of the library." About *Beyond* the *Boston Evening Transcript* was not charitable: "Although problems of sex have been utilized by Mr. Galsworthy in . . . his novels, never before has he been so obsessed by them. But for the graces of its style, 'Beyond' would be utterly negligible." Quietly the board "decided not to purchase the book mentioned." Instead trustees preferred to address more mundane matters that brought positive attention to the already venerable institution. On May 7, 1920, for example, Bryant Librarian Eva Davis attended the Lake Region Library Club meeting in Fergus Falls and gave "the Librarian's view of the school library." *Library News & Notes (LN&N)* noted that it "was one of the liveliest discussions of the program—for the trials and tribulations of the librarian with the school and the public library combined are many."[40]

MAIN STREET

When Sinclair Lewis's *Main Street* was published in 1920—it sold 180,000 copies in six months—Sauk Centre drew national attention that has influenced its self-image ever since. On the one hand, the small-town values that Lewis excoriated in his critically acclaimed novel angered local citizens; on the other, the fame it brought Sauk Centre invited unexpected opportunities. In part, reaction to *Main Street* forced Sauk Centre to become the voice of small-town America. Analysis of local newspapers and remarks made by Sauk Centre leaders gives the clear impression that civic leaders willingly assumed that responsibility, for they regularly applauded small-town values and benefits to anyone who would pay attention. "Did you ever stop to consider what an exceptionally good town you live in?," the *Herald* asked its readers in 1921. But for "a want of manufacturing institutions," it was "an ideal community, one of the finest places in the world to live," where schools were above average, churches were "exceptionally strong," a "modern and well-conducted show house" entertained, and prosperous lodges and fraternal organizations thrived. "Then too there is the library. As modern and well-equipped an edifice as any in the country of its size." Two months later the *Herald* acknowledged Lewis's fame in another editorial. "The entire East has literally gone crazy over the book," it wrote of the novel, which, when closely perused, "makes it possible for one to picture in his [or her] mind's eye local characters having been injected boldly into the story."[41]

Controversial locally, *Main Street* also became a topic for discussion at several local clubs, including the Gradatim. Bryant Library patrons seldom found any of its seven copies on the shelves (several citizens purchased their own copies, then donated them to the library). The novel circulated widely in public libraries across the country, but not nearby Alexandria, Minnesota. After Alexandria apparently banished *Main Street* from its public library, it was criticized widely. Twin Cities dailies assumed it was "because Alex was jealous of the advertising that Sauk Centre was receiving from the book." The *Milwaukee Journal* was less kind. "Critics may exhaust their superlatives and a reading public stand in awe of the genius who created such a novel, but there ain't going to be no such book on the shelves in Alexandria—not while the board of censors retains its consciousness, courage, and authority. No sir!" The real story about Alexandria may be less compelling. The Alexandria public library board president noted to reporters who bothered to ask that the library had "received a copy of the book, but that it was found defective and returned to the publishers." Multiple copies arrived weeks later, and immediately began circulating to Alexandria patrons.[42]

When Lewis returned home for a visit in 1922, the *Herald* noted, "The usual equilibrium of the community was not disturbed by the arrival of the famous author nor were the dogs of war unchained." His friends were glad to see him and glad at his successes. By this time the *Herald* banner was advertising Sauk Centre as "The Original 'Main Street' in the Heart of the Dairying and Lake Region of Minnesota," many local merchants and groups had changed their names (to Gopher Prairie Inn, the Main Street Café, the Gopher Prairie Shriners Club, and the Gopher Prairie Card Club, for example), and the local drugstore boasted a "Main Street" rack of local views and postcards—including one of the Bryant Library.

By mid-decade, the *St. Paul Dispatch* noted, "Thousands of summer tourists on their way to the lake region make it a point to drive through Sauk Centre, though it may be miles out of their way, to visit Gopher Prairie, and Sauk Centre is willing at last to accept that coin." Local merchants pointed to the prosperity on display on Main Street every Saturday evening. "We feel as if our little town of 3,000 people is really atop the whole world," the local Boston Store manager told the *Minneapolis Journal*, "and our Main Street really the main street of the world." All these phenomena showed that Sauk Centre wanted to capitalize on its fame, and perhaps show the world it was not particularly offended or angry at the novel. For example, at a meeting of the Lake Region Library Club hosted by the Bryant Library on May 21 and 22, 1925, board president Dr. E. J. Lewis gave a cordial "Welcome to Main Street" message to all visitors.[43]

In June 1928, the Bryant Library had 12,331 volumes to serve thirty-five hundred citizens, and a circulation rate of 8.6 per capita, which compared favorably with other public libraries from similar-sized Minnesota towns. A year later, the *Herald* began running library acquisitions lists of "high class fiction," "choice literature," and books for people with "discriminating literary tastes." Profiling "choice books," however, seemed to have little impact on the circulation of popular fiction; at five cents a week per loan, a "Pay Shelf" rental collection that featured popular fiction generated more revenue. And although the local movie house began running talkies about this time, this had no negative impact on Bryant circulation.[44]

THE GREAT DEPRESSION AND WORLD WAR II

The Great Depression had a huge impact on the Bryant Library in many ways. With more people out of work, Main Streeters (by 1929 the high school had adopted this nickname) gravitated to the library in greater numbers, and pushed up the circulation rate. By 1931 circulation per capita was 10.7, in 1935 it was 12.8, in 1938 it was 22.3. Like other Minnesota public libraries, the Bryant Library struggled to meet new demands with diminished budgets. Acquiescing to big government and growing state bureaucracies provided some relief. Despite its Republican loyalties, for example (in 1932 Sauk Centre gave Franklin Roosevelt 55 votes, Herbert Hoover 521; in Stearns County, FDR received 18,313, Hoover 4,498), the board successfully sought federal funds to hire two assistants to keep the library open longer hours. With other federal funds the board hired local labor to redecorate the basement, replace floor coverings, and build more shelves.[45] On January 25, 1934, the board met with State Department of Education Library Department officials, who made several suggestions for improvement. They were particularly forceful about recommending the purchase of a new set of encyclopedias (the library's most recent was dated 1905). The officials also noted that although the Bryant Library had a good circulation rate, its collections lacked "quality" and "up-to-date" fiction for children and young adults. To address this shortcoming, they recommended "a complete checking first with the Minnesota School Library lists and supplements, and with the ALA *Catalog* and Wilson Standard catalogs." And when they addressed cooperative efforts between the school system and library, the Department of Education officials argued for hiring a "trained librarian" (to state library officials the connection between upgrading the collection and the need for a professional was not coincidental). The officials suggested several names. Trustees agreed that they needed to hire a professional.[46]

While Sauk Centre's first and second graders competed for the honor of who could read the most books during National Library Week (March 19–23), Bryant Library trustees reviewed applications for the upgraded librarian position. On July 31 they hired Mynette Lindeloff to replace Eva Davis, who retired after twenty-nine years. Lindeloff was a 1931 graduate of the University of Minnesota Library School, and for the previous three years had been employed in a Minneapolis Public Library branch. She came to Sauk Centre "highly recommended and well qualified for the position," the *Herald* said. Within a year Lindeloff became a member of the Gradatim Club.[47]

Weeks later the Bryant began to look more professionally run and up-to-date. In September it got its first telephone and typewriter. The board also approved Lindeloff's recommendation to use the community room "for school and small community gatherings." Within a month the League of Women Voters began meeting there; a year later so did the Sauk Centre Country Club Women's Auxiliary. Recognizing the value of library as place, Lindeloff arranged for several hobby exhibits contributed by high school students for Children's Book Week (November 11–17), including model airplanes, radios, stamp collections, drawings, and electrical projects. All drew family and friends of the students into the library. In addition, she mounted an exhibit of books to mirror the Children's Book Week theme, "Ride the Book Trail to Knowledge and Adventure."[48]

On December 5, Lindeloff addressed the Gradatim Club. "What books mean in an organized society cannot be measured, but a progressive society without books cannot be imagined," she said. "If our minds are filled with trivialities, vulgarities, and dishonesties, we expect our lives to reflect those qualities. On the other hand, if our minds are filled with beauty and significance, we may expect our lives to grow richer and stronger." Her words echoed the professional rhetoric she had read in library literature and heard in library school. In the same issue that reported Lindeloff's address, the *Herald* also noted the Bryant Library's desire to increase non-fiction circulation. "All is being done that readers in this city may have available the best of contemporary non-fiction," the *Herald* said. Over Christmas, Lindeloff weeded regular collections and began reregistering local borrowers. Both initiatives had been recommended by state Library Department officials as part of making the Bryant Library management more "professional."[49]

The practice of book selection also changed under Lindelhoff. Rather than a library board committee making selections from scratch as had been done, the librarian prepared a list of recommendations based upon reviews in standard bibliographic guides, then presented the list to a board committee that selected from the list. Thus, selection effectively passed from trustees to a professional librarian. At Lindeloff's request the *Herald* published monthly a list of new Bryant Library books, with annotations largely extrapolated from *Booklist*. And always Lindeloff followed good professional practice by listing more nonfiction than fiction, despite the fact that the latter still accounted for 70 percent of circulation. If Bryant Library trustees recognized their diminished authority over this Main Street public library, they said nothing publicly. On April 18, 1935, the *Herald* summarized Lindeloff's annual report. Bryant Library had 35 percent of Sauk Centre's citizens registered as borrowers. Annual circulation was twelve items per capita, better than the ALA standard of ten per capita for a city of Sauk Centre's size. Although fiction circulation increased by two thousand, the *Herald* found another fact more important. "Probably the most notable increase is in the circulation of nonfiction books. There is an urgent demand for literature on vocational readjustment and books on trades and occupations."[50]

Two weeks later Lindeloff announced that the Bryant Library would begin sending boxes of books selected from State Library lists to rural schools in Stearns County, and exchanging them every month. Unlike her predecessors, Lindeloff wanted to better serve her profession by pushing Bryant Library services beyond Sauk Centre, into the more Democratic rural communities of Stearns County. "If this plan is successful," the *Herald* noted, "there may be a county library in the future." On May 28, 1935, members of a "Rural Library Association" consisting of representatives of eleven Stearns and Todd County rural schools met in the Bryant Library to select books Lindeloff had assembled. Each school was allowed up to nine boxes of thirty-five to forty titles, for which host schools paid an annual ten-dollar fee. "A circulation list of the books will be kept in each school to determine which type of books are the most popular," the *Herald* reported. "This circulation list will serve as a guide in preparing the book lists for the next year." The *Herald* was excited: "This is one of the greatest things that the Library could offer to the rural schools."

In June Lindeloff attended a Lake Region Library Club meeting to report on rural library service. "Books for all phases of reading were gone over [by attendees]," the *Herald* noted, "and it was pointed out the best in literature." Stearns County children were now receiving professional reading guidance from the new librarian. Lindeloff had even prepared an exhibit of the service for the Stearns County Fair, where fairgoers could "see just what is taking place." In early October she attended the MLA conference, which focused on certifying public librarians and establishing county library services across the state. "The rural service offered by the local library was cited during the convention as an example for the establishment of county service," the *Herald* noted proudly. About the same time, Lindeloff convinced city officials to ask the Works Progress Administration (WPA) to hire five people. "This project will include repair work on books at the public library, the school library and the eleven rural schools. . . . The work will be done by local labor and will be cared for at the Bryant Library."[51]

Also in October 1935, Lindeloff acquired Sinclair Lewis's latest novel, *It Can't Happen Here.* "A complete works of Lewis' books are now on the shelves," the *Herald* reported, "and it is the custom of the board to be among the first with the latest of his books." To celebrate Children's Book Week November 11–17, Lindeloff arranged for "several gala days" that featured children's books and their characters. On Friday that week the junior high school conducted a contest in which pupils portrayed book characters in costume. Books were given to three students who did the best job. On Saturday a regular children's story hour was supplemented by a "Children's Book Circus," in which children dressed up as their favorite animal book characters. But the showiness of such events was at odds with certain realities. Male patrons still alive in 2009 who were third and fourth graders in November 1935 recalled covert defiance of library rules: taking from the adult section books on World War I fighter planes that they were not allowed to check out and hiding them in the children's section behind books on the lowest shelf "where old ladies were unlikely to be able to bend." Once finished with them, lads returned them to their original place.[52]

Lindeloff's annual report the next spring documented what she saw as progress: almost half of Sauk Centre's citizens were registered borrowers, the rural library service accounted for a increase in total circulation of three thousand, and nearly three hundred pupils in fourteen rural schools had borrowed over four thousand volumes since the service started. She especially trumpeted the increased circulation of juvenile nonfiction literature. But the *Herald* noticed something in the numbers that Lindeloff had not emphasized in her annual report. "A shift of more than a thousand volumes has been made from the nonfiction to the fiction group by the adult readers," it noted. Lindeloff's professionalism obviously had limits. In a civic institution people did not have to use they exercised personal power by selecting books they wanted to read, not necessarily titles being pushed by a state bureaucracy or national profession. That annual report was Lindeloff's last, however. On May 21 she announced her engagement to Phil Steiner, president of the Sauk Centre Country Club, member of the American Legion and Rotary Club, and owner of Steiner Lumber Company. They married in the Congregational church on October 3, 1936, a month after trustees had put Lindeloff on the board to oversee the rural library service she had started. Thus, by marrying, Lindeloff—now Mynette Steiner—stabilized her position among Sauk Centre's leading families, and easily fit into a board consisting entirely of social peers. [53]

To replace the librarian, Bryant Library trustees hired Eloise Ebert, another University of Minnesota Library School graduate. Within weeks of her arrival she became a member of the Gradatim Club. That Ebert's librarianship differed little from her predecessor was soon obvious. For Children's Book Week in 1936 she exhibited Newbery Award–winning books on one table in the children's room, science books for intermediate pupils on another. In glass cases elsewhere were a local patron's stamp collection and a display put together by a puppet club run by a local teacher.[54]

But Ebert did try new things. She began to subscribe to *Children's Catalog* (an acquisitions guide professional children's librarians regarded as their bible) and mounted a "World Peace" display that the *Herald* lauded. "At a time when Europe is again the tinder box only awaiting the match to ignite, Miss Ebert deemed it a pertinent time to display materials designed to better acquaint persons with the international peace movement." But the *Herald* was quick to reassure its readers that "the display does not disregard the factor of patriotism." In her annual report several months later, Ebert proudly noted that the Bryant Library held twice as many volumes per capita as recommended by the ALA for a town of Sauk Center's size (six to three) and spent 40 percent more per capita ($1.40 to $1.00, ranking third in the state); in circulating twelve volumes per capita, the Bryant Library tied with Grand Rapids for the highest circulation per capita in Minnesota. What the report did not say was how much these figures had been influenced by the Bryant Library's relationship with the local and rural schools. In the summer of 1937 Ebert resigned to become director of the public library in Great Falls, Montana.

In September trustees hired Bernice Finnegan of St. Cloud. Although not a library school graduate, she did have an engaging personality and commitment to community service. Under her direction, the Bryant Library significantly expanded its reach. In October Finnegan announced, "We have now placed on the rental shelves many new western, mystery, and romance novels, which we are sure you will find very interesting."[55] That she specifically mentioned popular fiction suggests her attitude toward it differed from that of her professionally trained predecessors. For National Library Week Finnegan put together an exhibit of local authors. When she asked Sinclair Lewis for an autographed copy of his latest book, Lewis returned five autographed titles with a note: "To the Bryant Library, Sauk Centre, with love and with lively memory of the days when its books were my greatest adventure." Within months, Lewis donated twenty-four more books. Finnegan also solicited James Hendryx, son of former *Sauk Centre Herald* editor Charles Hendryx and author of the Connie Morgan series of boys' books, who also sent autographed copies of his books. In March she worked with the local Rotary Club to solicit dolls from foreign countries for a world unity display. "This will stimulate the public in acquiring a better knowledge of your life and thus bring a stronger bond of friendship and good fellowship," they wrote. The Rotary Club also donated display cases for the doll exhibit and an exhibit of the books Lewis had sent.[56]

In 1938, town officials used WPA funds to redecorate and relandscape the library. Spirea and other ornamental shrubs replaced rosebushes on the north side "so as to balance the landscape." Inside "a cheerful canary yellow . . . replac[ed] the dark green on the walls and ceilings," and the woodwork and fireplace were refinished with a walnut stain. Just before Christmas Finnegan hosted a grand opening tea for the redecorated Bryant Library, at which she accepted the gift of a fireplace mantle lamp from the Gradatim Club. (By this time she had become a member of the club.) Library patrons later remembered that they were "always welcome there," and that there was "no discrimination by social class." Thus, the Bryant continued to function as an attractive and inviting public space that served to knit the Sauk Centre community together in multiple ways.

By then the Bryant's rural library service had expanded to twenty-two schools. In March 1939 Finnegan reported that circulation in 1938 had been 60,521, nearly double that of a year before. Per capita circulation was now twenty, up from thirteen the previous year, which placed the Bryant Library first in per capita circulation for Minnesota public libraries of its size. At that rate Bryant's fifteen hundred registered borrowers averaged forty books checked out per year. "Juveniles" accounted for the largest gain, in large part because a summer reading program conducted through the rural library service was so popular. Fiction accounted for 75 percent of total circulation. If there were complaints about the popular fiction driving the library's circulation, they never showed up in *Herald* columns.[57]

Finnegan continued to promote the library as a community space. In March the library exhibited twenty-five paintings that the Gradatim had obtained through the Fine Arts Program of the Minnesota Women's Federated Clubs. Weeks later the library displayed a replica of a late-nineteenth-century Sauk Centre store, as well as a replica of a stockade built there in the 1860s. In April Finnegan asked Sauk Centre citizens to exhibit local historical photographs at the library. In October she invited them to "lobby for your hobby" by featuring a local philatelist's stamp collection. "Anyone who has what they believe to be an interesting hobby collection suitable for a display is asked to contact the Bryant Library," she said. The following spring Finnegan initiated a program to get library books to shut-ins by asking Sauk Centre Girl Scouts to identify "those who are ill or too aged to get out," and then deliver and retrieve books shut-ins requested.[58] Finnegan was proving very good at involving the community in Bryant Library activities.

Main Streeters were especially proud of the Bryant Library children's room. "Did you ever go into the children's room and . . . look around and enjoy the hospitality and warmth of that room?," the *Herald* asked in 1940. "[It] is very colorful with bright posters on the walls. On each radiator is a small pot with a plant in it. There are three tables in the center of the room with eight chairs at each, where the small children may sit and read. Of special interest . . . is the big picture which was made by the fourth grade. It consists of four individual pictures, each on a different subject but framed into one. The four subjects . . . are: an ox cart, early Minnesota Indians, Fort Snelling, and a covered wagon. Very nice work, children."[59]

Finnegan reached out to the community in other ways. In August 1940 she announced that the library had set up a Carnegie Corporation–funded "International Mind Alcove" of one hundred titles "discussing countries other than our own and by authors with widely divergent viewpoints." In October she announced that the Bryant Library would host one of three WPA-funded State Board of Education Library Division demonstration projects. The library would distribute books from its collections to inhabitants of rural Stearns County through substations in village stores, halls, "even farmhomes." "To Sauk Centre's library it will mean the greatest widening of the scope of its service in its history," the *Herald* trumpeted. Because the grant would match funds equal to the value of additional titles donated, Finnegan arranged a "Give a Book to the County Library" week in November in cooperation with the Sauk Centre Community Club, the American Legion, the Rotary Club, Black Cats (a young men's organization), the Sauk Centre Welfare Council, the Boy Scouts, and the Gradatim Club. "The project is interested in getting numbers of books," the *Herald* announced. "They are not so concerned over types of reading matter." Each member of the Gradatim promised to donate at least one book, and challenged other Sauk Centre residents to do the same. Under five "patrol leaders," the Boy Scouts moved "about the city in plotted districts" to collect books one Saturday morning. People had been told that they could "call the library in advance to arrange for books to be picked up." The community effort showed what the *Herald* called a "sunny side of Main Street" that contrasted sharply with the gloomy picture of small-town America that Sinclair Lewis had painted twenty years earlier.[60]

By the beginning of 1941 the WPA-funded project had collected four hundred books, just under one-third the total for all of Stearns County. All were housed in the St. Cloud Public Library, where a director monitored the project.[61] After Finnegan issued her annual report in March, the *Her-*

ald proudly announced that "for the second successive year" the Bryant Library not only ranked first in circulation for thirty-two Minnesota cities with populations of 2,500–5,000, but also now averaged twenty-four books circulated per capita, eighteen ahead of the median. And all this went against a nationwide trend of decreasing library circulation. Although the Bryant Library now had 85 percent of Sauk Centre's citizens registered as borrowers, juveniles accounted for the largest circulation increase, assisted in large part by the summer reading program and a "Champ of the Week" contest which Finnegan administered throughout the year in each grade of Sauk Centre's schools to recognize its most prolific readers. Winners saw their names and pictures on a bulletin board when they visited the library, oftentimes coming with parents and siblings.

Finnegan's report provoked an editorial on the subject of reading. Books were but "another of the agencies for molding public opinion," the *Herald* said, "else why should Germany ban such anti-war documents as 'A Farewell to Arms' and 'All Quiet on the Western Front'?" Sauk Centre, the editorial continued, "is no remote village or city that can shut its gates." It has to "take the long view." And the right books connecting local citizens to outside worlds answered that need. As an "antidote" to the "possible filtration of works that may extend faulty points of view, the library presents the International Mind Alcove, . . . a group of one hundred books assembled about different peoples about various countries by experts." By making these books available, the paper concluded, the library was contributing to "national defense."[62]

The *Herald* also thought "youth reading" was a "real problem," however. Years later young patrons recalled stumbling over several "steamy" novels. Rather than risk the disapproval of the librarian by checking them out, they hid them in the stacks, exchanged them at the library, made sure librarians did not observe them reading the forbidden fruit, and returned the books to their rightful place when the fantasy passed. As long as they behaved and were quiet in the library, librarians gave them considerable freedom. Others recalled meeting dates there in the early 1940s. "Going to the library was always an excuse for getting out of the house at night," Richard Hedin remembers, and it was certainly easier than asking parents for permission to go to the movies or the roller rink at the local armory. On occasion teenagers would sneak into the stacks when librarians were not looking and engage in some passionate kissing and light petting. "Couldn't get much petting done, though," Hedin recalls, "because in Sauk Centre winters we all wore a lot of clothing."[63]

In June 1941 Finnegan resigned to become librarian at Fort Leonard Wood, the army base in Missouri. "Sauk Centre is cosmopolitan and cultural," Finnegan told the *Herald* on the eve of her departure. "It's been a real pleasure to work with both the board and the people here." During her three and a half years in Sauk Centre, the *Herald* reminded its readers, Finnegan had presided over the largest circulation rate increase in the library's history. Two months later the board hired Mary Ann Skinner of Fairmont, Minnesota, daughter of the superintendent of schools there and not only a graduate of the University of Minnesota Library School but also a state-certified high school teacher.[64] Programs started by Finnegan continued under Skinner. In October high school art students placed posters they had made for Children's Book Week in the library and around town. Some addressed the theme "Come See Our 100 New Books"; another, with the title "Under the Silver Umbrella," displayed a series of poems featured during the Saturday morning children's story hour.

After Japan attacked Pearl Harbor on December 7, 1941, Bryant Library programming changed significantly. In January Skinner posted maps of the Pacific theater of war, made available pamphlets prepared by the Information Bureau of the American Nurses Association, and noted for the *Herald* that the Bryant Library had maps, books, and periodical literature providing background information on the war. A week later it joined the ALA's nationwide Victory Book Drive to collect ten million volumes for U.S. troops. Main Streeters were asked to conduct an "attic survey" of books no longer needed, which Boy Scouts promised to pick up while conducting a paper drive. The war affected Bryant Library services in other ways. Although Skinner's annual report still showed that Sauk Centre was the "readin'es town in the state," circulation figures had dropped 17 percent in a year. "War and the attending press of duties . . . is believed responsible in some measure for the circulation slumps," the *Herald* reasoned. By that time, however, the Bryant Library had collected four hundred books for the Victory Book Drive, acquired materials from the Office of Civilian Defense, and prepared a bibliography of magazine articles for local clubs wanting to study the war campaign.[65]

Skinner did not stay long in Sauk Centre. In June she resigned to join the WAVES, the U.S. Navy's division of women. The Bryant board replaced her with Elenora Gralow, another University of Minnesota Library School graduate (1941). Like her predecessor, Gralow acclimated quickly. For Children's Book Week in November 1941 she assembled one hundred titles to support the theme "Better Understanding Between Nations and People," organized two puppet shows ("Fraidy Cat" and "Cinderella"), and brought out the Rotary Club's doll display, which, except for a donated Mexican doll, had not grown due to the war. In subsequent months Gralow solicited more donations for another Victory Book Campaign. "Escapist books are welcome," she told the *Herald*, "but so are the classics." Boy Scouts promised to pick up all donations.[66] In the spring of 1942 Gralow reported circulation at 41,428, more than 5,000 fewer than 1940 but still sufficient to rank Sauk Centre first among Minnesota communities of its size in total circulation. In its analysis of Gralow's report the *Herald* noted "an increase in the percent of nonfiction" circulated and "a sizeable group of library patrons who do not appear in any part of the statistical report. They are the people who come in frequently and regularly to read the current magazines and newspapers."

In April 1943, the Bryant Library had new shelves installed in its reading room, reference materials were moved there, and the room was renamed the "Reference and Reading Room." In the space formerly used for the reference collection a "Young People's Room" was set up for junior and senior high school students. Work with local schools continued. In addition to sending collections of books to all local public and parochial schools, students in each grade school and junior high school class came to the library once a week.[67] For the 1943 summer reading program Gralow adopted the theme "Bomb Tokyo." On charts in the Reading and Reference Room the names of students enrolled were placed on "battleships . . . and for each book they read they [got] closer to Tokyo." Each child joined at the lowest rank as a soldier, sailor, flyer, or marine (Gralow showed gender sensitivity by including WAVES), and Gralow promoted them in rank as they read a certain number of books. Months later Gralow announced that the summer reading program had been highly successful, "with Tokyo having been repeatedly bombed by the older school children and the younger children backing the attack by building battleships." Gralow also announced plans for an honor roll containing names of all local servicemen, and solicited Sauk Centre citizens for names, pictures, and war souvenirs to be kept in a locked exhibit case "so that nothing will happen to them."

"She guarantees the safe return to the folks who bring them to her," the *Herald* assured its readers.[68]

In the fall of 1943 Gralow asked the library board to revise the circulation policy for the rental collection by charging five cents per week instead of ten cents. She also worried that reprinted westerns cost too much at $1.20, but the board believed "the demand for this type of book was sufficient to warrant the increase in price." Their action—they agreed to lower the rental fee—is an example of a library board helping to define a center of local literary culture that conformed to the reading interests of some local patrons, in this case library users who found in westerns a set of values consistent with the demands on citizens in a time of national crisis.[69] In March 1944, the Bryant Library became one of the five distribution centers of the new Stearns County Library system, and the rural library service that the Bryant had been running for a decade was subsumed by the county library. When the Stearns County Library announced in April that it would take over responsibility for book boxes, Bryant Library trustees countered that they would increase fees for the book-box service to $15 "payable in advance"—five districts were already in arrears.[70]

When Elenora Gralow resigned in the summer of 1944, the Bryant Library trustees hired Aagot Hoidahl, who at her first board meeting showed a curious antipathy toward youth. First she suggested "that no small children be allowed in the library in the evening." Reluctantly the board agreed. Three months later she complained about "many youngsters who do not pay fines," and suggested that rural students "should be charged 25 cents per quarter." The board agreed to deny service to youngsters who had not paid fines, but refused to charge rural students for use of the library.[71]

The town to which Hoidahl moved in 1944 differed in many ways from the Sauk Centre of preceding generations. Its three thousand citizens lived in just over six hundred houses, "most of them white." On its streets were 125 new parking meters accepting pennies and nickels. The local power company supplied electricity to one thousand accounts and city mail carriers had 600 stops, up from 250 when the service started in 1927. In Sauk Centre, locals bragged, "butter is the hero and the dirty old villain is oleomargarine." The *Herald* carried a regular wire-service-provided "Book Review" column, but the paper did not connect this to Bryant Library acquisitions. The *Herald* also carried a movie review column. Local churches included St. Paul's and the Church of Our Lady of the Angels (Catholic), Westport Methodist, Church of the Nazarene, Gospel Tabernacle, First Congregational, Church of the Good Samaritan (Episcopal), Trinity Lutheran, Elon Lutheran, First Lutheran, and Little Sauk Lutheran. By this time Sauk Centre had a J. C. Penney and a Gambles store; an A&P, a Supervalu, and a Red Owl grocery; a Ben Franklin discount store, and a Coast to Coast hardware shop. Chain gas stations dotted Main Street, and the town was served by a Greyhound bus station in the Waldorf Hotel & Café.

The Bryant Library board of trustees in 1944 showed similarities to the boards of previous decades. Board Chairman Winfield D. Gallup was owner and manager of the Ben Franklin store, a member of the American Legion and Community Club, and on the board of directors of the local chamber of commerce. Mildred Thielen had been on the board since 1939 and had organized the Sauk Centre effort to start the Stearns County Library system in 1940. She worked closely with Mynette Steiner, who remained on the board. When board members Chuck Rathe and Lyle T. Johnson returned from World War II service, Rathe went back to his position as a columnist for the *Herald* and Johnson resumed his dentistry practice. Both were American Legion members. Richard Bushey owned the local Rexall drugstore, served as director of the chamber of commerce, and was a member of the Rotary Club and Masonic Lodge. Hattie Hedin, who had been a trustee since 1929, was a cashier at the First State Bank of Sauk Centre and a DAR member. She was a Sauk Centre native, daughter of Erik and Ida Hedin, both Swedish immigrants. Louise Thomas was a member of the Gradatim Club, the League of Women Voters, and the St. Michael's Hospital Auxiliary. All were leading members of their community, but most were no longer connected to Sauk Centre's pioneer families. It was to this board that Hoidahl reported in April 1946 that annual circulation had dropped to 26,636.[72]

A SETTLED EXISTENCE

In 1946 the World Publishing Company reissued Sinclair Lewis's *Main Street* as part of its Living Library series and supplemented it with Margaret Lowengrund sketches of Sauk Centre in the 1920s. "Her sketches are undeniably faithful," the *Herald* noted. "The fact that it says Gopher Prairie on the depots doesn't fool anyone." The newspaper noted that the novel was "still a widely read book in the local library"; the Bryant then had three copies: two were in constant circulation, while the third—autographed by Lewis—was locked in an exhibit case. The library continued its practice of buying multiple copies of every novel Lewis published, including *Kingsblood Royal*, which appeared in early 1947, and for which, Hoidahl announced before the book had been received, "a list of prospective readers ... is already forming." With columnist Chuck Rathe on the library board, *Herald* coverage of the library increased. "Sauk Centre has had its nose in a book almost as long as it's been Sauk Centre," he editorialized, but "the war ended the era of reading prosperity."[73]

In May Hoidahl resigned—"to continue her library education," it was said. The board may have forced her to resign. Circulation had so decreased that Sauk Centre's ranking had dropped to fourth for Minnesota towns of its size in 1946. While per capita annual circulation (9.5) was just short of the ALA standard (10), programming lacked the previous decade's zest. In August, trustees hired Alice Dystad, a graduate of Carleton College who had been a librarian in the Northfield, Minnesota, schools. At a September 27, 1947, board meeting, however, members discussed her frequent absences and occasional practice of closing the library during times it was scheduled to be open. After she overstayed a Christmas leave without authority, on January 5 the board demanded her resignation.[74] Dystad refused to relinquish the library keys, argued that she had been terminated for insufficient cause, and returned to work on January 6. In response, the board demanded the keys and directed her "to stay out of the Library Building." Her lawyer suggested that further trouble might be averted if Dystad was permitted to keep her job through June 1. The board refused. "Her re-employment as Librarian could only lead to further difficulty; ... the public is entitled to better library service than she furnished." Dystad held out for five days, and only after the city attorney had the locks changed did she surrender her post. On January 15 two trustees "were appointed to gather Miss Distad's [*sic*] personal things still in the building, inventory them, and send them to her." Days later the state attorney general validated the board's action. It had been an ugly incident.[75] For six months an assistant ran the library.

A month after the *Herald* announced on June 24 that the Bryant Library had recently acquired a copy of Tennessee Williams's controversial *A Streetcar Named Desire* (1947),[76] trustees hired Lewis Olds as librarian —the first man to direct the institution. Olds did not have a library degree, but was enrolled in a four-summer curriculum at the University of Minnesota Library School. That he was community service–oriented quickly became apparent. By October he had put together a display of Native American curios, including colored beads from a Crow Indian reservation in Montana; wooden boots carved by Indian children at a Busby, Montana, school; headpieces made by Cheyenne on the Tongue River Reservation in Montana; and pottery fashioned on the Pine Ridge Sioux reservation.[77] In December Olds asked the board for permission to use the library's basement room for hobby clubs that needed public space for their meetings. The board approved. A week later the *Herald* carried Olds's appeal for adult supervisors for hobby clubs—"especially in stamps and coins"—who wanted to meet in the library.[78] Olds also began a *Herald* library column entitled "Book Trails," and used it to promote the library. In January 1949, "Book Trails" announced the organization of the Sauk Centre Stamp Club, scheduled to meet in the Bryant Library community room every Monday night. A month later nine high school girls organized a library club under the direction of an English teacher. As reported in the *Herald*, "The girls will meet once a week . . . to learn more about the library, to help the students make more and better use of the library, and gain experience in library work for possible future employment."[79]

As usual, the library hosted a summer reading program, and to this added a Wednesday afternoon story hour for children from kindergarten through the third grade. As a result, monthly circulation of juvenile books doubled over the summer. Perhaps Olds's efforts were too successful. In fall of 1949 the mayor of Sauk Centre told the Bryant Library board that he had been asked if the local Girl Scouts and 4-H clubs might use the library's community room. Because of lack of space and staffing, trustees had to turn them down. The library had limits imposed by budgets and past collecting practices which effectively filled much of the library building with books and magazines acquired for decades.

On October 27 "Book Trails" reported that the library had subscribed to a bimonthly that evaluated current motion pictures. "These [evaluations] give a short review of the movie and how it is rated as to suitability for adults or for family," Olds noted. For Children's Book Week in November he announced a "holiday" on children's fines and asked for adult volunteers to tell stories and read books. "Of late the trend has been to make [story-telling] a family affair, not connected to the libraries and the bookstores alone."[80]

In the new year Olds continued his outreach efforts. In January 1950 he showed trustees a circular he had distributed "around town" that listed "outstanding new books of 1949." In February he put together an exhibit for Boy Scout Week (February 5–12), and began distributing bookmarks to all children "to encourage them to use library books and keep books in better condition." In March "Book Trails" noted a growing interest in science fiction, and indicated that "your public library has a number of interesting books . . . with imaginary discoveries based on acceptable scientific fact or theory." In May the St. Michael's Hospital Auxiliary was given permission to use the library community room to sew tags on hospital linens needed for a new facility just about to open. As Auxiliary members entered the library they passed a special book and pamphlet exhibit that Olds had put together for Mother's Day. Olds's efforts paid dividends; circulation increased from 25,552 in 1949 to 29,133 in 1950. The popular fiction rental collection (Olds publicly referred to these as "run of the mill books") continued to receive heavy use.[81]

In observance of United Nations Week in October 1950, the library sported a special display of pamphlets, books, and "colorful flags." For the Christmas and New Year holiday season, "Book Trails" reported it had acquired new copies of *The Betty Crocker Cook Book*, the *Singer Sewing Book*, *Crafts for Everyone*, and U.S. government tax forms. Olds also announced that the Bryant Library had received a copy of *The Willow-Bender* (1950), a new novel by former Sauk Centre resident Helen Rich, thoughtfully inscribed "To the Bryant Library—where I had so many happy hours."[82] It was the fifth Rich title in the Bryant's collection; Olds placed it in the locked exhibit case with books autographed by Sinclair Lewis and James Hendryx.

Sinclair Lewis died in Rome, Italy, on January 10, 1951. Within forty-eight hours his body was cremated and his ashes sent back to Sauk Centre in a silver urn, where on February 1, "in the glittering bitterness of the year's coldest Sunday," his brother Claude deposited the ashes in the family cemetery plot as five hundred people watched. Between the novelist's death and the ceremony, several local citizens decided to establish a memorial for Sauk Centre's most famous native son. Claude consented, and requested that the memorial be located at the Bryant Library, site of some of Lewis's happiest times as a youth. At the service following the graveside ceremony, Claude gave the silver urn to the Bryant Library as "a permanent shrine." Board President Winfield Gallup also announced that a bronze plaque would be prepared for permanent mounting outside the library. The plaque was unveiled on May 31—Memorial Day. Laurel Kells, a prominent local attorney and a former library trustee (1912–1935), noted how frequently Lewis had acknowledged his debt to the library. "Just which book so inspired Sinclair and our other authors we do not know, but most certainly our library did." On cue, eighty-seven-year-old Minnie Mullin—who had been Bryant librarian when Lewis was a young patron—pulled the cord that dropped the cloth covering the plaque. It commemorated Lewis as author of *Main Street* and above his signature reprinted words he had inscribed in books he had donated in 1937: "To the Bryant Library with love and with lively memory of the days when its books were my greatest adventure." By that time *Main Street* had sold over two million copies in the United States.[83]

Lewis Olds's 1951 annual report noted that circulation had increased from 29,133 to 32,165, with heaviest circulation in adult fiction (65 percent of the total). In the *Herald* Olds also announced that the summer reading program would be entitled "Reading Roundup at Your Library," in which the reading progress of enrolled "cowboys" and "cowgirls" would be recognized in "three corrals." Every book read would "be another step toward a higher corral," various cattle brands would be used to mark progress, and diplomas would recognize accomplishments. Fifty-five children enrolled; by the end of the summer twenty were eligible for awards and recognition. About the same time the Bryant Library became the site for the written portion of driver's license examinations.[84]

Sauk Centre celebrated the fiftieth anniversary of the Carnegie building during an open house at the Bryant Library on November 19, 1953. The Gradatim Club arranged the exhibits, which consisted of several Sinclair Lewis manuscripts loaned by the University of Minnesota, oil paintings of a pioneering Sauk Centre couple donated by their son for the library's permanent collections, and historic pictures of the library and Sauk Centre points of interest. Local florists provided flowers paid for by the chamber of commerce and the A. C. McClurg Company, the wholesaler through which the Bryant Library obtained most of its books. Girls from the high school Home Economics Club served refreshments they had made. Minnie Mullin and Dr. and Mrs. Claude Lewis visited, and recalled memories of the old library; and the *Herald* put a picture of the library on its front page that day.

Despite the fact that televisions were increasingly invading the living rooms of Sauk Centre homes at mid-decade, circulation at the Bryant Library continued to increase. From 40,964 in 1953 it climbed to 42,667 in 1954. Juveniles accounted for the largest increase, which may explain why Olds continued to push summer reading programs. For 1954 the theme was "The Bookworm," and those enrolled were given a card with a bookworm pictured on it. For every book read the library would add a section to the worm. Seventy-three children signed up, thirty-two finished, and twenty-five even went beyond the fifteen sections required to complete their worm.[85]

Like any good librarian, Olds persistently warned against book mutilation. One bookmark handed out during Children's Book Week (November 14–20) contained a poem:

> I'm always quiet
> As can be
> When I am at
> The Library.
> I'm always careful
> With each book,
> Especially with
> The one I took.
> I'm always sure
> My book is clean.
> No turned down page
> Or mark is seen!
> I'm always back
> On time with mine,
> So I'll be sure
> To have no fine.

Bad poetry, yes, but a public text nonetheless that delivered an important lesson in good citizenship—a civic responsibility that the Bryant Library had been fulfilling in multiple ways for generations. In 1955, library circulation increased again; fiction accounted for two-thirds of the total. In late July, Olds resigned to take a position in Coleraine, Minnesota.[86] By that time the Bryant Library was so embedded in Sauk Centre's local culture that no one questioned its value to the community as a public place and as a source of stories and information.

CHAPTER TWO

A Credit to the Place

The Sage Public Library of Osage, Iowa

On January 9, 1871, seven prominent men of Osage, Iowa, gathered at the Center School House "to establish a Library of general reading matter suitable for persons of all occupations and professions." To raise money, members pledged that capital stock should "not be less than 100 shares nor more than 500 shares of $5.00 each." An executive committee was charged to select books and magazine subscriptions, and to select a librarian to care for and catalog the collection. Each shareholder had a vote and could draw one item from the collection for every share he owned.[1] Charter members of the Osage Library Association (OLA) resembled their counterparts in Sauk Centre, Minnesota. Most had emigrated to Mitchell County, Iowa, from the East to set up banks, practice professions, manage schools, or establish businesses essential to rural populations. Osage was settled largely by families "of the calculating and conservative character," the *Osage News* noted. OLA board members came from this group. All were Protestant men, and most were Republican, with many Civil War veterans and GAR members.[2]

On May 27, 1872, the Osage city council appointed a committee of "old settlers" to meet "on his arrival" Orrin Sage, a wealthy Ware, Massachusetts, banker who five years earlier donated a bell for Osage's Congregational church.[3] In 1856 Sage had worked through Iowa agents to purchase a Mitchell County plat. "Old settlers" agreed to name the town Osage, after Sage, and on April 14 voted to make Osage the county seat. Within three years all the land in the plat was sold. In 1856 Osage boasted a population near fifteen hundred. In 1869 the Illinois Central Railroad connected Osage to the outside world. A year later, a Women's Christian Temperance Union (WCTU) chapter formed the First Congregational Church; about the same time Hamlin Garland's family moved there when his father became elevator manager for a local Grange organization.[4]

It is not known what transpired at the 1872 meeting between Sage and the "old settlers," but subsequent events suggest that several OLA leaders discussed a lack of good books in town and suitable space for a library. In his autobiographical *Son of the Middle Border*, Hamlin Garland noted that McGuffey Readers he used "were almost the only counterchecks" to sensational novels, but that as a lad he regularly traded scores of "Beadle's Dime Novels" and borrowed twenty-five to thirty numbers of the Seaside Library series from a harvest hand his father hired. "The pleasure I took in these tales should fill me with shame, but it doesn't—I rejoice in the memory of it."[5]

The OLA had none of these novels. Perhaps that explains why it sold only eight shares in two years. To generate more revenue it allowed non-share-holders to use the collection "by depositing with the Librarian the retail price of the books they wish together with fifteen cents for reading of the same." Better news came in June 1873, however, when Orrin Sage wrote to the Osage city council that he was prepared to deed the city 669 acres he owned in Missouri if Osage agreed to establish a "Public Library" to increase "the intelligence" and address "the moral and religious welfare" of "all Osage inhabitants."[6] Although town fathers welcomed the offer, they could not act immediately. First they had to find a site, which they hoped sales of the Missouri property would cover. In the interim the OLA continued to struggle. But Sage proved impatient. "Have you ever made an estimate of the building which you propose to put up for a Library?," he wrote in December. "I may be disposed [to help]," he said.

In January 1874 the mayor of Osage appointed a committee to find a site. A month later the committee recommended a two-story building; the "Sage Public Library" would be located on the second floor, and the first would be rented to generate library revenue. On March 11, Sage offered $2,500 to help purchase the property. The city council happily accepted, then authorized a special election to discern "the expediency of forming and maintaining a free public library." The vote was sixty-five for, four against. (Women, children, and propertyless men could not vote.) As a result, the Sage became the second tax-supported free public library in Iowa under an 1872 state law.[7]

Construction began that summer. In January 1875, the city council ap-

2. Sage Public Library, Osage, Iowa, 1960s. From "Little Bird Watchers"
by David Rottinghaus. Used by permission of the artist.

pointed a committee to draft rules for the "Free Library of Osage." On
January 2, Orrin Sage sent a copy of the Ware (MA) Library Association
catalog. "It is not to give information of what you ought to have in your
library. It is a memorandum for you and those interested to select from if
you think proper." That same month the Chicago newspaper *Inter Ocean*
carried a story about Sage's gifts to the town that bore his name. "They are
not a class to prosecute a work of this kind in a slipshod style. They have a
good deal of literary taste, culture, and enterprise, and will not stop short
of a splendid library."[8]

The Osage that the *Inter Ocean* described in 1876 had experienced considerable growth after 1856. It was still a "prairie city" with few manu-
facturers, but it already had several notable educational institutions. The
Union School provided elementary education for all Osage children. The
Cedar Valley Seminary had been open for thirteen years, and boasted a
student body of one hundred, with nine hundred alumni. In addition to
the library building and many "elegant dwellings," three new structures
were planned for Osage's Main Street that year. The *Winnebago (IA) Summit* complimented Osage on having no saloons, "which speaks well for the
refinement and morality of the people." Hamlin Garland later recalled a

vibrant town supporting county fairs, Fourth of July celebrations, itinerant circuses and—especially after an opera house opened in 1879—scores of traveling shows and lecturers.[9]

The new Sage Public Library was not the only place where citizens could access print. "The reading room of the Y.M.C.A. over Scofield & Stacy's store is well patronized," the *Mitchell County Press* reported in 1879. It was also reported that H. Z. Shipherd had "opened [in his store] a new library of late works, which he will rent on favorable terms." At his drugstore J. F. Dailey offered "more school books than all the other book stores in the county put together." Frank Atherton (brother of Postmaster T. H. Atherton, also a *Mitchell County Press* editor) operated "a first class stationery stand" at the post office, which in most small midwestern towns was a heavily visited community site. Two local Grange libraries routinely purchased books in bulk from Atherton. "Just received," he announced in December 1877, "100 volumes of popular books; an assortment of over 200 volumes to select from." Among them were works by Sir Walter Scott, Charles Dickens, Charlotte Bronte, Mary J. Holmes, May Agnes Fleming, and E. D. E. N. Southworth, and—for "young people of all ages"—Oliver Optic books, titles in the Cozy Nook series and the Jack Hazard series, and the "Famous Ballantyne Land Stories." Likely it was here that Hamlin Garland and his friends bought "Beadle Dime Novels."

The town was also served by two newspapers, the *Osage News* and the *Mitchell County Press*. "The citizens wisely regard it as their first duty to take a county paper," the *Inter Ocean* noted. Pesky traveling salesmen also regularly visited. "Don't purchase books of agents who travel around the community," the *Press* warned. "People frequently subscribe for a costly book that they do not need or want, simply to get rid of the impudent agent." On the other hand, an American Bible Society agent complained in January 1884 that Mitchell County subscribers still owed $422.97 for Bibles purchased the previous year. Finally, like those in Sauk Centre, Osage churches disseminated their own printed materials.[10] In the midst of this active culture of print the Sage Public Library began carving out its own niche.

On May 6, 1876, the city council met in newly completed "Library Rooms" to appoint a committee "to canvass the town for funds to be used in purchasing books, periodicals, etc., to be placed in the reading room," and also to confer with OLA stockholders about "turning over their stock in the town."

On May 15 the committee reported that a "Miss Williams" had agreed to monitor the library. In August the council proposed a one-mill tax "for the maintenance of a public library." The measure carried unanimously.[11]

A CREDIT TO THE PLACE

On December 18, the Sage Public Library opened, as planned, on the second floor of a two-story structure located on Main Street. The building cost $5,700; Orrin Sage had contributed $2,500. A city council library committee reported that the OLA had donated its collection, of which 210 books were "fit for circulation," an additional fifty said to be worth rebinding, and the remainder "unfit for circulation and of no value." One by one the council then approved "Library Rules." The library would be open Saturdays, 3:00–9:00 P.M., and—provided they gave "satisfactory security"—any Osage resident might "draw books from the Library." All borrowers would need a library card to check out books. Cardholders could draw one book per week, renewable if not in demand. Reference works would not circulate. Delinquent borrowers were to be fined ten cents per week, and could not check out books until all fines were paid. Anyone writing in or injuring a book was responsible for paying for its replacement. Finally, "the use of tobacco and all conversation and other conduct not consistent with quiet and orderly use of the Library Room [were] prohibited." After the council unanimously adopted all the rules, it appointed Naomi Moran as librarian (what happened to "Miss Williams" is not known) and authorized a salary of one dollar "for each day the Library was kept open." It also instructed the mayor to collect six month's rent from the first-floor tenant. Finally, the council authorized its library committee to "report a list of $250 worth of books for the Library, for the approval of the Council."[12]

The *Mitchell County Press* was lukewarm about council action. First, OLA books, it argued, were "generally not of the most valuable and popular class." Second, the $250 the council authorized to buy new books "will not make a library at all credible for a city of this size." The only immediate solution, the *Press* concluded, was in the hands of Osage citizens. "There are probably fifteen hundred books in the city that could well be spared and given" to the library, it said. "The people . . . can make the Library a credit to the place." Two months later, the *Press* announced that the Sage Library had received "a large addition . . . of new books embracing latest works by popular authors."[13] That the *Press* repeatedly used the word "popular" to describe works it considered most valuable for a public library sent a clear message to its readers about appropriate community literary standards. But those standards were nonetheless mediated with other community groups. While members of the Osage chapter of the WCTU happily hosted library benefits, elsewhere in Iowa WCTU chapters routinely monitored local stores for copies of *Police News*. In April the *Press* announced, "the public library is well patronized by all classes of our citizens."[14]

As long as the Sage Library was not causing problems and as long as the building's first floor was drawing rent, the city council's library committee saw no need to push the library as a more active force in Osage's cultural activities. As council members saw it, culture surrounded them—literary events at the Cedar Valley Seminary, plays and musical presentations at the new opera house, and organizations like the Shakespearean Club (established in 1881 by local women), the local Comet Band, and the Osage Lecture Association. In March 1878, for example, Elizabeth Cady Stanton gave a lecture entitled "Our Girls" to "a splendid audience" at the Congregational church. The Sage Library existed within this mix of forces, and presented Osage with another choice—"desirable" books readily available and a library functioning as another symbol of local culture. Once a year the library committee presented the whole city council with a list of recommended books, and the council regularly authorized the committee to select from it $250 worth of books "as will please the taste of all."[15]

In 1887 not only did the Sage Library get new bookcases, a coat of paint, and 250 new books, it also got a new librarian. By this time the librarian position had become a political football. It once took the council forty-eight tries before successfully electing a librarian. Every election provided opportunity, and perhaps cause, for the city council library committee to appoint a new librarian whose loyalties seemed more important to a majority in power than did any professional expertise. In a contest between three candidates, Mollie Atherton—from the same family as T. H. and Frank Atherton—was appointed librarian on April 5, 1887. Her selection provoked comment from the *Osage News* about potential conflict of interest, since on occasion the library purchased books from Frank Atherton's post office store. The *Press* responded immediately. Mollie Atherton was just as qualified as her predecessor, it said. The *Press* did not say why her predecessor was not rehired. Atherton resigned in October, however, and was replaced by Mrs. L. M. Abbott. At the time Osage's population was twenty-five hundred, and Mitchell County's was fifteen thousand; the rural environs were largely populated with hard-working German, Norwegian, Bohemian, and Irish immigrants, who were transforming the county from grain to livestock and dairy production. Although Osage had been served by a north–south Illinois Central line since 1869, in 1890 it also welcomed an east–west Winona & Southwestern line.[16]

That the Sage Library had a low community profile in 1888 was obvious from a January 12 *Press* editorial on church lending libraries. At the time, Osage churches represented six denominations—Methodist Episcopal, Free Methodist, Roman Catholic, Baptist, Universalist, and Congregationalist —all making efforts to engage the interest of their youth. "Young people will read whatever they can lay their hands on," the *Press* commented. "Should it not be a pleasure as well as a duty to put good reading in their way?" Ironically, the *Press* made no mention of other agents in the local culture of print, including the Sage Library, the YMCA reading room, Mitchell County's Grange libraries, the recently opened Osage Public School Library, or the book stocks of retailers like Dailey's Drugstore or Atherton's post office book and stationery store, where young people like Hamlin Garland obtained their series fiction. Although the *Press* editors seemed much interested in getting young people to read, they did not look to the Sage Library as a conduit. That same month Mattie Powers replaced Mrs. L. M. Abbott as librarian.[17]

Powers lasted until the next council election, when Mary Pearson was appointed. In September 1889 Pearson presented the council with the Sage Library's first-ever annual report. She noted that fifty new volumes had been added and that total circulation for the year was 435, only 45 of which were renewals. Compared to Sauk Centre's Bryant Library in 1889 (1,044 volumes; 7,484 circulation), these statistics were dismally low. A month later "literary ladies" of the town's fourth ward formed a "reading circle" to meet weekly "and discuss everything from a literary point of view." When the *Press* announced the formation of "the Carey Chautauqua Reading Circle," however, it made no mention of the Sage Library.[18]

That the librarian position was so openly political may explain the Sage Library's low profile in Osage cultural activities. If librarians participated in such organizations as the Osage Lecture Association, the Shakespeareans, or the Carey Chautauqua Reading Circle, they maintained a low profile. Examples of lost opportunities abound. In November 1890, the *Press* announced a Young People's Literary Society. Again, it made no mention of the Sage Library, despite the fact that the city council's library committee had expressed "an urgent and special need of improving and replenishing the City library, . . . especially [for] the young people who desire to avail themselves of the privileges of a good library." The council responded to its library committee's report by increasing the library's annual acquisitions budget from $250 to $300.

In February 1893, the Sage Library showed signs of improvement. The council library committee chairman, Cedar Valley Seminary Principal Alonzo Abernethy, authorized a new printed catalog. A month later Mayor J. W. Annis reported his belief to the city council that the library was "in good condition," but criticized it for not spending "more money for new books." Although the council then authorized an additional $90 to the annual acquisitions budget, Abernethy and Annis had put their colleagues on notice—they thought the library was not getting adequate funding. In 1891 the Sage Library was one of only fifteen Iowa public libraries supported by local taxes, but a public library movement was building momentum. The Iowa Library Association (ILA), established in 1890, the Iowa Federation of Women's Clubs (IFWC), established in 1893 with a "Library Committee" as its first standing committee, the State Teachers Association, and several other groups were lobbying for statewide legislation to establish separate boards of trustees for local public libraries. In May 1893 Abernethy and Annis argued that because the city council had been borrowing from interest on the library fund for years, it owed the Sage Library one thousand dollars plus 6 percent interest. At the very least, Abernethy and Annis said, the council needed to credit these sums to the library.[19]

The legislation anticipated in 1893 became reality in 1894. In February 1895, Mayor Annis appointed a Sage Library board of trustees to comply with the new law that required nine-member boards to control each public library and its funds, appoint librarians, select and purchase books, craft all regulations, and submit annual reports. Receiving appointments were Alonzo Abernethy, Dr. W. H. Gable, Clarinda Hitchcock, local home builder Oliver Cole, Laura Eaton (the mayor's sister and wife of three-time mayor W. L. Eaton), real estate developer William Moss, Amelia Lohr (whose father had been a councilman in 1874 when Osage had accepted Orrin Sage's offer), local businessman Albert W. Tallman (an OLA charter member), and Frances Owen.[20]

Four women and five men made up the first Sage Library board. All were Protestant (most Congregational); two were Democrats, seven were Republicans; all were connected to their community through a network of organizations and associations. Through their membership in women's groups associated with the IFWC and its library committee, Eaton, Hitchcock, Lohr, and Owen were learning how to remake their local public library into an active agent for change. Wives of male trustees were part of these same organizations and probably echoed these sentiments at the family dinner table and Sunday morning church services. Together, trustees represented a subset of Osage's leading families. At their initial meeting they elected Eaton president and Hitchcock secretary. Both had ties to the women's suffrage movement, the Shakespeareans (which had joined the IFWC), and the Women's Christian Temperance Union (Osage boasted the largest chapter in the state). Two weeks later trustees approved an organizational structure to include four standing committees: Buildings, Finance, Administration, and Books. The last would "select and recommend books and periodicals for the library and its reading room." To that committee President Eaton appointed Abernethy, Hitchcock, Lohr, and Cole. The board also unanimously selected as librarian Augusta Hitchcock, daughter of trustee Clarinda Hitchcock.[21]

On April 8, 1895, the Committee on Books reported that the Sage Library needed three "consulting and reading tables" and four dozen chairs, book stacks to hold one thousand volumes, and "sufficient light" so "that books may be read in any part." The library also needed a magazine rack for fifty periodicals, the committee said, a copy of the latest edition of *Dewey Decimal Classification*, and subscriptions to *Inter Ocean, Youth's Companion, North American Review, Atlantic Monthly, Cosmopolitan, Review of Reviews, Chautauquan, Literary Digest, Forum, Harper's Weekly, Public Opinion, Scientific American*, the *Woman's Journal, Arena*, and the *Midland Monthly*. When the committee added *St. Nicholas* and *Harper's Young People* to the list a week later, it showed that the Sage Library board was going to address the reading needs and desires of Osage's young people.[22]

To highlight changes under the new board, a public opening was held at the library in August. Visitors could access the building from Main Street on a new cement sidewalk, and once inside they could view newly installed electric lights. In November, the *Press* assessed the changes. "The visitor to the library at almost any hour during the week will usually find a number of people occupying the reading room. The young people go there to read the young people's magazines and newspapers. Books are also taken out daily for home reading in increasing numbers."[23]

At its November meeting the board's book committee reported that it had "made a list of books and obtained prices" from the American Baptist Society, Montgomery Ward, and the A. C. McClurg Company of Chicago. After some discussion trustees placed an order with McClurg (at the time the largest book wholesaler in the Midwest). By going through McClurg, adopting the Dewey Decimal Classification system, and purchasing accessions books, a circulation system, and a public card catalog from the Library Bureau (a library supplies company favored by library leaders), Sage Library trustees modeled most practices advocated by library professionals, but not all of them. Although they had acquired an ALA catalog in 1894, trustees did not allow it to dictate selection. In December 1897, the *Press* reported that "the Sage Library has recently added $100 worth of new books by the latest popular authors."

Thereafter, business around the Sage Library assumed a routine. News items about it appeared regularly in local newspapers, tidbits like this: "A number of new books, chiefly in the line of fiction, have been added to the library." Readers soon came to recognize what that meant: popular fiction, just what they wanted. In June 1898 the board extended hours greatly— to 2:00–6:00 P.M. and 7:00–9:00 P.M. daily, except Sundays. In 1899 it added to its subscription list two local newspapers plus the *Chicago Daily Record*, and periodicals *Popular Science Monthly, Ladies Home Journal, Scribner's, McClure's, Saturday Evening Post*, and *Public Libraries*, the latter a Library Bureau publication loaded with practical information specifically intended for small public libraries in the Midwest. That summer Hitchcock resigned. To replace her, trustees selected Ella Stacy, a Mitchell County resident since 1856, an alumna of Cedar Valley Seminary, and a Congregationalist "greatly devoted to her church."[24]

Soon thereafter the *Press* gave Stacy a regular column titled "Sage Library Notes." On January 4, 1900, she reported that 1,142 people had visited the reading room the previous year and for the three months ending Saturday, December 30, the library had loaned 2,769 books (roughly equal to the Bryant Library's per capita circulation during the same period in Sauk Centre, Minnesota). But Stacy did not select books. In February the Sage Library board agreed to purchase thirty from a list that Clarinda

Hitchcock had generated. In her May *Press* column, Stacy noted that the library owned copies of "the seven most popular books quoted in all late book reviews."[25] As in Sauk Centre, Osage's public library was connecting local users to a national culture of print, mostly through popular fiction.

Public library services that Stacy and her board implemented were increasingly affected by an emerging library profession. Much of this influence was overt. In Iowa, for example, the Sage Library was one of forty-eight public libraries in 1900—certainly a critical mass to draw the attention of the library profession and state government. With pressure from groups like the IFWC, the ILA, local and state newspapers, and periodicals like *Public Libraries* and *Midland Monthly*—all seeing in public libraries solutions to problems variously brought by immigration, urbanization, and industrialization that they perceived as particularly manifest in a restless and undisciplined youth—the Iowa legislature established the Iowa Library Commission (ILC). From its beginnings the ILC advocated for public libraries by pushing for the creation of new ones, identifying the best means to administer and organize them, and especially to help them select books—the right books. At the time, most Iowans involved in public library advocacy possessed ideologies of reading that argued that good books effected good behavior and bad books led to bad behavior. But determining the difference between "good" and "bad" books was not a science, nor a task that community leaders would willingly relinquish to outsiders.

Along with the ILC came the *Bulletin of the Iowa Library Commission* (*BILC*), a quarterly publication delivered free to all Iowa public libraries and their trustees. When Ella Stacy opened her copy in April 1902, she saw an article entitled "Fiction in Public Libraries" that quoted several library authorities. "A free library cannot supply the demand of current novels 'hot from the press,'" argued Librarian of Congress Herbert Putnam. "The latest novel is not necessarily entitled to a place in the free public library because it is popular," said Iowa State Librarian Johnson Brigham. "I have been thinking that it might be a good plan, as we all realize where this flow of fiction is leading us, if the libraries would say, 'We will buy no work of fiction until it is at least a year old,'" suggested library philanthropist Andrew Carnegie. The same issue of the *BILC* carried another article suggesting that one solution to demand for popular fiction was the practice of maintaining a rental collection.[26] Herbert Putnam, Johnson Brigham,

Andrew Carnegie, and the *BILC* notwithstanding, the Sage Library unapologetically continued to circulate mostly popular fiction.

In 1900, the Sage Library board took no public notice of recently passed state legislation mandating that every Iowa public school have a library. Osage already had a school library. That this school library existed—by this time a high school library in a high school building—and was receiving community support helps explain why the Sage Library did not participate in formal education the way the Bryant Library and other small midwestern public libraries did. It may also explain why the Sage Library trustees and librarians concentrated so easily on popular fiction. In her December 19 "Sage Library Notes" column, Stacy noted that "the list of fiction is up to date" and that circulation for November 1900 had been 1,285, or 364 more than the previous November.[27]

But the drumbeat against popular fiction continued. Waterloo's J. M. Brainard wrote to the *BILC*: "The deplorable squandering of public money to provide the public with a free fiction pasturage, and the prominence that the current popular fiction has assumed in public libraries, are deplored by every librarian and true lover of literature, but they alone are unable to break the chains that bind them to this 'body of death.'" Only public library trustees could address this problem, and Brainard called on all to pledge "not to buy any book of fiction for six months after its publication."[28] What Brainard saw as a problem, however, Sage Library users saw as an essential service.

In September 1906, the *BILC* carried a story about books that were "never in" (always checked out), noting a propensity for those running some Iowa public libraries to satisfy immediate demand instead of stocking multiple copies of books that "have stood the test of time." In the latter category it mentioned Louisa May Alcott's *Little Women* and *Little Men*, Lewis Carroll's *Alice's Adventures in Wonderland*, and Harriet Beecher Stowe's *Uncle Tom's Cabin*. "If a book is really good and you know it is good and the people want it," the *BILC* concluded, "why not duplicate, yes, *multiply*?" In 1906 the Sage Library had six copies of *Little Women*, five of *Alice in Wonderland*, and five of *Uncle Tom's Cabin*. A month later the *Mitchell County Press* ran an ad for Cromer's Store. "Books, hundreds just opened now on sale at popular prices," it announced. "We also have 100 Alger books for boys and new stories for girls." On that date the Sage Library had twenty-four Horatio Alger books on its shelves. But up-to-date, "useful" information was also a priority. In April 1907, the Sage Library purchased J. Nelson Larned's eight-volume *History for Ready Reference* (1901); in November it bought the *Encyclopedia Americana*. Thus, for Osage youth, in 1907 the Sage stocked titles considered "best" by library professionals backed by the nation's literary establishment; popular series fiction; and sources of ready reference information that supported formal education's "official knowledge"—all evidence of a civic institution negotiating a set of demands from inside and outside the community to satisfy patrons whose use was largely voluntary.[29]

CARNEGIE BUILDING

In February 1903, Sage Library trustees appointed a committee "to secure money from the Carnegie fund for the erection of a new library building." A month later, Alonzo Abernethy wrote to Carnegie that although Osage had "for many years" had a public library, it was not well located. "We can probably secure a central and choice location 100 × 100 feet," he wrote, "with streets on two sides and alley on a third side if we can secure the means to erect a good fireproof building."[30] Abernethy's letter was not a community secret; in April the *Mitchell County Press* surmised that if the library could sell its Missouri land, it could generate an annual income between $1,500 and $1,800, which "would enable us to secure $18,000 or $20,000 from the Carnegie fund." Unbeknown to the *Press*, however, Carnegie had already responded. If Osage agreed to "maintain a Free Public Library at . . . One Thousand Dollars a year and provide a suitable site for the building," James Bertram wrote, "Mr. Carnegie will be pleased to furnish Ten Thousand Dollars."[31] Although trustees now had a commitment from Carnegie, they were disappointed with the amount and decided to press for $15,000. In Iowa there was precedent. Davenport had convinced Carnegie to increase his gift from $50,000 to $75,000, and Dubuque had convinced him to increase a $50,000 gift to $60,000. On April 23 the city council resolved "to support a library with a two mill tax that would annually yield $1,500," to which, Abernethy wrote Carnegie the next day, would be added $200 rental charges from the old building and $1,000 from interest on sale of the Missouri land.[32]

Weeks passed with no answer and on June 3 Abernethy wrote to Carnegie again. "Our citizens have come to take quite an intense interest in the matter, and I am waylaid about every time I appear on Main Street to learn what reply I have received," he said. "Prominent citizens," he noted, had also told him to mention that Osage had banished saloons in 1876 because "such a fact would commend itself to you as a good place for a library."[33] Abernethy forwarded to Carnegie diagrams showing that all available space in the current building was occupied by shelves "already well filled." In addition, he told Carnegie, the building housing the second-floor library could be reached "only through a dark and narrow stairway of twenty steps from the street" and was located next to a steam laundry "with its smoke stack, its noise, and escaping steam a few feet only from the rear corner of the building." The location made library quarters especially hot and uncomfortable during the summer. Finally, Abernethy noted, the building did not have space to accommodate other needs, including County Historical Society collections and an art gallery. But Abernethy's efforts failed; Carnegie refused to grant $15,000. At the same time, however, trustees still had not accepted his original offer of $10,000. On December 18, Abernethy again wrote to Carnegie "to renew our application," again asking for $15,000. Carnegie did not respond.[34]

In December 1904 the board tried to pressure Carnegie. When Iowa's Senator William B. Allison visited Osage that month, trustees asked his help. "Our people were much disappointed that our application was not granted," Abernethy told Allison, "especially as Mr. Carnegie had so generously responded to like applications from all parts of the state." Although Allison asked him to reconsider, Carnegie would not budge. The *Osage News* worried over trustee intransigence. "Let the people do the proper act by accepting this magnanimous offer immediately," it argued. "Here is the opportunity for those who have passed beyond school age to secure the advantages of advanced education without extra expense. It is the poor man's college, and its influence cannot be calculated."[35]

Finally the board buckled. Although trustees voted unanimously to accept the gift the day after the *News* editorial, they also agreed "that a further effort be made to have Mr. Carnegie add $5,000 to the donation." Within the week Allison wrote another letter to Carnegie ("it is a little difficult to build a fireproof building of approved architecture with the small sum," he noted), and days later Iowa's other senator, J. P. Dolliver, endorsed Allison's request, but to no avail. On April 24, 1905, Bertram responded: Carnegie "thinks that $10,000 is enough to erect an adequate library building for the people of Osage."[36]

Although the board accepted Carnegie's offer, Osage still had not settled on a site. On May 17 the *Press* reported, "a prominent citizen of Osage is considering the donation of a building site." It was later learned that W. L. Eaton, a local lawyer and politician, was being pressed by his wife Laura (Sage Library board president from 1895 to 1901) to donate a corner lot next to the courthouse square. But Eaton "refused to confer" with a library board committee, the *Press* said. Another possibility was the "Barrett corner" on Main and Eighth Street. Board minutes noted that members were "having considerable difficulty deciding on a site." Votes on choices became a consistent 4–3, too close to force a decision, trustees concluded. The *Mitchell Country Press* expressed frustration. "The summer is being wasted. What a disgraceful business it has been!" Two weeks later the *Press* attributed the board's indecision to "outside pressure . . . undertaken to force the selection of an east location. . . . We ought to get together at once and agree upon any suitable site that can be secured without expense to the city," the *Press* concluded. "If this cannot be done without taxing the people, the offer of Mr. Carnegie should be declined."[37]

Months went by without any action. Some hope arose in March 1906 when the Osage Women's Relief Corps chapter offered land and an additional $3,000 for a building if the library board gave "perpetual use of a story of said building . . . for a G.A.R. and W.R.C. Memorial Hall." The board agreed and sent notice to the council. In June, however, the council refused because it feared perpetual commitments. In protest, trustees Abernethy and Clara Merrill resigned. To make matters worse, the *Press* ran a July 4 editorial noting that several midwestern communities had accepted Carnegie grants but had been subsequently unable to meet the annual allocations he required. "As a result, the property has reverted to Mr. Carnegie. The taxpayers cannot help but feel elated that such a library project was not carried out in Osage." At the moment, the *Press* said, Osage had higher priorities. "The present building will answer for all purposes until after the city has given us that which is of more vital importance— a sewerage system."[38]

In July 1906, Ella Stacy retired. To succeed her, trustees chose local high school graduate Etta Westlake. Board members "are pleased to be able to fill the position," the *Press* reported, "by one whom it is thought will be entirely capable." It was hardly a ringing endorsement. Westlake was not a member of Osage's leading families, and had no library training. In

May 1909, the *Press* announced that the public library had been "wonderfully improved" by recent changes, including the construction of a "little alcove" out of a corner closet to create "a cozy nook for the children's books and reading table," but the quest for a Carnegie building continued to languish.[39]

In September 1909, trustees tried to reopen the issue. They asked the city council to "act without delay" on its four-year-old resolution to fund the library at $1,500 per year, but also pledged that the board would be "fully satisfied" with any location the council selected. Only Charles Sweney —an OLA charter member—disagreed. In October the board president appointed W. H. Gable, Herbert La Rue, and George Genung to a committee to represent the library at a council meeting considering a site. To Genung and La Rue, location was secondary to obtaining Carnegie funds. In this sentiment they found allies with two other recent appointees to the board, Grace Scofield and Fred Moss. "The elimination of four firebrands, two for and two against," local historian Charles Wells later wrote, "had reduced the torrid heat at board meetings."[40]

The committee met with the council on October 11. A lack of room and a "great increase" in use mandated action, they argued. In addition, Carnegie was getting old, "and may die before Osage is ready to take advantage of his offer," they said, "if indeed it still holds good." Some council members suggested that Carnegie's gift represented "tainted money." Others thought that accepting it "was not honoring the memory of Orrin Sage, who gave, in proportion to his wealth, a great deal more than Carnegie is giving." Still others worried that Osage could not afford to subsidize the library and also pave Main Street. But "the library may still be called the Sage Library," committee members responded. To move the issue along, the council resolved to purchase a site and to first approach several parties owning desirable lots. "Osage may be assured that they have a council that will do more than talk," the *Press* concluded, "and the prospects are bright for both paving and a new library."[41] At a meeting three weeks later the council agonized over the site. Had the matter been brought to their attention earlier, some argued, they might have proposed a tax to purchase a lot and included it in a levy for that year. Now, however, they could only foresee "trouble ahead" over legal points that would be "hard to straighten." "The new library looks farther away than before," the *Press* noted. The *Osage News* expressed hope that "the library should be as near the center of town as possible. We also think it should be where it will be seen by those who visit the town."[42]

On November 16, 1909, La Rue reported to trustees that the city had agreed to levy a tax "not to exceed one mill each year" until the site was paid, but because the council was wary of its legal right to buy a site, council members recommended that trustees "use powers given them by the law" to purchase property. Trustees then decided to consult the city attorney to clarify the board's authority to purchase land. The board president also appointed a committee "to investigate the question of a library site, get prices &c., and report at the next meeting." At the council meeting the next evening members endorsed the board's plan of action. "The library board will probably choose a site immediately," the *Press* reported. At its November 29 meeting, the board considered two properties, the Barrett site for $2,000, and another site more distant from the town center for $1,400. "Board voted unanimously for the Barrett site."[43]

After trustees heard that the city attorney had negotiated a ninety-day option on the Barrett property, Sweney resigned in protest. Two days later—nearly seven years after Alonzo Abernethy first wrote to Carnegie —Sage Library trustees again contacted him. "We can now secure a fine piece of land, and are prepared to go on with the project and write you at this time to ascertain if your offer is still open." Days later Carnegie said yes. Under the headline "Library and Paving Assured," the *Press* summarized a January council meeting at which library trustees announced that they offered $2,000 for the Barrett site, but because of legal questions they asked the city to purchase it jointly with the library. The council agreed. When trustees presented the mayor with a contract for joint purchase of the property, he signed it immediately. "It now appears that the library men will have clear sailing and may go forward as rapidly as they wish," the *Press* reported. "A beautiful library building on that corner will improve the appearance of Main Street vastly."[44]

In March trustees hired an architect. A month later they solicited construction bids. By June trustees had selected a Mason City construction company for the work. "The new Sage-Carnegie Library [its official name] is rising rapidly into the shape of a beautiful building," the *Press* reported July 20. "Foundations, steps and sills have been laid and it will be ready for the important event of laying the cornerstone next Friday." Trustees asked the local Masonic Lodge to conduct the ceremony (almost all male trustees were members). Seated on the dais were librarian Etta Westlake, members of the library board and city council, and women of the local Eastern Star chapter. The Knights of Pythias band played while Masons marched in. The board president introduced a local judge, who gave a speech "dwelling on the importance of the public library." Thereafter a female choir sang Masonic hymns, and Masons laid the cornerstone. Enclosed were Masonic lodge records, library records, and the December 20, 1907, souvenir edition of the *Mitchell County Press* that contained early histories of the library, town, prominent businesses and people, and chief points of interest. Local Masons then tested the stone, found it to be "square, level and plumb, and laid in accordance with the rules of our ancient craft. Then the corn, the wine and the oil, symbols of peace and plenty were scattered upon the stone."

To all communities receiving a Carnegie grant, where to locate the new public library was a matter of vital importance—it symbolized the cultural value each community placed on this civic institution. In some, like Osage, the decision occasioned much debate. For seven years, debate over the size of a Carnegie grant and location of a building site divided the town. On this occasion, however, the library brought the community together. "The foundation for the splendid library, the rush of work on the new paving, and other evidences of activity about town seem to betoken an awakening in Osage, which is hailed with joy by every wide-awake citizen," the *Press* gushed. "It is a source of deep satisfaction that the public library, the great school for the people, is to be one of the foremost of the new improvements."[45]

Construction progressed more slowly than expected, however. One trustee made carpenters take brass spikes out of supporting timbers and replace them with steel spikes; another made masons tear the brick front off because, the trustee said, the bricks did not line up properly. The structural part of the building, including the tile roof, was completed in October 1910, at which time the contractor announced that the library would be ready in January. In November craftsmen installed and stained the shelving. In December the board authorized purchase of the "Harvard Classics," a fifty-volume set of "best books" offered by a local colporteur for fifty-one dollars.

On November 30 the local high school burned to the ground, and until Osage could build a new one, classes met in the new library and the Congregational church. Not until July 1911 was the Sage-Carnegie Library officially opened, despite the fact that the basement was still unfinished. The board presented the property to the mayor, who accepted on behalf of the city. The local Methodist minister gave "the address of the evening," telling the gathering "of the great value of the public library to the community, its uplifting influence, and inspiration for nobler living." Books were finally moved into the new building on August 1.[46]

At the time the Sage Library ranked second in volumes per capita for Iowa towns of similar size. The library also subscribed to four newspapers (two local) and twenty-five magazines, most of which were indexed in *Readers' Guide.*[47] Westlake also wrote a monthly *Mitchell County Press* column to let "people know what we have in our public library and to encourage the love of good reading among all ages." In these columns Westlake did not echo the attitude of the professional library community toward series fiction. Instead she promoted "good books" largely by replicating annotations in *Booklist* and ALA catalogs. Her strong Congregationalist background also showed in frequent references to the Bible and reading recommendations for holidays like Christmas and Easter.[48]

The town that gave birth to the Osage Library Association in 1871 was significantly different in 1911. "A resident wasn't an old-timer," one citizen noted, "unless he was here before the Civil War." Several years earlier, local women's clubs had opened a "Rest Room" at the National Bank to accommodate farmwives on their Saturday trips into town (many club members were married to professionals who benefited from these visits), and like small towns throughout the Midwest, Saturday evenings in Osage buzzed with activity. Out on Main Street visitors could frequent businesses with attractive store windows (still no saloons) that made Osage a Mitchell County "trading point," including two department stores, four banks, four drugstores, seven grocers, two tobacconists, three clothing stores, two hardware stores, and a variety of liveries, harness makers, barbershops, and shoemakers. Beyond the business district, scores of sugar maple trees lined Main Street in front of handsome homes, most with "neatly mowed and green lawns," the *Press* noted. "Our residents have enough pride in their city and in their possessions to keep their residences up in first class shape."[49]

Osage boasted five lodges and many church members in 1910, including 411 Methodists, 254 Baptists, 240 Lutherans, 233 Congregationalists, 195

Catholics, 74 Universalists, 18 Christian Scientists, and 8 Jews. Eight pas-senger trains a day served the city. Although ten blocks were paved, Main Street was still lined with hitching posts (only a dozen citizens—mostly doctors—owned automobiles) and at night was illuminated by flaming arc lamps on each corner that crackled and sizzled (and often burned out). A sanitary sewer system was still eight years away. The Sprague Opera House hosted traveling troupes of acrobats, actors, and trained animals. Osage's first theater opened in 1908; the manager announced new films by shout-ing through the front door.[50]

RENA GRAY, LIBRARIAN

Etta Westlake resigned in 1911. To replace her, trustees hired Rena Gray, former *Press* linotype operator. The appointment surprised Gray—she had not applied. Although the *Press* did not identify why she had been selected, it noted: "Miss Gray is in every way qualified for the office. She is a capable and conscientious young woman and can always be depended upon to do her best." Little did board members or the *Press* realize that al-though Gray had no formal library education or college degree, she would occupy the position for the next thirty-six years. Between Westlake's res-ignation and Gray's hiring, the new library became a site for a touring sculpture exhibit by E. Louise Guernsey of Chicago, a former Osage resi-dent who had studied under Lorado Taft. At its December meeting, the board unanimously voted to accept the *Catholic Encyclopedia* as a gift of the local Roman Catholic parish.[51]

On April 8, 1912, trustees considered a request from the local WCTU chapter. Members were worried that Osage's young men had too much idle time, and hoped Sunday library openings would address the problem. A month later the board complied: the library would open on Sundays from two till five, "for reading purposes only." In her first annual report two months later, Gray noted that visitors had increased from 5,599 in 1910 to 11,351 in the reporting year ending June 30, 1912. In addition, cir-culation had increased from 13,079 in 1911 to 15,268 a year later. The new building was obviously attracting more traffic, despite some competition from libraries at the Cedar Valley Seminary and the Osage High School. And when a second movie theater opened in Osage (on Thanksgiving Day, 1913), circulation still did not suffer.[52]

Not only did the Sage Library have local competition, board members also got plenty of advice from inside and outside the community. "What books do we want in our library?," the county superintendent of schools wrote in the *Press* on October 22, 1913. "It is time that parents realized the great importance of the reading habit upon the minds of their children. Many a boy has taken his first steps towards a criminal career from a bad book." In March, the *BILC* published "How Shall We Select Our Books?" by *Booklist* editor Elva Bascom. Peppered throughout her remarks were references to the ALA catalog, *Booklist*, and the H. W. Wilson *Book Review Digest*, each of which, she said, would help librarians select the best fiction. Six months later the *BILC* listed twenty-four "Boys' Best Books" that Chicago Public Library (CPL) Director Henry Legler thought every public library ought to have. (The Sage Library had them all, many in multiple copies.) Three years earlier Legler had pulled all Horatio Alger and Oliver Optic novels from CPL shelves. "Alger and Optic are just as bad as nine-tenths of the nickel novels now extant," he said. Despite Chicago's lead, however, the Sage Library librarian and trustees pulled none of their Algers and Optics.[53]

While war raged in Europe, the Sage Library seemed barely affected. In March 1914, Shakespeareans offered to finish one of the two lower-level community rooms if they could use it "as a ladies club room." In September the school board offered $20 a month if it could use the other community room "for school purposes." To both proposals the board said yes. Several years later the board also permitted the Social Service Club to use one community room (the Shakespeareans still met there) as "a club room," and allowed clubwomen to shift the Saturday "Rest Room" for farmwives from the National Bank to the library's other community room. When the American Legion Auxiliary organized in 1921, it also held monthly meetings in the library. That the board continued to believe the library was valuable as public space was obvious. Five years earlier it had purchased an adjoining lot "to preserve the symmetry of the grounds and prevent the erection of a building too near the library."[54]

Post–World War I Osage saw few changes at the library. The town's two theaters were drawing larger audiences, Osage citizens supported five public lectures annually between September and April and a series of Chautauqua programs during the summer, there were now 816 telephones to connect local citizens, and use of the Sage Library continued to grow. Although Rena Gray no longer distinguished between fiction and nonfiction in circulation figures she reported to the Iowa Library Commission, columns she ran in the *Press* continued the practice. The former conformed to ILC recommendations that helped disguise the circulation of popular fiction in Iowa public libraries; the latter addressed patron demand, which consistently showed a preference for fiction. The compromise worked for everyone, albeit with subtleties reflected in *Osage News* coverage of the library. On the one hand, the *News* noted that an ILC biennial report showed "that Osage folks rank right up near the top as readers of literature from the public library, there being only six towns in our class in the state having a greater circulation of books per capita than this city." On the other, it connected Osage readers to the nation's literary establishment by noting that the Sage had the ten books a *Literary Digest* readers' poll identified as the best published between 1900 and 1925. Although the *News* never mentioned it, the popular fiction Sage Library patrons wanted most still dominated circulation.[55]

At the beginning of 1922, a Saturday children's story hour was inaugurated, but the Sage Library was not involved. Clubwomen organized it and scheduled it to be held in the old library building. "These story hours are very popular in many towns in this size, and it is believed they will be so here too," the *Press* reported. One session drew over two hundred children. Although the Sage Library did not participate, it continued to function as important community space. In the building's lower level, clubwomen hosted a reception for the Episcopalian Upper Iowa conference. Several years later they began a book club that met in the library's boardroom to discuss titles like Erich Remarque's *All Quiet on the Western Front* (1929). In 1925 they had convinced trustees to place community rooms "at the disposal of the citizens in which to hold committee meetings" when the library was closed.[56]

Rena Gray continued to run acquisitions lists in the local newspapers. In September 1928, the *Osage News* complained that because "people prefer to sit at home and listen to their radios," attendance at local Chautauquas, baseball, basketball, and football games had noticeably decreased. On June 30, 1929, Gray submitted her annual report. Circulation had increased to 39,133 (up from 26,262 five years earlier) and number of visitors to 12,097 (up from 9,928 in 1924). Obviously radio was not having the same effect on library use. The same day that Gray issued her annual report, a local theater introduced talkies to Osage citizens.[57]

Like Sauk Centre, Minnesota, during the Great Depression, Osage was forced to pare funding for its library at the same time that usage was increasing. More and more Osage citizens used the library—and for more purposes than ever before. In January 1930, for example, the WCTU asked the Sage Library to put up "good citizenship" posters. Months later the new Osage Women's Club held meetings in the library's boardroom. The year following county 4-H club leaders met there, as did township representatives of local girls' clubs. And on occasion the Shakespeareans sponsored library teas to raise additional funds.[58] Two weeks after Mitchell County voted to repeal the Eighteenth Amendment in June 1933 (Osage overwhelmingly voted against the repeal), Rena Gray took a 20 percent pay cut.

On April 23, 1936, the *Mitchell County Press News* (the *Press* and *News* merged in 1931) reprinted a *St. Paul (MN) Daily News* story featuring Mrs. Marshall Sweney, a former Osage resident who with her husband operated the First Arcade Bookshop in St. Paul. "Older office women like nice love stories," she said, "younger women prefer mystery stories, the bloodier the better. Nearly all men readers think western stories are good relaxers." After a customer visited her shop several times, she said, she generally knew what he wanted. "It's surprising," she noted, "how it pleases a reader to have you suggest the kind of book he most often reads." In commenting on the story the *Press News* argued: "Don't blame the writers—blame yourselves! The writers are doing it for a living. They've got to write what you'll read or they can't sell their products." Of the thirteen titles Sweney specifically mentioned as popular First Arcade selections, the Sage Library held ten. Gray and her trustees likely empathized. That she was not listed as an ILA member nor the Sage Library as an institutional member probably reflected their relative indifference to ILA and ILC pressure to "elevate" local reading tastes.[59]

In 1940 the Sage Library board still represented Osage's leading families. Most were old-timers used to a particular set of library practices. Unlike in Sauk Centre, however, the board continued to make all acquisition decisions through its "Book Selection Committee." Of Iowa's 212 public libraries, only 25 then employed librarians with professional training. Iowa had not yet implemented a certification process to give librarians professional standing. Although many Iowa libraries availed themselves of New Deal programs to repair books, maintain buildings, and hire staff,

Sage Library records give no indication that its trustees ever applied for or received federal funds. That Osage's founding families (from which the library drew its board membership) were conservative Republicans may explain this.[60] Local community groups continued to use the library. In February 1939, clubwomen moved the children's story hour they had been sponsoring for seventeen years to one of the Sage Library's community rooms. In December, the library was "entirely redecorated inside," the *Press News* reported.[61]

From afar, the nation's library profession pushed for the kinds of change Mynette Lindeloff and Bernice Finnegan had already implemented in Sauk Centre, Minnesota. In March 1940, the *Iowa Library Quarterly* reprinted a letter from an Oregon public library director arguing that "small libraries" needed to incorporate into larger county systems to improve service and efficiency. "Frequently jealousies between communities account for an unwillingness to unite in a larger service," she argued. "These are the things which retard library progress and perplex a state agency." That the *Quarterly* thought the letter "so applicable to the Iowa situation" suggests a set of priorities dictated by a professional agenda that looked upon service priorities manifest in local libraries as something to be corrected. In the 1930s the Sage Library made no effort to extend its service beyond city limits.[62]

As in papers in other small towns in the Midwest, Osage's local newspaper regularly hosted an "open forum" column, and on occasion a regular library user attached himself or herself to the library's cultural authority to pontificate on particular issues. In March of 1940, "C. N. W." cited a Sage Library book he or she had been reading, in order to rail against urbanism, the availability of liquor in the United States, and the need to eliminate the "cleavage between religion and education." Two months later C. N. W. complained that *Press* readers were "absorbing a lot of misleading statements that perhaps we can correct" regarding John Steinbeck's *The Grapes of Wrath*, which the writer then proceeded to attempt to do, despite not having read the book (the Sage Library owned three copies). In December C. N. W. was back at it. This time the self-appointed expert added *Gone with the Wind* to *Grapes of Wrath*, arguing that both were "saturated with pure fiction, plastered with lewd, licentious situations as degrading as the most famous French novels," but complained about still being unable to check out any of the library's three constantly circulating copies of the Steinbeck novel (perhaps because both were being read by members of three newly organized women's book clubs). Other regular patrons reflected stereotypes familiar to all twentieth-century librarians. Rena Gray described one particular patron—"a quite old man, who is forever wishing to know this and that for no good reason; he is no more or less than an old nuisance." But this "nuisance" met no resistance, Gray noted. "All who come to the Osage library, prince or beggar, are received with courtesy and the valuable services of this democratic institution dispensed with a smile."[63] Evidence of yet another community role for the local public library.

The Sage Library assumed a much larger community role during World War II than during World War I. In January 1942, the *Press News* announced a county committee "to collect good books" for soldiers. "Good fiction of all kinds is wanted," it was stated, including "adventure, aviation stories, historical novels, humor, mystery, sports, and westerns." Donations could be left at Osage Cleaners or the Sage Library, or could be picked up by Girl Scouts. Mitchell County eventually sent 1,618 books to Fort Smith in Arkansas. The Sage Library also opened community rooms for Red Cross work, and sold some of the Missouri land given by Orrin Sage decades earlier, using the proceeds to buy war bonds. In late October, Osage hosted an ILA meeting for officials and librarians from Mitchell, Floyd, and Worth Counties to discuss ways libraries could disseminate war information. Representatives of the Red Cross, the Iowa Federation of Women's Clubs, the Iowa Farm Bureau, a regional rationing board, the American Legion (and its auxiliary), and the Works Progress Administration, among others, offered "many many suggestions," the *Press News* noted, "which can be carried out by our local librarian."[64]

Two months after county officials announced that they would join a second campaign in support of the war effort, the *Press News* ran a piece headlined "Sage Library is Doing War Service." After referencing the October ILA meeting, the article noted that the Sage Library was building a file of local servicemen (citizens were invited to donate pictures and biographical data), had acquired federal war bulletins, and was displaying war-related materials in changing monthly exhibits. In addition, titles like Joseph Grew's *Report from Tokyo* (1942), Richard Tregaskis's *Guadalcanal Diary* (1943), Frances C. Coulter's *A Manual of Home Vegetable Gardening* (1942), and juveniles like Helen Nicolay's *MacArthur of Bataan* (1942) and Harley F. Cope's *Serpent of the Seas: The Submarine* (1942) were available for checkout.[65]

In January 1945, the *Iowa Library Quarterly* ran an article entitled "On Defending the Freedom to Read in Libraries." "Every librarian hates censorship," it began, and it went on to report that the ALA Committee on Intellectual Freedom wanted to compile "a record of attempts, successful or not, to interfere with the library's provision of any book or periodical." Librarians across the country were encouraged to communicate with the committee, and assured "we shall not make this information public without your permission." But the Sage Library had nothing to report. For decades old-timers on its board had responded to the reading interests that local patrons clearly demonstrated in the books they checked out, and in the process legitimized the slowly shifting set of community-based literary values reflected in library collections. The library represented a filtering system that Sage patrons had grown to accept and support over the decades, and thus rendered censorship efforts unlikely and largely unnecessary.[66]

The problem that caused the board most concern in 1945—"as usual," minutes recorded—was disagreement between the librarian and the janitor. Three board members "had a talk with the Librarian, trying to impress upon her the fact that it's easier to secure a new Librarian than to find a new Janitor. Results to be seen." When the board met in July, it noted that circulation and library visits were down considerably from previous years. Minutes also record the following: "Miss Gray having filed no application for Librarian, she was called in, and finally consented to take the position for another year."[67]

In January 1947, the board agreed to allow the Osage Junior Chamber of Commerce to establish a youth center in the library's community rooms. Within weeks the "Hep Hide Out"—later renamed the "Teen Tavern"—opened for one night a week, later for two. The *Press News* noted that this was part of a statewide movement to provide recreational facilities for local youth. Planning use of the space was a committee of eight high school students. "It is hoped that the center will be equipped with adequate facilities for dancing, including a juke box, and a milk and Coke bar in addition to several booths placed in the main room." By May, 129 students had become members of the youth center.[68]

Rena Gray got her wish in May 1948. After thirty-six years of service she effectively resigned. She had repeatedly tendered her resignation since 1940, but until 1948 the board had always convinced her to stay "for one more year." "During her long service, Miss Gray has seen many changes," the *Press News* noted. "Demands for library service change with the times. When times are not so good, there is greater demand for books. Periods of prosperity find fewer readers." To succeed Gray, the board chose local resident Mrs. Flora Danforth, who had no library training.[69]

When Danforth was appointed as librarian, Osage had just installed parking meters on three blocks of Main Street. The *Press News* continued to run lists of the library's fiction and nonfiction acquisitions, but other participants in Osage's culture of print also found a place in the local newspaper. The Literary Department of the Osage Women's Club recorded its activities, the Lashbrook Drug Store announced it had school supplies and textbooks on hand, and the local high school had a library where students could complete most of their homework under the supervision of a "teacher-librarian." A 1949 state report in *Iowa Library Quarterly* noted that 64 percent of Mitchell County's residents were effectively without library service, and that only 23 percent of the country's residents had access to the Sage Library.[70] In May 1949 the board sent the librarian's annual report to the city council with a request for increased funding. The library had been operating on the same appropriations for several years but salaries had not kept pace, and revenue generated from the old library building was not sufficient to cover necessary repairs. But the council refused. In December, Teen Tavern managers asked to open more nights per week. For lack of funding the board denied the request. Within a year the Teen Tavern closed.[71]

As librarian, Danforth was not proactive or community-oriented. When the board tried to persuade her to attend a 1950 ILA district meeting, "closing the library if necessary," she declined. Two months later, her annual report showed circulation at 23,075 (6.7 per capita, 2.3 less than the ALA standard at the time). The library's registered borrowers accounted for 23 percent of Osage's population; ALA's standard was 45 percent.[72] When Danforth told the board in March 1951 that she felt "forced to resign her position" (records do not indicate why), the board "decided to advertise for applications in our city papers." On May 1, they hired Mrs. Ingwald T. (Nellie) Iverson, another Osage resident with no formal library training.[73]

More than her predecessor, Iverson projected the Sage Library into the public eye. Columns carrying lists of recent acquisitions appeared weekly in the *Press News*. For National Book Week in November, Iverson told the paper's readers that "the complex problems of the present time" gave Book Week "added significance." She then listed new titles just arrived, including J. D. Salinger's *Catcher in the Rye* (1951). Announcing Salinger was an act of courage: upon publication, the book had been immediately controversial across the country. Iverson also began attending University of Iowa Library School workshops for rural librarians. A November 27, 1952, *Press News* editorial listed forty factors that identified "what makes a good town." Number twelve read: "There's a library with a good collection of 1952 books."[74]

The editorial ran a day after Osage exhibited a bookmobile for rural teachers and librarians sponsored by the Iowa State Education Association (ISEA). "The bookmobile carries the entire collection of over 1,700 titles recommended for purchase in 1951–52 by the ISEA library service," the *Press News* noted. "Many of the same titles found in the bookmobile will also be found in the OHS [Osage High School] Library, since the approved list for high schools is ordered from the ISEA library service each year." That the Sage Library had squandered opportunities to attract local youth was obvious. "The Osage Jaycees are helping to stock the library shelves with funds left over from the Hep Hideout fund, originally set up for the benefit of the high school recreation room in the basement of the Sage Library," the *Press News* reported again.[75]

In May 1953, librarians from the ILA's second district met in Osage; eighty-five representatives from forty-eight libraries attended. By this time the Sage Library was one of 366 Iowa public libraries. Besides discussing common library problems, attendees saw a film "about the importance of a county library," the *Press News* reported. "Several librarians also commented favorably on the number of books in the shelves of the Sage library" (14,414, 1.2 per capita above the ALA standard of 3.0). In an editorial published the next day, the *Press News* noted that one librarian was "greatly surprised" at the Sage Library circulation rate because her library, which served a city of ten thousand, could not match it. "It appears that not only are our citizens progressive, they are also thoughtful," the *Press News* noted. They "take time to read quite a few books each year."[76] Ironically, Sage Library's circulation rate had dropped the previous year to 5.4, 3.6 below the ALA standard, and only one-third the average rate of other Iowa public libraries. But no one in Osage seemed to notice. A decades-long pattern of reading sufficient to sustain community support of the public library had so stabilized the institution that few questioned whether it might be doing better. Board minutes indicate that—except to authorize emergency repairs or replace resigning librarians or board members—trustees had for some time been meeting just once a year, to receive the librarian's annual report and address routine matters.

But pressures to change continued from outside. In June 1953, the ILC warned Iowa public libraries against carrying a balance into the next fiscal year. "The money allotted for library purposes should all be spent if you wish to have as much, or more, next year." The ILC also urged Sage Library trustees to press for more funds, and said that at a city council meeting considering the library budget "one or more of the members of the board should appear in person when presenting this request." A month later ILQ issued a fifteen-question "Self-Rating Sheet" that sought to assess library policy on censorship pressures. "[Have you] read the ALA Library Bill of Rights?," it asked. "[Do you] have a book selection policy?" "[Do you] assist individual readers in purposeful reading?" It is not known if Iverson or anyone on her board responded. Iverson did, however, continue to celebrate National Book Week, conduct tours for local grade school and high school students, and publish recent acquisitions lists in the *Press News*. For 1953–1954 she also reported a circulation of 29,547—up by more than three books per capita from two years previous. Leadership was making a difference.

A photograph the *Press News* published on November 17, 1955, to profile National Book Week showed Nellie Iverson watching Ed Scofield (whose wife had been a Sage Library trustee from 1907 till her death in 1945) read to a five-year-old in the library's children's nook. "The two represent the older and younger generations as the most frequent users of the local library," the caption read. Accompanying the photo, the *Press News* quoted two students. From the outside, said one, the library looked like "a stuffy, cold place. Then one day I went in and got between the covers of a book. I found a real warmth and deep pleasure exists within our city library." The other student said, "It's a refuge from noise, an excellent place in which to study." A *Press News* editorial also declared a direct connection between Iowa public libraries and the fact of the state's high literacy rate, saying that "no state in the nation can equal Iowa in the percentage of its citizens who know how to read and write."[77]

CHAPTER THREE

Tourist Attraction

The Charles H. Moore Library
of Lexington, Michigan

A s the first settlement on the Lake Huron shore north of Port Huron, Michigan, Lexington Township was organized in 1837. At the time Sanilac County was covered with forest; much of the interior was swampland.[1] In 1846 the village opened its first sawmill; shortly thereafter, lumber products were loaded onto sailing vessels called "hookers" off Lexington's three permanent docks. In 1848 Lexington became the county seat, and in 1855 it incorporated. With lake access and productive sawmills processing lumber from surrounding forests, Lexington trade grew. In the 1880s Michigan supplied one-fourth of the nation's lumber, a sum equal to that of the next three states combined. In 1879 a railway linked Detroit to nearby Croswell, and twice a day another train connected Croswell to Lexington. But the arrival of trains came too late to affect the transportation of local lumber. On September 5, 1881, a huge fire in Michigan's Thumb Area all but eliminated the lumber industry there. Thereafter citizens invested in agriculture, and the Lexington docks that formerly transported lumber were loaded with locally produced farm products —especially sugar beets—for shipment south. By that time, most Michigan towns had a few citizens whose wealth had been made by lumber.[2]

In the autumn of 1870, prominent Lexingtonians started a Lexington Library Association. Together they raised $150 for books, and invited citizens to contribute. Few did. Without stable funding, the association failed its second year. Books were eventually stored in a public school, and over time they disappeared. In 1885 prominent women organized the Lexington Atheneum Literary Society. They held monthly meetings at the newly constructed Cadillac House, which, by hosting lectures, political rallies, concerts, and touring minstrel shows, became the village center of social life and the principal site for community involvement.[3] Like women's clubs elsewhere, the Atheneum looked for ways to improve local culture.

On October 18, 1899, Atheneum members opened rooms above the Lexington State Bank to house a thousand-volume library that lumber baron J. L. Woods had left to his sister, the wife of Charles Moore (Woods's business partner for thirty years), and Charles's three daughters, Emma, Ella, and Mary. All three were Atheneum charter members.[4] Initially an Atheneum Library Committee staffed the subscription library, and made sure rules were enforced. For twenty-five cents a year, village residents had access to the collection every Saturday from nine in the morning until noon, and from one until nine in the evening. Children under fourteen needed permission from parents or guardians. Patrons could check out books for a two-week period, were fined ten cents per week for their late return, and had to pay damages for books they injured, the full cost of books they lost, and the full cost of a series if they lost one volume from a series.[5]

When Charles Moore died shortly thereafter, his daughters purchased a law office building just off Main Street, and, after naming it for their father, immediately remodeled it into a library on the first floor and Atheneum club rooms on the second. They refashioned the facade to resemble classical architecture, installed stained glass and leaded glass windows, added several hundred books, and established a $2,500 endowment for operating expenses provided the books would always be free to village residents. On November 3, Charles H. Moore Library trustees held their first meeting, asked the local marshal to tend the fire each day the library was open and collect fines incurred by patrons, gave the Atheneum use of the building's second story "as long as they remained in active existence," and began cataloging books.[6]

The list of board members appointed (they would have to run for office at the next election) read like a Lexington social register. For president the trustees elected Circuit Judge Watson Beach, a Connecticut native who had arrived in Lexington in 1859 to practice law, but left to fight in the Civil War shortly thereafter. He was a Republican, a Mason, a Congregationalist, and a GAR member, and between 1865 and 1886 he owned the weekly *Sanilac Jeffersonian*. Daniel Clarke was elected vice president. A native of Vermont who had moved to Lexington in 1869 to start a dry goods store,

3. Pen and ink drawing of Moore Library of Lexington,
Michigan, ca. 1910, taken from library bookplate.
Used by permission of Moore Library.

he was a Mason, an Episcopalian, and a Republican. John Norman was elected secretary and treasurer. Born in Canada, he had moved to Lexington in 1867 to start a dental practice. He was a Democrat, an Episcopalian, a village trustee, and member of the local board of education. Other trustees included D. C. O'Brien, a Catholic physician who had arrived in Lexington from Massachusetts in 1858, and Charles S. Miller, bond salesman for a Detroit company. Miller was an Episcopalian, a Mason, and village trustee. All these male board members were married to Atheneum charter members. To run the new facility the board selected Anna Henry, daughter of Lexington pioneer George Henry, a prominent local Republican who at one time had been the school board president. Anna Henry was also a member of the Atheneum, and an Episcopalian.[7]

On Saturday, January 17, 1903, Mary Moore Sleeper presented the Charles H. Moore Library to Lexington on behalf of herself and her now married two sisters, Ella Hanley and Emma Myers. That morning the library received local schoolchildren from ten till noon (two boys raced from school to be the first to register), and presented each with a bag of candy. From two till four that afternoon, Mrs. Sleeper and her husband Albert hosted a reception. From six till ten that evening, Atheneum members welcomed friends and trustees. All day long patrons checked out books. On their way to the Moore Library, many traversed new cement walks lining Lexington's main streets. Progress seemed everywhere in evidence.[8]

In subsequent years the Moore Library settled into a routine that drew community pride but little community attention, in large part because it fit a pattern common to other small-town midwestern public libraries. The *Sanilac Jeffersonian*—with its office and press in nearby Croswell—ran a "Lexington" column detailing activities in that community. On December 4, 1908, the column recognized the Moore Library as "one of the institutions of which we are justly proud. It contains all the standard and classical works, as well as a regular supply of monthly magazines. It is a regular mine of useful information and pleasure, and one our citizens most heartily appreciate. Its destinies are presided over by Miss Anna Henry, who performs her duties most gracefully and to the eminent satisfaction of the public." Among Henry's duties was shared responsibility for collection development. On the one hand, individual trustees often presented recommendations for purchase, but at the same time, the *Jeffersonian* said, Henry "carefully reviews every new work brought in and sees to it that nothing of a doubtful or harmful character is placed before the young." Two years later the *Jeffersonian* announced the new works of popular fiction acquired by the library. "They were selected by Anna Henry," the paper noted, "whose literary taste is a guarantee that the works are of a high order."[9] While some in the Michigan library community might have disagreed that any popular fiction was "of a high order," in Lexington the Moore Library showed a different set of standards, locally determined.

In March 1909, John Bell replaced John Norman on the Board. Bell was a local druggist, village trustee, Mason, and Episcopalian. Socially he was little different than the man he replaced. Two years later the board welcomed Charles Crosby to its ranks. Crosby, a local businessman and president of the Lexington Improvement Association, had helped organize the Lexington Beach Association in 1908 as a summer home cooperative. He was an Episcopalian, a Mason, and a member of the Knights Templar. His wife was also a member of the Atheneum. With Bell he formed a committee to investigate whether the Moore Library could garner larger discounts for book purchases if it worked through book suppliers.[10]

If the Moore Library was a popular place in Lexington, it was hardly

noticed elsewhere in Michigan's library community. In 1899 the state authorized a Board of Library Commissioners (BLC) to advocate for public
libraries across the state and set up travelling libraries of 100 books each
for six-month loan periods. In April, 1907, the BLC appointed a county orga-
nizer to help towns establish or improve library services. Records suggest
no one from the Commission ever contacted the Moore, which was absent
from a list *Michigan Libraries* carried in 1911.[11]

The Moore Library experienced its first significant shift on October 14,
1911, when the board appointed Florence Walther to succeed Anna Henry,
who resigned to marry. Walther (whose appointment the Moore sisters also
approved) was daughter of Mr. and Mrs. Frederick L. Walther, both "Lexington pioneers." Florence Walther was an 1898 Lexington High School
graduate, and in 1911 was thirty years old. She was also an Atheneum member, and an organist at the village's Episcopal church, where she taught
Sunday school. As compensation for her work at the Moore Library she
was paid six dollars monthly, plus four dollars twice a year for cleaning the
building.[12] Unlike Henry, however, she did not select books; trustees did.

When she became librarian, the Lexington that Florence Walther served
was shifting away from a past that Anna Henry had inherited and moving
into a future Charles Crosby already recognized. Road improvements and
installment-plan payment for automobiles increased travelers in the state,
and many middle-class Detroiters with cars found Lake Huron beaches
ideal for summer vacations. Many built lakeshore cottages; others rented.
Collectively they established summer colonies that patronized local con-
gregations and businesses. Seldom did the Cadillac Hotel experience a
summer vacancy; permanent residents often rented out rooms to tourists
by the night or week. When a November 1913 storm on Lake Huron sank
eight ships and drowned 235 people, it also destroyed Lexington's docks
and killed its lake trade. Tourism may have been more seasonal, but it
was less subject to natural disaster, and city fathers began investing in it.

In the summer of 1914, for example, Lexington brought in variety shows
(the "Freed Trained Animal Show" was especially successful) and sponsored regular band concerts every Saturday evening, when the town was
"lined with rigs and lanterns bearing loads of people who appreciate good
music," the *Jeffersonian* noted. "The Lexington band is an institution of
which we are justly proud." Community leaders were eager to satisfy
tourist needs in order to keep them coming back, and the Moore Library

provided an important service that addressed what many regarded as essential recreational reading needs. As a result, the library assumed an important role in the local economy, and village fathers recognized the need to maintain it. A new coat of exterior paint applied in 1912 made the library look "as clean and sweet in its new dress as a summer girl in a fresh calico."[13]

Inevitably, however, outside pressures to professionalize Moore Library services encroached. For example, in the early twentieth century the Michigan Federation of Women's Clubs adopted library advocacy as a goal. "The Federation wishes to increase the interest in libraries as an educational and civic asset, among club-women in every county in the state," noted the *Detroit Tribune*, "through the study of library conditions in every town and county, and through an understanding of library methods." Lexington's Atheneum, which continued to meet monthly on the second floor of the Moore Library, could not have missed the message.[14] Nonetheless, records for 1915 indicate that no one associated with the library was a member of the Michigan Library Association (MLA); the librarian and trustees must not have received its publications. Thus, the Moore Library was run in relative isolation from Michigan's growing library community. Walther followed her predecessor's practices and never attended a professional library meeting or visited other libraries to review newer methods (board minutes indicate she made no suggestions for changes or improvements), nor did she actively provide reference work or solicit BLC help. No one from Lexington attended a February 18, 1915, roundtable meeting the MLA and BLC hosted in Port Huron "to bring together a small group of librarians . . . where they may meet such citizens, club members, school teachers and students, as are interested in the discussion of the use of books, and the influence and administration of libraries."[15]

But the isolation would not last. In June, the Moore Library received its first visit from a BLC commissioner, who "tried to emphasize the necessity of carefully kept records, caution in buying books, the importance of attending library meetings and visiting other libraries, the value of reference work, and the willingness of the state to help."[16] Some changes followed. In late 1916, at a time when Lexington screened its first moving picture (Mary Pickford starred in *Ramona*), trustees hired a local carpenter to install new shelves for growing collections. About the same time the *Michigan Library Bulletin* (MLB) reported on the Moore Library's first story hour, held Saturday, February 24, 1917. The occasion was planned, the *Bulletin* noted, "with final valuable suggestions obtained at the Round Table at Port Huron in February." Because the Moore Library had no separate children's room, the seven youngsters who attended sat in the main room, where they listened to stories told by local teachers. At first the Moore restricted story hour to children under ten; later it was extended up to age fourteen. Except for hosting, Florence Walther did not participate.

The Moore Library diversified services in other ways. With the help of a raffle for handcrafted pillowcases and of a series of benefit dances at the local opera house, the library raised enough funds to purchase an Edison diamond-disc phonograph. Thereafter, the Moore Library hosted a musical program each day it was open. With help from the Lexington Woman's Civic Improvement Association (most members were wives of Moore trustees), the Library also sponsored a birdhouse-building contest that ended with an exhibit. "This is the first time since the library was established 15 years ago," *MLB* told its readers regarding the Moore Library, "that there has been a departure from the regular routine of the loaning of books."[17] Like other Main Street public libraries, the Moore was beginning to expand its community reach and influence.

Except for D. C. O'Brien (who became president in 1918) and Charles Miller, the rest of the board membership turned over in the 1918 election. Still, wives of all new married trustees were Atheneum members. Banker Grant Smith became vice president. A village clerk, a Methodist, vice president of the Lexington Band that performed for local citizens and tourists on summer Saturday nights, he also served on the Lexington Improvement Association executive committee. Theodore Wixsom became secretary-treasurer. He was a bank cashier, a Congregationalist, a Mason, and president of the village trustees in 1918. The widowed Oliver Yake was a Civil War veteran and GAR member, served as minister of the Advent Christian Church, and in 1918 was village assessor. Board membership may have changed but its socio-demographics had not.[18]

But the Moore Library itself experienced significant change in 1919. As the town was wired for electricity, the library was among the first to install electric lights. That made it even more "attractive to lovers of good reading," the *Jeffersonian* noted. "More new cards were issued to tourists Saturday than on any one day in the history of the library," it noted in one issue, proving, the *Jeffersonian* said, "that the library is one of the

town's principal attractions." Finally, with the arrival of women's suffrage, the board's gender composition shifted, and the library became a
site for women to display their leadership skills. The 1919 Lexington voter
registration book reflected the impact of women's suffrage. It was divided
into two alphabetically arranged sections, the front for men, the back for
women. In the March 1920 election, the town split its political loyalties into
two groups. One—called the Victory ticket—argued that certain parties
had pushed too hard for electric lighting systems. The other—called the
Village ticket—supported the increased pace of change. Because women
could now vote, and because library trustees were still elected officials,
the Moore Library inevitably was caught up in the battle. Charles Crosby,
Nellie Emigh, and Margaret Nichol ran for library trustee on the Victory
ticket; Grant Smith, D. C. O'Brien, and Mrs. Michael (Dora Paisley) Meyer
ran on the Village ticket.

When Dora Meyer won, she became the Moore Library's first female
trustee.[19] She was Catholic, and with her husband (owner of a local fish-
ing firm) lived in a home overlooking Lake Huron. (Flowers from Meyer's
garden regularly adorned the library's circulation desk.) Two elections
later, the board was entirely female, including Dora Meyer (president),
Secretary-Treasurer Lillian Fraser (an Episcopalian married to a local
physician), Jamesena Norman (a Methodist married to a local drugstore
owner), Abbie Sheldon (an Episcopalian married to the president of the village council), and Helen Schell, an employee of the Lexington State Bank,
a Catholic, and a daughter of a Lexington pioneer. Like all other board
members, Schell was a member of the Atheneum. On May 12, 1922, Fraser
and Schell accompanied Florence Walther to the Port Huron Round Table
meeting, where Lexington was complimented for its consistently increasing annual attendance.[20]

The first week in October 1922, the library closed for redecoration. "The
work is under the supervision of the new library board of women," the
Jeffersonian reported; "the renovation has long been needed." Ceiling and
walls were cleaned and the stove repaired. Once it reopened, the Moore
Library trustees reported a number of new books. "It has become a problem to select books these days," the *Jeffersonian* noted, "as the publication
of any of those who have hitherto been considered among the best authors
are, to say the least, questionable for general circulation." Fortunately,
however, Moore Library trustees exercised responsible leadership. Acqui-

sition lists, the *Jeffersonian* said, would "be published as soon as they have been approved by the board and made ready for circulation."[21]

By 1923, summer tourists were making such demands on Moore Library collections that trustees decided to assess nonresidents a fee of fifty cents per year. Although the library remained open year-round on Saturdays until 9:00 P.M., trustees also extended hours to 9:00 P.M. every Wednesday during July and August "to accommodate resorters and others who do not care to get out in the heat." For additional summer work Walther received an extra $10. By that time Lexington had developed a twenty-seven-acre campsite to accommodate, free of charge, the campers who drove up from Detroit on Huron Shore Pike to visit "the cleanest, coolest, and most convenient tourist town on the East Shore," the *Jeffersonian* noted. Because they were grateful for the Moore Library's service, several regular tourists annually donated money, books, and phonograph records.

Trustees later judged the schedule change "well worth the while. Summer patronage has gradually increased, when more books were loaned than during the same time of any previous summer." And it was the summer circulation that drove the annual circulation reported to the state library commision. Averaged against a census population of 519, as Walther was required to report, the Moore Library's per capita circulation was 16.4, nearly three times that of other Michigan public libraries. To meet this demand, the library had on its shelves 4,800 volumes which, when calculated against its 1920 census population, averaged 9.2 per capita, or three times what ALA standards called for when established ten years later. Once local officials decided to craft the library's collections and services for the summer tourist population, the Moore Library became an aberration among small-town Heartland public libraries. For the next three decades, the Moore statistically spent more per capita, owned more books per capita, and had a higher rate of circulation per capita than any other Michigan public library, according to formulae developed by library professionals. But the formulae were too inflexible to accurately explain what was happening to library services experiencing demands unique to Lexington and its Moore Library.

Despite the impact of summer tourists, Moore Library trustees did not neglect local citizens. In the fall of 1925 the board opened the library "one extra afternoon each week in order that the school children could get the necessary books needed in their work." In summer of 1926 the library hosted two benefits. With the $180 realized they purchased "attractive new editions of old favorites," plus "such popular authors as Joseph Lincoln and Zane Grey, written some time ago but never before on the Library shelves and which complete the collections of novels by these authors." In 1929 the Moore Library owned twenty-nine Zane Grey novels.[22]

On January 17, 1928, the twenty-fifth anniversary of the Moore Library was celebrated with an open house. Posters made by local schoolchildren adorned the walls, and "gifted story teller" Mrs. George Stokey "entertained the younger children." Florence Walther treated them all to nuts and candy. Surviving Moore sisters Mary Sleeper and Ella Hanley donated "a lovely bouquet of flowers in a silver vase" that sat upon the circulation desk. Visitors also toured Atheneum rooms, where they were served refreshments and treated to "an attractive program" by Atheneum members. They were also greeted by new board president Margaret Nichol, an Atheneum member married to the village assessor. She was joined by five other board members; only one was male. At the Moore Library, women continued to dominate.[23]

In the summer of 1929, Nichol and Walther attended a Port Huron Round Table meeting, where they heard that the radio was "an important means of reaching a wider public." By the time the stock market fell later that year, most Lexingtonians owned radios that brought into their homes soap operas, music (classical and popular), Hollywood gossip, up-to-date weather reports, lectures, and sermons. To get to Port Huron, Nichols and Walther traveled by automobile; passenger rail service in Sanilac County had stopped years earlier. Automobiles also enabled Lexingtonians to attend a growing number of area movie theaters, which by the end of the decade all had "talkies." Not everyone was happy with the quality of these films. Father Joseph Luther, member of the Detroit chapter of the Roman Catholic Legion of Decency, told a Lexington Town Hall audience in 1934 that movies had become "dangerous modes of entertainment because 25 percent of the shows picture[d] vice as attractive and solicited sympathy for the wrong ideals of life." With automobiles, radio, and talkies invading the local culture, the Cadillac House was less able to support itself from live music and drama, and increasingly relied on its restaurant and hotel.[24] But the newer media had no impact on Moore Library circulation, which continued to grow.

The Great Depression was not kind to the library. Shortly after it hit, trustees found themselves in a dilemma. They wanted to give Walther a raise, but could not while still meeting other obligations with a shrinking budget. The two Moore sisters came to the rescue; each gave one hundred dollars, and promised more if necessary. With that money, the board raised Walther's monthly salary to twenty dollars. Records show that for 1932, Lexington, population 350, used a one-mill tax rate to raise $350 for the library; another $150 came from other sources (subscription fees for nonresidents and endowment interest). From this income trustees paid $50 for books and $154 for salaries ($120 for Walther; $34 for an assistant who substituted when Walther vacationed or was ill).[25]

At the January 1934 meeting of the Moore Library board, its president read a letter from the state librarian asking whether the library had applied for federal relief funds "for improvements of any kind to the building, etc." The board quickly identified several projects—rebinding twenty-five books, recataloging the collection, redecorating the library, and installing a more efficient water system for the toilet—and sent two members to the county seat, Sandusky, to solicit funds. Their efforts were largely unsuccessful. The only federal money given the Moore Library during the Depression was spent to repair the library driveway.[26] The Depression affected the library seriously in June 1934, when the Lexington State Bank was placed in receivership and, in effect, froze the Moore Library's endowment. Because village leaders recognized how valuable the library was to summer tourists (by this time Lexingtonians regularly referred to their town as "a resort village"), the council immediately levied a two-mill tax to compensate for the loss. Immediately, to meet the anticipated summer traffic, the board authorized Walther to take that tax money plus money from dues and fines to purchase used books from a Port Huron bookstore.

By the 1930s Lexingtonians had made it a practice to gather in mid-May for an annual "Clean-up Day" (Memorial Day formally kicked off tourist season), to support weekly summer dances and concerts at the town bandstand, lease beachfront land for public use, and monitor a self-supporting trailer park and a tourist camp (the Eastern Michigan Tourist Association pronounced it "the best one on the eastern shore"). In July 1935, the *Jeffersonian* reported that "the warm weather has filled Lexington to capacity and many tourists were unable to find rooms in or near town."

During summers, cars parked on Lexington streets routinely sported license plates from states as distant as New Jersey, Maryland, California, and New York.[27]

For all this the library was prepared to meet the demand. In 1935–1936 its collections grew to 5,800, but only by 229 volumes (19 were purchased, 210 donated). Circulation was 9,232. Although the local population was 350, total number of borrowers was 2,588. Obviously, summer tourists drove circulation. For the most part, those running the Moore Library took little notice of what was happening in other public libraries around the country. A state aid bill had been proposed for Michigan public libraries in early 1937, and the board did write for more information but took no action. It did not participate in library advocacy events like National Book Week or Children's Book Week. And as of 1936 it still had not cataloged or classified its collection as recommended by the ALA. In April 1936 the Moore Library board wrote to the Michigan state welfare director to find out if federal funds could be used to hire a cataloger, but in the absence of a response dropped the matter. Except for deaths, board membership seldom changed.[28]

In May 1938 the Moore took part in Clean-up Day. For a week it remained closed while walls were repainted, a new rug added, water piped into a room under the stairs (a toilet and sink were not added until 1941), and electricity installed in the back shed. Hardwood floors were sanded and revarnished, bookshelves were rearranged, and Walther was authorized to spend fifty dollars for "new fiction and biography." That fall the board began an annual contest for schoolchildren "to increase interest in good literature and use of the library." Trustees authorized Walther to craft a series of questions to be answered by library materials, and then offered as prizes four books. Three trustees served as judges.

In April 1939 the board discussed the merits of joining the Book-of-the-Month Club (BOMC). Later that month trustees voted to join the club under the president's name "in order to receive an extra premium." At monthly meetings thereafter, trustees decided whether to take the BOMC selection. Perhaps unknowingly, they thus acquiesced to a filtering process in which BOMC judges attempted to craft the middlebrow reading tastes that had taken root before the Depression, but had become dominant in public library circulation in the decade following. What BOMC judges "were after," argues historian Janice Radway, "was a reading experience that promoted interest in an object or situation beyond the self and that dialectically evoked in the reader a sense of being recognized by another. This mutual regard in literary form created excitement, they believed, as well as hope and the possibility of commitment to the future."[29] By making this commitment the Moore Library board unwittingly enrolled all its patrons—year-round and summer—in these reading experiences. But that did not mean the board automatically abdicated selection responsibility to BOMC judges; they still mediated literary values for their local community. At their January 30, 1940, meeting, for example, the board president asked each member about the BOMC's controversial selection *Christ in Concrete* (1939) by Pietro Di Donato; unanimously they agreed to put it in circulation. Their patrons—and especially their summer patrons—wanted it.

Two months later Walther reported that in 1939 the Moore Library had purchased 105 books and had another 23 donated, bringing the collection total to 6,315, or 19.4 books per capita (6.5 times the ALA recommended average). The library had also registered thirty-two new local borrowers for a total of 326, while the 5,940 books circulated the previous year had been checked out by 2,781 people. (Thousands of tourists were still carrying library-owned novels to local beaches.) Calculated against the population of local borrowers, circulation came to 18.2 per capita, almost twice the ALA standard of ten.[30]

Although not active in World War I fund-raising or book collecting efforts, the Moore Library did participate in the Victory Book Campaign. On January 16, 1942, the *Jeffersonian* told Lexingtonians to bring "acceptable" books (not magazines) on "current affairs, military publications, up-to-date technical books, grammars, science, foreign language and fiction" to the library. Books were forwarded to the Port Huron Public Library, where they were later shipped through a distribution center to GIs in training camps and overseas.[31] Moore Library trustees also tied the war to efforts to bring more youth into the library. In December 1942, local teachers were encouraged to "bring the titles of three good books for recommendation to the librarian." A month later the Moore Library informed teachers that they could take out a number of books for classroom use on their own cards. For the library's annual literary contest, judges awarded one book to the first-place winner, twenty-five-cent defense stamps (paid from the dues and fines collection) to others. In October 1943, the board authorized twenty-five dollars to purchase children's books, and to adjust the library's open hours so pupils "might derive more benefit from the library." Officially the library took no notice of June race riots in Detroit. That it had a copy of *Native Son* is probably because Richard Wright's recently published work (to be discussed in more depth in chapter 5) was a 1940 BOMC selection.[32]

In many respects, the Moore Library still existed in isolation from public librarianship elsewhere in Michigan. No one connected to the library (including Florence Walther) belonged to MLA, which by 1935 had 350 personal members. In the 1930s MLA pointed out that one-fourth of Michigan's citizens had no library service, and that at thirty-eight cents per capita Michigan was way below an ALA recommended minimum per capita of one dollar spent annually. In 1937 the Michigan legislature passed a State Aid for Libraries Act, which created a General Library Fund to be distributed on an equal per capita basis to all qualifying libraries, and a Library Equalization Fund to organize and establish new county libraries. Within eight years thirteen new county libraries opened, per capita funding increased from thirty-eight to fifty-five cents, and 269 libraries qualified for grants. But because the Moore Library's practice of providing reading materials to summer tourists effectively skewed its statistics, the library automatically disqualified itself from this funding. In 1941, for example, it reported a local population of 326 and total expenditures of $594, for a per capita income of $1.82, more than three times the rate for the rest of Michigan and nearly twice the ALA benchmark.

With this new legislation, MLA membership shot up to twelve hundred and its Round Tables Committee arranged five short institutes around the state for in-service training of librarians. By the summer of 1942 the MLA required completion of two technical-level workshops within three years for library employees to be issued first- or second-grade certificates. Florence Walther did not participate in any of these workshops. A modification to the law said that after 1948 any public library whose annual support was less than $6,000 might "participate in the apportionment of the General Library Fund only by uniting with another library, or becoming part of an approved county or regional library."[33] Those running the Moore Library were uninterested.

For nearly half a century the Moore Library—a community project— had its own identity in Lexington, one that did not fit the formulae developed by the Michigan library establishment or necessarily follow the lead of the American Library Association. Trustees did not feel the need for or perceive the benefits of participation in the broader library community. On January 19, 1945, the *Jeffersonian* noted that the Moore Library had recently acquired a walnut "combination book case and magazine rack" designed and built by a local craftsman. Three years later the board formally voted to purchase a plunger and "Saniflush" for the library's new toilet. Through its board president, the Moore Library continued its BMOC membership. By that time services and traditions set in place generations earlier kept some substantial issues from even appearing on board agendas.[34]

In 1947 the Moore Library reported to the state library that it had 6,788 books, and, according to the form the state library required, its population of 390 accounted for a per capita rate of 14.4. No other Michigan public library came close to that figure. Because several trustees retired that spring, board leadership changed but not its socio-demographics. All new members were heavily involved in local churches, Catholic and Protestant. If female, all were married to prominent local businessmen and were members of the Atheneum. If male, all were prominent local businessmen and married to members of the Atheneum. Most were connected to pioneer families; two, however, had summered in Lexington for years before moving there at retirement. As summer visitors, both had been Moore Library patrons.[35]

At its annual meeting held April 7, 1949, the board congratulated itself for new building decorations and increased use by local youth. "The juvenile department," the *Jeffersonian* reported, "is said to compare favorably with the other libraries of its size, and is liberally patronized by the younger readers." Years later one patron especially recalled "the heavy front door. When you opened it and closed it behind you, you knew you were on solid, almost sacred territory." Jim Sullivan's "happiest memories there were on cold and snowy winter days. Few came to the library during that season. And I'd sit by her library check-out desk and chat with Miss Walters [*sic*] about everything under our star." Sullivan remembers Walther as "polite, but somewhat frosty. . . . Her stern looks broadcast to one and all that she would brook no misbehavior." As an adolescent he discovered *National Geographic* "in the back room. There I must have spent hours learning about the native populations of Africa." Walther also gave him open access to adult books about World War II, like Herman Wouk's *The Caine Mutiny* (1952) and Robert Scott's *God Is My Co-Pilot* (1943). "Miss Walters [*sic*] never deterred me from reading any of these rather adult books. In fact, she used to kindly point out new war books that she thought I'd enjoy." At the 1949 board meeting Walther reported that the library had purchased 112 new books the previous year ("a rate of ten a month," the minutes reported proudly), and was ready for summer traffic. "The ever popular fiction department is up to date with current books," the *Jeffersonian* noted. The board also announced that the library had telephone service for the first time in its history.[36]

On January 17, 1953, the fiftieth anniversary of the Moore Library was celebrated. "In spite of the sleet storm," the *Jeffersonian* reported, "a large attendance was at the open house." At the time Sanilac County had no bookmobile service, and no one connected to the Moore Library was an MLA member. For her years of service, Florence Walther received a corsage "and lovely plant."[37] Nine months later Walther was hit by a car and suffered a broken leg. It marked the end of an era. For the next few years the board met irregularly, while an assistant filled in for Walther. In 1955 the village council failed to place library trustee names on the spring ballot, so two new members had to be selected from "scattered votes." Sometime during this decade, board members also decided to replace a fifty-year-old set of encyclopedias. Although televisions had become commonplace in Michigan homes and while Sanilac County had become the state's number one milk producer, Michigan's economy had taken a downturn. The village of Lexington was losing population, while the Township of Lexington was gaining. By that time Michigan state aid to libraries had reduced the number of residents without public library service from 27 percent in 1937 to 13 percent in 1955, established sixteen new county libraries, and supported thirty-seven bookmobiles. For the year 1955, Moore Library trustees reported its per capita tax support at $1.77, its per capita book stock at 13.1, and its per capita circulation at 9.1.[38] Statistically, the Moore Library continued to look like one of the best-supported and most-used public libraries in Michigan.

CHAPTER FOUR

Those Commission Ideas

The Rhinelander Public Library
of Rhinelander, Wisconsin

O n February 9, 1898, citizens of Rhinelander, Wisconsin, gathered at the courthouse to hear Lutie Stearns of the Wisconsin Free Library Commission (WFLC) speak about the value of public libraries. Stearns's visit was sponsored by the Rhinelander Women's Club (RWC). "This is a start in the right direction," said the *Rhinelander Herald.* "There is no way in which the city can better invest a small amount of money than in maintaining a library and reading room."[1]

The new Rhinelander Public Library (RPL) for which Stearns advocated emerged out of local and state forces. The town was named after Milwaukee Lake Shore and Western Railway President F. W. Rhinelander when the railroad reached the Upper Wisconsin River in 1878 to service lumber pioneers, including the Brown family, whose members purchased thousands of acres from the government for logging pine, birch, maple, and spruce. Within a decade Scandinavian immigrants shipped seventy million board feet to Chicago. After the trees were harvested, the Brown Brothers Lumber Company sold what remained as farmland—stumps and all—to recently arrived immigrants for up to $500 per forty acres. When the city of Rhinelander incorporated in 1894, Webster E. Brown became its first mayor. In November that year, influential citizens eager to import culture into their backwater settlement pooled their resources to open a subscription library in a small gymnasium owned by Brown Brothers, which the lumber company offered rent-free. A general subscription from influential citizens yielded $109.

The next summer Rhinelander's WCTU chapter, which made no secret of its desire to "steer the lumber jack" away from the "liquid refreshments so abundant at the gilded palaces of drink," assumed responsibility for the library. On July 27, 1895, the *Herald* reported that a "Library and Reading Room Association" constitution provided a fifteen-member board of directors, "all of whom are to be women, and an advisory board of an equal number of gentlemen who are to meet with the directors ... and give them counsel and financial aid." Not surprisingly, board members represented leading Rhinelander women.[2] To sustain itself the association relied upon donations. By February 1896, however, members began a campaign for a public library. On February 29 the *Herald* endorsed the initiative, but on March 14 the town's common council tabled a resolution calling for its establishment. Advocates for a public library redoubled their efforts.[3]

A year earlier the Wisconsin legislature had authorized the WFLC to provide advice "to all free libraries in the state, and to all communities which may propose to establish them as to the best means of establishing and administering such libraries." Shortly thereafter the commission hired Lutie Stearns. On October 21, 1896, influential Wisconsin women organized the Wisconsin Federation of Women's Clubs in Milwaukee, where they identified public libraries as their highest priority. It was no coincidence that the president of the Rhinelander Women's Club also sat on the board of the WFLC, nor that her friend Lutie Stearns was in an audience that also included RWC officers. Stearns realized how valuable women's clubs could be as she crisscrossed the state advocating for public libraries. Little wonder, then, that on November 27, 1897, the Rhinelander common council approved a resolution from the RWC to establish a "free public library and reading room."[4]

Rhinelander's new public library opened on February 27, 1898, in the second floor of a local bank building. Trustees appointed by the mayor included Mrs. Webster E. Brown, her sister-in-law Mrs. E. O. Brown (both married to Brown family lumber barons), Mrs. F. L. Hinman (married to a local physician), Mrs. Joseph C. Wixson, Mrs. John Barnes (married to a local attorney), the Rev. George H. Kemp (a Congregational minister), local businessman S. S. Miller, Alderman Jacob Klumb, and local businessman Charles F. Barnes. The superintendent of public schools served ex officio. The board's makeup: five women, four men; eight Protestants (most Congregationalist), one Catholic; eight Republican (or married to one), one Democrat. All board women were RWC charter members, all the men married to one. Like the Bryant Library in Sauk Centre, Minnesota, and the Sage Library in Osage, Iowa, the Rhinelander Public Library undoubtedly

4. Circulation desk at the Rhinelander Public Library, Rhinelander, Wisconsin, ca. 1910. Used by permission of Wisconsin Historical Society.

was a subject at dinner tables, church events, and associational meetings where trustees gathered.[5]

A constitution provided three standing committees, including a Book Committee, which "shall control and supervise the buying," it was stated, and be responsible for "exchange and binding of the books and periodicals." A board-selected librarian, it was stipulated, "shall have charge of the library and reading room and be responsible for the care and safety of the books and other library property; classify and arrange all books and publications." On April 4, 1898, the board gave its Book Committee an additional $50 to purchase new books from the A. C. McClurg Company.[6] By February 1899, the collection had grown to over one thousand titles, and the library was forced to move to a larger room in the bank building. The RWC deserved much credit for collection growth. In February it hosted a "book reception" at the home of A. W. Brown (yet another brother); each invitee was requested to "bring an old or a new book suitable for the Public Library." For their efforts, the club received 128 books, and $8.43 in donations, which it promptly turned over to the library. Upon the recommendation of the WCTU, the board also hired local citizen Inez Van Tassell as librarian. Like her counterparts in Sauk Centre and Osage at the time, she had no formal library training.[7]

For its five thousand citizens in 1900, Rhinelander was home to eight churches, including a Free Methodist, Methodist Episcopal, Episcopal, Congregational, Baptist, Roman Catholic, and two Lutheran churches (one serving Norwegian immigrants, the other German). It also hosted six societies, including Foresters, Masons, and Knights of Pythias. However, unlike unindustrialized Sauk Centre and Osage, Rhinelander's lumber industries gave rise to labor unions, to which newly immigrant employees regularly gravitated. Often they brought with them well-developed political ideologies that lumber barons and industrialists found threatening.[8]

On July 1, 1899, the board submitted its first annual report. During the previous year the library had spent 80 percent of its budget on books, which now totaled 1,103 volumes; 68 percent were fiction. "The demands on the library are steadily growing and the interest is increasing amongst every class in our city," the board reported. Trustees also solicited citizens to notify them "on slips provided for the purpose, of their wishes respecting desirable books," saying that the board desired, "as far as possible, to accommodate all classes." The *Herald* complimented the library on "a very good showing. In fact, we doubt if there is another one of the same age in the state that has been the success ours has." In the previous two years philanthropists across the state had gifted money for buildings and endowments to found twenty other public libraries. During the same time the WFLC increased its traveling libraries from 32 to 189.[9]

When Van Tassel resigned in March 1900, the board hired a local high school graduate to replace her. But the board also recognized that its growing collection needed to be recataloged and contacted Lutie Stearns for advice on hiring a cataloger to put the library "in proper condition." Stearns recommended a Wisconsin Library School (WLS) alumna who had taken cataloging and classification courses in Madison.[10] In July, the alumna supervised a team that included library board members Mary Shelton and Mrs. E. O. Brown as they reclassified the collection using Dewey Decimal Classification and recataloged the books by ALA rules into a new card catalog. "It will be seen that the system is a perfect one," the daily *Vindicator* reported. On February 20, 1901, the *Vindicator* also noticed Andrew Carnegie's growing library philanthropy.[11]

RPL was not the only source of reading materials available to turn-of-the-century Rhinelander citizens. Certainly local churches provided multiple texts, but the high school also had a two-thousand-volume library. In addition, the Rhinelander Book Club, a men's club, met monthly. Members purchased the latest editions of popular titles, then auctioned them off at the end of the year. Local merchants also stocked printed materials. C. D. Bronson advertised that his store offered all the "late books"; these could "be found on our shelves and no other place in the city." Lola Beers Deyo remembered a "grand rush" with her friends to Bronson's store to obtain *Arabian Nights*. She also remembered "waxing indignant" with others in her young adults' circle "over the vicissitudes of Elsie Dinsmore" and becoming "jubilant . . . over the moral victories of Horatio Alger" (neither the Elsie Dinsmore series nor Horatio Alger books were represented in the RPL collection). Although Deyo's mother had warned her daughter that *Police Gazette* would "pollute the morals" of Rhinelander's fire chief—she had seen him reading it—"she little knew that Papa would buy it and she was blissfully unaware it was under the buggy seat later to be read in privacy."[12]

Also available was the serialized fiction the *Vindicator* regularly ran in its weekly edition. "Make books your friends," it urged both men and women. "Every good book read makes you a better and abler man." At the same time, however, the newspaper recounted a Seattle story "in which a woman after reading one of Marie Corelli's novels arose and killed her husband. . . . While censorships are to be disapproved on general principles," the *Vindicator* opined, "it is obvious that some restrictions may yet have to be placed on publications of this form." (In 1902 RPL carried no Corelli novels.) Books were thought to be harmful in other ways. In October 1901, the Rhinelander Health Department closed the library during a scarlet fever outbreak "as the exchange of books was considered a possible means of spreading diseases."[13]

CARNEGIE BUILDING

Unlike trustees in Sauk Centre and Osage, RPL trustees took a major step toward modern library professionalism by contacting the WFLC in September 1901 about hiring a "trained librarian." This action preceded a decision to raise money for a separate building and make the new library "a monument to the effort and industry" of the Rhinelander Women's Club members. In January 1902, the club hosted a "Library Day" and later that month had a "Library Party" at the home of "the Misses Brown."[14]

All these activities were part of a larger agenda. On January 24, 1902, E. O. Brown wrote to Andrew Carnegie on Brown Brothers stationery that although Rhinelander was a "thriving city" with a public library of two thousand volumes, the latter had "outgrown its present quarters." If the philanthropist would be willing to give Rhinelander twelve thousand dollars for a "suitable brick building," he said, Brown Brothers would donate a corner lot two blocks from the business district center, and he was sure the common council "would agree to raise by taxation ten per cent of this amount annually for the maintenance of the library." With his letter, Brown included a resolution the RWC had passed pledging one thousand dollars to furnish the new building.[15] For months, however, Carnegie failed to respond.

But trustees pressed on. On February 24, 1902, they resolved to "close arrangements" for a "trained librarian." Two months later they hired Mary S. Smith, a WLS graduate who, the *Vindicator* said, "comes to Rhinelander well recommended" and "thoroughly competent for the position." Smith was on site April 26 when the library expanded hours from three afternoons a week to Monday through Friday, 2:00–6:00 and 7:00–10:00 P.M., and Saturdays from nine till noon. A month later the library subscribed to *Readers' Guide*, and adopted new rules limiting children to two books a week and adults to one work of fiction per visit.[16]

In May, 1902, the *Vindicator* began a monthly column entitled "Library Notes." Its first column reported that May 24 would be "Magazine Day," when eighth graders from local schools would circulate around the city to collect magazines for the library. "A file of magazines is a most important part of a modern library," the column asserted. The newspaper noted that the library already subscribed to *Harper's Weekly, McClure's, Outing, St. Nicholas*, and *Youth's Companion*, while board members loaned it *Country Life in America, Frank Lester's Monthly, Ladies Home Journal, Lippincott's Magazine, Municipality Outlook, Review of Reviews, Table Talk, Wisconsin Journal of Education Weekly*, and daily newspapers. The effort generated six hundred magazines that the library later bound into thirty volumes for circulation.[17]

"Library Notes" also reported recent acquisitions, circulation statistics (May's circulation was "the largest number ever issued"), and exhibits. "An exhibit of the drawing work of the Public Schools will be held at the Public Library during the week," the *Vindicator* noted on June 4, 1902. "All are invited to visit it and see what the children have been doing." And just before the fall term opened, the board issued special cards to teachers. Few would dispute that RPL was fast becoming a local force for the construction of community. On September 30, Smith submitted an annual report that gushed with excitement. Since April more than twice as many people had used the library than had visited during the entire year previous, and circulation had increased by nearly 100 percent. "The increase in the number of children using the library has been especially noticeable," Smith remarked.[18]

In October, board member Mary Shelton decided to contact Carnegie again. The library rooms in the bank were so cramped, she said, that men and boys stood during evening hours "wherever they can find a place to use the material upon the reading table. . . . We have room for [only] four chairs." On November 26 Lutie Stearns attended a board meeting, congratulated the library on its "efficient librarian," and urged "the great necessity" for more space. Stearns estimated that Rhinelander had the smallest quarters of any library in a Wisconsin city of comparable size.[19] Several weeks later Carnegie requested further information. Within days Shelton responded. She thanked Carnegie for giving "this notice to our appeal" and expressed hope that Carnegie would find RPL "worthy of your further consideration." Rhinelander had finally hooked Carnegie's attention. His answer came the first week of 1903. "If the City agrees . . . to maintain a Free Public library at . . . $1,250 a year and provide a suitable site," Carnegie's secretary James Bertram wrote, "Mr. Carnegie will be glad to furnish twelve thousand five hundred dollars to erect a free public library building for Rhinelander."[20]

Four days later the board urged the city to accept, but at the same time sought to increase the library's annual appropriation from the city to $1,500 in order to press Carnegie to increase his gift to $15,000. The Rhinelander Women's Club also promised to raise $1,500 for furniture and fixtures. The local press celebrated the news. "For over a year Mr. Carnegie has been reminded" that Rhinelander needed a new library, noted the *Vindicator*. On January 7, 1903, the city accepted Carnegie's gift, and promised $1,500 per year. That evening Shelton wrote to Carnegie to accept, but she also asked him to increase his gift. "We realize that to ask for more when

you have been so generous is a delicate matter," she wrote, but she surmised that Carnegie might have been concerned that Rhinelander could
not afford a $1,500 annual appropriation. She told Carnegie that construc-
tion costs in northern Wisconsin were higher than elsewhere because so
many building materials had to be shipped there, and she requested that
he send any "plans, specifications, forms of contract, and material" necessary "so that the contractors may begin work as soon as the weather will
permit." On January 12 Bertram responded bluntly: "Mr. Carnegie does
not see his way to make any increase in the allowances for the building."[21]

At month's end trustees engaged a Milwaukee architect, and several
weeks later he presented a plan for a one-story building with a basement
that would house a twenty-seven-by-thirty-two-foot assembly room with
a separate entrance. On either side of the main floor would be a children's
room and general reading room, each with a fireplace. Elsewhere the plan
showed a book delivery room, a librarian's room, and an open-access
stacks section capable of storing seven thousand volumes. On February
11, Lutie Stearns visited Rhinelander to confer about the plans. A week
later trustees approved them.[22]

In 1903 Rhinelander had reason for optimism. The previous year had
been a gloomy one for the local economy. The Wabash Screen Door fac-
tory, which had burned down earlier, would not be rebuilt, it was announced. The weekly newspaper *New North* believed local officials needed
to bring in more outside investment. City businessmen agreed. They understood that the logging era was passing, and to replace it they looked
to an emerging paper industry. In February, an Oshkosh firm contracted
with the city to construct a paper mill employing two hundred men; the
plant would produce newsprint and wrapping paper. Rhinelander's lumber barons were among major stockholders of the new Rhinelander Paper
Company. Later that year several other prominent businessmen reorga-
nized the Wisconsin Veneer Company into a plant that employed seventy
men.[23]

In July, after the architect selected an Antigo, Wisconsin, firm to construct the building, a Milwaukee firm to furnish it, and the Rhinelander
Lighting Company to wire it, trustees approved a contract calling for completion in January 1904. But efforts to keep costs below $12,500 continued
to frustrate. On July 2 trustees acknowledged that they had been "unable
to materially modify the specifications so as to reduce" the cost, and so

resolved to go back to Carnegie. To add weight to their request of Carnegie, trustees convinced Congressman W. E. Brown to endorse it. On July 27, Bertram wrote to Brown, "Mr. Carnegie will increase his donation . . . to fifteen thousand dollars." The *Vindicator* celebrated the news. "The city is now assured of a perfect library building." By August, foundation walls were complete. Assisted by the local Masonic Lodge, the cornerstone was laid on September 25.[24]

But the summer did not pass without a major disturbance. To build the new $800,000 paper mill the contractor hired fifty Italian immigrants from Milwaukee. Because living quarters near the construction site were not finished when they arrived on July 9, they were instead housed in a large shed behind a bank. Young Rhinelander males gathered near the shed, shouted "down with the Dagos!," and threw rocks through shed windows. Police rushed in, restored order, and arrested five youths. Next day businessmen spent several hours convincing Italians to remain on the job. Their success was temporary; two months later the immigrant workers left Rhinelander after they were divided into separate crews, each of which had been placed under a boss who spoke only English. Local unions looked on with grave concern.[25]

Work on the library continued over the winter. By December the slate roof was completed, wiring begun, and the heating system installed. At their December meeting, trustees approved use of the new library's community room for RWC meetings. Later it extended use privileges "for school purposes."[26] In the meantime the old library continued to struggle under cramped conditions. During the summer trustees had shifted circulation rules. Borrowers were allowed two cards—one for either nonfiction or fiction, the other for nonfiction only. Upon request, special-privilege cards would be extended for nonfiction. Books could be kept for two weeks, and renewed once if not in demand. Books marked "Seven Days" could not be renewed. Children could take out no more than two books per week. As an unwritten rule, patrons could not check out a book, return it the same day, and then check out another. Most of these circulation rules reflected an ideology of reading—held dear by WLS graduates and RPL trustees—that the reading of popular fiction needed to be controlled.[27]

On November 1, 1904—less than three years after E. O. Brown had first contacted Carnegie—the board opened the new building to the public. A dedication ceremony was held that evening, and all two hundred seats were occupied. Another seventy people leaned against walls and book-shelves; others listened as best they could from halls and adjoining rooms. Women's Club members provided piano and choral music, and served re-freshments. Board President Samuel S. Miller (local district attorney, Re-publican, and Congregationalist) thanked founding trustees, the Brown Brothers Lumber Company for the lot, Andrew Carnegie for the building, and the Women's Club for the furnishings. To the mayor he said: "We leave these treasures in your hands, confidently hoping and believing that they will be profitably used to the uplifting of the people, the promotion of pa-triotism, and the upbuilding of good citizenship in our community." Other dignitaries who commented included Congressman W. E. Brown, who particularly complimented trustees for placing the library "in [the] charge of a careful and competent librarian" and making sure that "children of tender years could go to the library and secure only such literature as they should read." In 1904 RPL was one of 123 public libraries in Wisconsin.[28]

PROFESSIONALIZING THE PLACE

In the spring of 1905, the Rhinelander Public Library got a telephone. A month later Mary Smith reported that German-language books from the WFLC traveling library system were now available at the library, and noted that for North Side people unable to come to the library because of weather she had located a case of thirty-five books in "Mr. Franklin's store." She placed another case of thirty children's books in "Miss Pugh's school room," and reported that twenty-one of thirty-one public and pa-rochial teachers had registered for teachers' cards. She also noted heavy use of WFLC bookmarks listing books recommended for children. "When a child completes one, his name is placed on a roll of honor. A large copy of the book-marks with call numbers opposite each title is posted in the children's room and is used by children in finding books." Her professional training showed in each initiative.[29]

In her 1905 annual report, Smith proudly announced a 4 percent de-crease in fiction circulation. She also noted heavy use of materials by the Monday Club and the Rhinelander Women's Club, thanked the Wis-consin Federation of Women's Clubs for a traveling library collection of art books, and thanked the Wisconsin Free Library Commission for an Italian book collection. That summer RPL borrowed a WFLC traveling library collection of thirty-six Scandinavian-language books.[30] Using these collections had two advantages: first, the library did not have to buy foreign-language titles; second, the commission assumed responsibility for their content. No book by a "modern degenerate" would find its way into any traveling library, the commission reassured Wisconsin librarians. Foreign-language traveling libraries were primarily designed to bring immigrants into the library, where it was hoped they would quickly learn English.[31]

When Smith resigned that summer to take a similar position in Eau Claire, Wisconsin, trustees hired Mary Bevans, a WLS graduate employed by the Decatur Public Library in Illinois. Among the first moves Bevans recommended was subscribing to two copies of the most popular magazines, and purchasing one extra copy of the most popular books to start a rental shelf (a practice increasingly popular in U.S. public libraries). She also thanked the local Children's Audubon Society for donating a collection of bird eggs. On February 14, 1906, the *Vindicator* reported that the library was exhibiting a model collection of children's books circulated by the WFLC. "The books will be exhibited for ten days and it is hoped that parents and teachers and all interested in children . . . will find this collection a great aid in planning for birthday and holiday gifts." Through its "trained librarian," the state library commission was much more involved in library practice and policy at RPL than it was at the libraries described in the first three chapters of this book.

On May 12, 1906, the library began a tradition. "At 10:30 about ninety children went from their own pleasant room down to the lecture room," the *Vindicator* reported. "Here all formality was done away with and they grouped themselves around Miss Gillespie [a local teacher], a few on chairs but nearly all choosing to sit on the floor. Then for three quarters of an hour they heard, many of them for the first time, of the heroes of the old German and Norse tales." In her annual report Bevans announced that story hour attendance averaged thirty-five, but she also noted that "the circulation of fiction has not decreased, being still 73%."[32] A trend Smith thought she had started by practicing the librarianship taught her at the Wisconsin Library School proved short-lived—RPL patrons mostly wanted fiction.

With the new building, the library found itself strapped for cash. The board contacted Carnegie yet again, this time to fund a collections endowment, but to no avail. "Mr. Carnegie . . . does not assist with books,"

Bertram snipped. The Women's Club again rallied support; its members pledged one hundred dollars a year for five years to purchase books, and in addition agreed to spend twenty-five dollars annually on art books. Despite this help, more funds were needed. Compounding its troubles, the board learned that Mary Bevans was going to resign. Again trustees turned to the WFLC.[33]

WLS student Ada J. McCarthy applied for the job. A graduate of the Milwaukee Normal School, she had taught for ten years in the Midwest and the Pacific Northwest. "I understand that a great deal of stress is put on work with the schools in Rhinelander," she wrote to the board secretary, "and I feel that my training and experience in both library and school work will enable me to fill the position to your satisfaction." When offered a job two weeks later, she immediately accepted, pending graduation from WLS. Her acceptance letter showed her training, as she asked some pertinent questions: "Who is your superintendent of schools? What percent of your population is foreign and what is the predominant nationality? Is there much done with the Women's club?" Shortly after she arrived in Rhinelander, McCarthy reported to WFLC officials that she had been "out to a lovely tea last night and met your friends the Browns."[34]

As a WLS graduate, McCarthy frequently wrote to former faculty members about her experiences. In addition, in 1907 the WFLC annually began visiting and evaluating Wisconsin public libraries. Because so much written material connected with the WFLC evaluations has been preserved, it is possible to write a fuller history of professionalizing influences on the RPL than on the public libraries written about in this book's first three chapters. For example, in a letter to WLS Preceptor Mary Imogene Hazeltine, McCarthy noted efforts to increase adult use of the library by locating signs in local hotels and stores, but said that these had only shown marginal results. The problem was young adults, she said, who came to the library "not to read or study," but "to visit and largely make dates." In early December she wrote to one Rhinelander parent: "I am sorry to report to you that your son William came to the Library Saturday night and greatly disturbed the people there. As you are responsible for his good conduct in the Library I trust that you will not let this pass." Hazeltine urged persistence: "While you cannot have a guard on your staff, I am sure you are doing quite right in calling the police to your rescue, because it dignifies the place. I agree with you that the place must be glorified, put on a pedestal, as it were."[35]

And McCarthy was persistent. In March she complained to Hazeltine: "It is the High School girl who gets the new fiction. Sometimes I am almost afraid I have set my standard a little too high for this community, but I can't bear to have it any other way." A month later she reported success. "Thursday night the reading room was just what I wanted it to be, for the first time since I have been here. It was almost full of older people as well as High School boys & girls, and all were reading and it was quiet and dignified. We have attained our ideal." Later that spring, the WFLC secretary complimented Rhinelander on its "library progress."[36] McCarthy was particularly good with teachers. By fall term in 1907 she had negotiated a reading program that required all fourth-grade through eighth-grade pupils to read four library books during the school year. The library also underwent some renovations, including cork panels on walls above shelves particularly useful for mounting student artwork. And on a fall Saturday the Women's Club began an annual event called "Tag Day." On Rhinelander streets, club members "tagged" people, "young and old," who were then expected to contribute to a new RPL endowment fund.

In her December "Library Notes" column, McCarthy made a special pitch to recently furloughed local labor. "Now that the working force of the mills has been reduced, it is earnestly hoped that those taking this enforced rest will find time to spend an hour or two in the evening in the cozy reading room in their Library."[37] Her words carried little sympathy for their plight. McCarthy's January 8, 1908, column focused on library serials, most of which were middle-class periodicals cited in a recent *Wisconsin Library Bulletin* (*WLB*) article entitled "Magazines for the Small Library" and indexed in either *Poole's Guide to Periodical Literature* or *Readers' Guide to Periodical Literature*.[38] The centralizing tendencies of professional practice were obvious. For leadership and guidance McCarthy looked mostly to her profession rather than to her local community.

In her 1908 annual report McCarthy proudly noted that 39 percent of Rhinelander's population had used the library the previous year. Although this seemed to give "an encouraging outlook," she still worried about nonusers like "men in our mills, more children in the schools and on the street, and mothers in their homes." In September she told *Vindicator* readers: "It is hoped that the coming school year will be another proof that the Library is more than a mere place of amusement, that it is a place for study and research." To reinforce this principle, McCarthy joined other Wisconsin librarians in removing comic sections from Sunday newspapers because laughter they evoked disturbed the dignity of the library.[39]

But labor particularly concerned her. At the city's Labor Day parade she noticed few familiar faces. This prompted her to send local unions a circular. "While watching the recent . . . parade, I notice[d] with regret that very few of the members of the different labor organizations ever visit the library." Months later she published an article in *WLB* entitled "The Library at Rhinelander and the Workingmen." Rhinelander had thirty-three saloons and but one public library, she said, and to reach the community's workingmen she had placed cards identifying library services and hours in boardinghouses, mills, and factories; she also had asked mill superintendents to put these cards in workers' pay envelopes. In addition, she slipped them into the books of workingmen's children, and asked them to give the cards to their fathers. In these notices she especially stressed the availability of Norwegian- and German-language book collections, which the WFLC continued to supply. "Our next move," she told *WLB* readers, "is to compile an annotated list of books concerning the kind of work each union is interested in." Days after the article appeared, Hazeltine congratulated McCarthy. "That was an excellent letter that you sent to the different unions."[40] McCarthy and Hazeltine could not see that an institution set up and run by Brown Brothers Lumber Company owners and their family members and funded by antilabor robber baron Andrew Carnegie might be held suspect by union men.

In April 1909 Rhinelander voted against the prohibition of alcohol (a political issue that divided Yankee founders and their churches from German and Scandinavian immigrants and their churches), the Bijou (the local theater) set up a "new moving picture" machine, and the RWC asked that its annual $100 library contribution be placed in an endowment. "It is hoped that the citizens of Rhinelander will follow the example of the club," the *Vindicator* said.[41] For her annual report, McCarthy cited progress. More than 40 percent of Rhinelander residents were now registered borrowers, and they checked out 26,512 books (60 percent of these were fiction titles). RWC members made regular use of the library assembly room, and did research there for twenty articles related to club activities.

Monday Club members used it for twenty-one presentations. Both had a shelf in the reference area set aside for information on club topics. In addition, the library had developed a collection of more than three thousand pictures for teachers' classroom use. Again, in her annual report, McCarthy mentioned workingmen and homemakers. In the fall of 1909 the board allowed the school system to use the assembly room for a kindergarten.[42]

In December 1909, McCarthy resigned to accept a similar position in Marinette, Wisconsin. Harriet Allen, another WLS graduate, succeeded her in January. A month later, for the "worthy poor of the city" the Rhinelander Salvation Army opened a lodging house with a reading room "where a few hours may be spent . . . in rest and mental recreation and improvement . . . reading the daily papers and current literature," the *Vindicator* said. For RPL the Salvation Army reading room was bittersweet news. On the one hand, it demonstrated that the library had not attracted workingmen; on the other, fewer "strangers" crowded the building. Allen continued McCarthy's monthly *Vindicator* columns; most were booklists with canned annotations.[43]

In her annual report for 1910, Allen noted that almost all library periodicals were indexed in *Readers' Guide*, that circulation figures for the German and Scandinavian collections showed that "this branch of the library has been well appreciated" (the library still refused to buy foreign-language books), and that Saturday morning story hours were well attended. Allen did not mention workingmen, but gave greater coverage to "children's work" than previous reports had given. "The work with children is one of the promising features of the library movement," she wrote, then repeated a professional conviction that Hamlin Garland would have disputed: "The reading habit and taste for good literature is formed while he is young and the choice of books in his mature years depends largely on what he had read as a child," presumably including girls in this analysis.[44]

The problem with teenagers did not go away. On May 18, 1911, trustees discussed "the matter of boys & girls making Library a rendezvous of an evening." One trustee wrote to local newspapers, others asked ministers to address the issue in Sunday sermons. In "The Library and the Social Center," Lutie Stearns gave WLB readers two pieces of advice on how to make the library a place to change youthful behaviors. First, "the leader of the boy gang may be persuaded to temporarily give up the reading of the lurid 'nickel library' in favor of Custer and Grinnell's truthful Indian experiences"; second, "boys that frequent the gymnasium may be won by [Ralph Henry] Barbour's latest football story." Ultimately, she said, library books had three purposes—"to inform, to inspire, or to refresh.... A novel should be loaned with a book for study." And the ambience of the library was very important. "The library and reading room should be well lighted and heated, and order and quiet should be insisted upon."[45] Thus, the RPL leaders' response to problem teenagers was in lockstep with WFLC advice.

In 1911, general circulation was up only slightly, and although Allen gave category figures in her annual report, she failed to mention that fiction had increased to 66 percent of the total. Librarians across the country also worried about declining circulation, Allen said. "One of the main attributive causes seems to be the large number of moving picture shows which have been opened up." Allen's remarks played to local concerns. In Rhinelander, guardians of local morals complained of several pictures at the Bijou, and in an editorial the new *Rhinelander News* reminded its manager "to see that his good reputation is maintained by cutting out all obscene allusions and indecent pictures." So that these "amusements" would "not be allowed to take the place of the reading of good literature," Allen argued that it was necessary to develop "the library habit," especially "among children and young people."[46] On an "Annual Statistical Report" sent to the WFLC she also noted: "Men's reading room discussed and hopes are entertained of having one opened at the library this fall." Part of the reason for the initiative was WFLC pressure. "It is because the library in its acquisition of books has heretofore paid too little attention to the needs of the worker that it now becomes so important to select utilitarian material," the commission said. Here the commission echoed the professional library community, which perceived labor unrest as a social problem the public library could address with the right information.

In her 1912 annual report Allen noted that the library had recently started "a small rent collection" so "the most popular books the patrons want may be more quickly accommodated." She also noted that circulation had increased over the previous two years. Although fiction now accounted for 70 percent of circulation, that figure did not appear in her newspaper report several months later. Allen also extended special thanks to one patron who "kindly remembered the library with cut flowers for the desk." Finally, she noted that the library would host a booth at the county fair, and that the board had given the local WCTU chapter permission to use the assembly room for its monthly meetings.[47]

In two newspaper columns, Allen proudly announced that the library had secured a "beautiful edition" of Charles Dudley Warner's thirty-one-volume *Library of the World's Best Literature* and "excellent editions of Shakespeare, Eliot, and Stevenson. . . . Readers will find these volumes much more attractive and easier reading than the old editions." These books, she noted, were "purchased with interest money from the endowment fund—money from Tag Day receipts." When the WFLC inspector visited in March, he "checked up ALA Supplement" with Allen, judged her use of it "pretty good," and noted that "Booklist is followed carefully."[48] Allen's training was obvious. In May 1914, however, as she put finishing touches on an annual report showing that fiction accounted for 72.5 percent of circulation, Allen resigned to take charge of the City and School of Mines Library in Houghton, Michigan.[49]

The transition to another librarian did not go smoothly. Two male trustees wanted to delay a hiring until fall, in part to save money. Allen pointed out that during the summer someone had to process new books and send large numbers of periodicals to the bindery. But "that was a very simple matter" an assistant could do at less cost, said one male trustee. To that two female trustees objected, arguing that the library needed a director. Allen was especially offended when one male trustee said her salary matched that of local policemen—"the first time I have been classed with them in my work," she complained to Hazeltine.[50]

The women got their way. In July the board hired Jessie W. Bingham, yet another WLS graduate, at the time working at the Chicago Public Library, where several years earlier Horatio Alger and Oliver Optic novels had been pulled from the shelves. Bingham came highly recommended. When she entered library school, a former employer noted that she came from "a home of culture; . . . her personality is exceedingly pleasing in its reticent approachableness, its gentleness, and dignity." Like all others who had weathered the WLS curriculum, she gained entrance only after an oral examination on her knowledge of authors like Charles Dickens, Nathaniel Hawthorne, William Thackeray, Victor Hugo, and Sir Walter Scott. To a recommended list of titles, however, WLS Preceptor Hazeltine also added Jane Austen and George Eliot, and even included Jane Addams's *Democ-*

racy and Social Ethics (1902) and *Spirit of Youth and the City Streets* (1909). The list reflects a gendered perspective on quality literature, and a middle-class white progressive's perspective on social reform. It did not necessarily reflect what circulated most at the Rhinelander Public Library.[51]

Days later Europe erupted in war. Rhinelander's population of New England Yankee transplants and European immigrants reacted with mixed loyalties. To address the situation the *Rhinelander News* ran a story entitled "Information on War at the Library," in which Bingham identified relevant magazine articles that intended to "aid one in getting an idea of the conditions over there." But the library carried on with other activities. It stocked a WFLC German and Norwegian collection, although Bingham was not happy with fiction titles. "Books are included which, if written in English, would be barred from the library without a doubt." Bingham continued to advertise library services in her monthly column, noted an exhibit of native butterflies put together by a local resident, and participated in the annual auction of books by the men's and women's book clubs. And she practiced librarianship just as she had been taught in Madison, where the WLS was situated. In early June, she ordered from the American Library Association copies of Theresa Hitchler's *Cataloging for Small Libraries* (1915), the *ALA Manual of Library Economy* (1911), Caroline Hewins's *Books for Boys and Girls* (1915), and Harriet Hassler and Carrie Scott's *Graded List of Stories for Reading Aloud* (1915).[52]

When the WFLC inspector came through Rhinelander in mid-March 1915, the library had just recorded its largest monthly circulation ever. Although Bingham "has been friendly and sociable, and has talked books," the inspector reported, reduced appropriations enabled her to buy only thirty new titles that year. "Instead of buying new books," Bingham "tied up six or more numbers of magazines containing a serial novel, and issued that as a book." The WFLC inspector also reported that she had met several trustees, including Mary Shelton, in whose house Bingham lived "and the one woman whose criticism she [Bingham] dreaded."[53] In her annual report, Bingham noted that RPL had enjoyed its busiest year ever, despite the fact that annual appropriations had not increased and several new establishments were competing for local citizen attention. Al Taylor's Billiard Parlor had opened, sporting "first class tables, a full line of cigars, tobacco, and soft drinks." And in addition to the Bijou, Rhinelander now had the Majestic, which in December 1913, showed Rhinelander its first "big picture"—*The Battle of Gettysburg.* The Majestic's owner told the *News*: "In my theater I am furnishing the people clean, wholesome entertainment for the small price of five and 10 cents."[54]

The opening of local billiard parlors and movie theaters did not affect library circulation, perhaps because in 1915 an increased appropriation enabled Bingham to buy more fiction. Newly acquired popular novels included Mary Roberts Rinehart's *K* (1915), Booth Tarkington's *Turmoil* (1915), Arthur Conan Doyle's *Valley of Fear* (1914), Honoré Morrow's *Still Jim* (1915), Zane Grey's *Lone Star Ranger* (1915), Samuel Adams's *The Clarion* (1914), and William H. Phyfe's *18,000 Words Often Mispronounced* (1889). "With the arrival of decidedly crisp evenings that make indoor entertainment much preferable to motoring," the *News* reported, "the demand for books at the Carnegie Public Library is being increased tremendously." But not without some worry. That fall the *News* reported that several rural youth "seduced" by "yellow backed dime novels" to "run away from home on a wild west trip" had been picked up by Rhinelander officials near the railroad station and quickly sent back home. Congregationalist Rev. W. C. Heyl also worried about the influence of media. Movies had the power to work "for good or for evil," he said in a Sunday sermon. On the one hand, "saloonists of many cities complain that the picture shows are ruining their business." On the other, "librarians announce that fewer books are being read."[55] Not at the Rhinelander Public Library, however.

Concern for these worrisome influences led Bingham to talk about "Why Some Books Are under the Ban of Libraries" at a Women's Club meeting. Because the library had an open shelf system, "censorship is necessary," she said, and the public had to be protected from "immoral books." What constituted immoral books? "Get-rich-quick" schemes, "everyone does it" tomes, and books "which leave us worse than [they] found us." The latter required special attention, she said, because they often confused "our ideas of right and wrong" or lowered "our mental tone by vulgarity of treatment or by sentimentality."[56] Of course none of these kinds of books were cited in *Booklist*, the *WLB*, or ALA catalogs.

Six months later, in 1916, a WFLC inspector conducted a routine evaluation of Bingham's performance. The librarian was "untiring in her efforts," "is extremely well liked," and "an excellent housekeeper," the inspector noted, but Bingham had "very decided ideas and is not easily convinced that her way is not always the best." Because her budget did not allow for many acquisitions, she could purchase books only three or four times per year. "Most of the fiction," the inspector reported, "is purchased from a Book Club in the town. In this way it is gotten for a small price and is comparatively recent." For Bingham, it also meant that these books came with prior approval by city leaders. Eighteen months later the 1917 inspector reported that Bingham was purchasing "current class books" through Western News of Chicago, where she obtained "prompt service and good prices." Bingham never visited local schools, in part because the school superintendent (an ex officio board member) had not worked well with her predecessor. On her board, according the inspector, President Judge Harold Steele ruled. "All questions not taken up first with him are doomed to oblivion. Not very interested in Commission because it does not contribute state aid." Obviously, Steele was not as inclined to take direction from the WFLC as Jessie Bingham was.[57]

In her 1916 annual report, Bingham reported circulation at 23,898, 66 percent of which was fiction, both about average for Wisconsin public libraries in communities of Rhinelander's size. By that time Rhinelander was readying for a new YMCA, which would be equipped with a gymnasium, free baths, a reading room, and a classroom for a night school intended "for young men who work in the mills and factories and have not had the advantage of an early education." Obviously, RPL librarians' efforts to attract workingmen had been unsuccessful; yet another civic agency emerged to address perceived social problems unique to this group.[58]

The debate about fiction refused to leave the public discourse. In January 1917, *WLB* reprinted a comment by prominent library publisher F. W. Faxon: "I wonder if libraries, by excluding *Munsey, Cosmopolitan*, and *McClure's* [all containing serial fiction], are helping the public, or driving the very people they hope to protect into a field of reading infinitely worse." RPL had none of the periodicals. Two months later, Helen Turvill of the Wisconsin Library School pressed a different point of view, asking *WLB* readers where their libraries stood on the issue of nonfiction circulation rates: "Is your percentage of non-fiction circulated as large as other libraries report?" In some Wisconsin communities, she noted "striking progress," nonfiction circulation rates above 50 percent. On April 6, 1917, however, the *Rhinelander News* reprinted a story from the *St. Louis Post Dispatch*. "Somebody has made the astonishing discovery that literary men as well as men of affairs are fond of reading detective stories," the paper noted, and mentioned several examples, including Charles Reade's *Hard Cash* (1913), Wilkie Collins's *Moonstone* (1906), and the works of Thomas W. Hanshew.[59] On its shelves at that time, RPL had twelve titles by Reade, nine by Collins, but none by Hanshew.

In 1918 Rhinelander was one of 211 Wisconsin public libraries, 89 of which occupied their own building; Carnegie had funded 63. Daily, Bingham and her staff changed date stamps, arranged book cards, entered circulation statistics, and shelved books. Periodically they read the shelves, often pulling worn books to be mended or unused books to be weeded. For acquisitions Bingham checked the pages of *Booklist* and other collection guides that the WFLC provided, and upon purchasing new books ordered Library of Congress catalog cards. She also responded to any letters, regulated the schedule for the assembly room (including citizenship classes held every Friday night), attended to small bills and petty cash, and ordered necessary supplies, all of which she dutifully reported to her board. Local citizens regarded the service her library provided as "highly satisfactory"; no one—including trustees—pressed her to reach further into the community.[60] By war's end, RPL had become a fixture with a set of traditions the community had come to expect. The Women's Club continued to support the library with Tag Day, rummage sales, Liberty Bonds, and endowment funds (Mary Shelton gave one thousand dollars in her husband's memory). After passage of the Nineteenth Amendment, the Women's Club used library rooms to organize a local chapter of the League of Women Voters. In December 1919, the *Rhinelander News* (which had just become a daily) started running Etta Verne Lyndon's serial novel *When Love Came*.[61] RPL never acquired a copy of the book after it was published.

On April 8, 1920, Rhinelander sent shock waves through the state by electing Socialist Party candidate Sam Perinier as mayor. Elsewhere in Wisconsin, Victor Berger, the socialist mayor of Milwaukee, was being prosecuted for sedition. In his inaugural address, Perinier acknowledged that "there are those who are filled with misgivings when viewing the action of the working class of Rhinelander in choosing an administration from its own ranks," but he reminded his audience that "by an overwhelming majority our people are of the class that toils." Given the absence of titles on socialism on RPL shelves (to be discussed in more depth in chapter 5), one wonders what the new mayor—and those who voted him into office—thought about their public library. That over the years no one from

labor complained to the newspapers about the dearth of socialist literature in the library suggests several possibilities: socialists relied on their
own resources for political information; laborers came to view the library
as a civic institution controlled by Rhinelander's major employers and
their families; and family members of the "class that toils" still used the library, but not for political information. Instead, they came to expect—and
insist upon—the popular fiction that drove the library's circulation rate,
and in the act of reading that popular fiction they not only connected to
other readers of all classes, they also appropriated models of behavior and
life lessons unique to their social and economic circumstances.[62]

For her 1922 "Annual Statistical Report," Bingham noted that of Rhinelander's 6,664 citizens the library had 3,260 registered borrowers who
withdrew 24,237 items from its collection of 7,961 volumes including the
rental collection. This represented the lowest circulation per capita of all
Wisconsin cities with similar populations. Of that total adults accounted
for 15,280 books circulated (80 percent of these fiction), children 8,957 (74
percent of these fiction).[63] At the time the library subscribed to thirty-
eight periodicals and seven newspapers, none of them socialist. In response to a local curfew "to control immorality among school children,"
the WFLC inspector noted, Bingham had established a rule "that children
under seventh grade could not come to the library in the evening." As a result, "her discipline problem" was made "easier," the inspector reported.[64]

In October 1922 Bingham attended a WLA conference, where members
were asked, "What is your outstanding accomplishment in making your
community conscious of your library service?" Answers included: activity in public affairs; bird records kept in library; book talks and exhibits;
a Christmas tree and evening programs during Christmas Week; civic
organizations; support by newspapers; exhibits, readings, and lectures
in library; extension service to rural teachers, pupils, and teachers; fac-
tory stations; a float in a Labor Day parade; "frequent book purchases well
advertised"; help to speakers; publicity through printed lists and movies;
special invitations to non-cardholders delivered by Boy Scouts; Sunday
opening; the training of schoolchildren in use of the library; window displays; and work with teachers and women's clubs.[65] Thus, in the early 1920s
many Wisconsin public libraries embraced their roles as community centers. Measured against this list, however, RPL was only moderately active.

On December 6, 1922, Rhinelander opened several community rooms in the City Hall basement. "The new rooms consist of a capacious reading room well stocked with carefully selected literature," the *News* reported, "and a large reception room, the floor of which is used for dancing purposes by the young folks who already throng the rooms every evening in the week except Sunday." Showers and bathtubs were also provided "for the free use of guests." Mayor Perinier expressed hope that one day the city could build a separate community building, but in the interim, he said, the rooms demonstrated a cooperative civic spirit. Although library board members had been on the committee planning these rooms, the library itself had nothing to do with its reading room collections or services.

In the early 1920s Rhinelander citizens had many opportunities besides the public library to participate in the local print culture. At home, they subscribed to periodicals and newspapers, and read the printed products of their churches, associations, and organizations. For popular fiction they could go Packard's Pharmacy or Koppa's Oneida Pharmacy ("Books make ideal Christmas gifts; We have the latest fiction at 75c."), and—for selected titles for youths—Kate McRae's gift shop. Other kinds of information and entertainment came from the radio, with a lineup of programs (national and local) that the *News* printed daily, and the Majestic and State Theaters, each showing the silent films Hollywood produced and circulated. In 1922 Rhinelander was also home to 842 automobiles, or one car for every seven people—an average, the *News* noted proudly, that ranked it with Los Angeles. The early 1920s brought other changes. In July 1923, the Rhinelander Country Club opened a short distance from the city, and in September the Public Welfare Department of the reconstituted Rhinelander Women's Club announced a program that focused on health issues, working conditions, and the employment of women and children. None of these endeavors involved the library.[66]

By this time the *News* had stopped reporting on board meetings, carried no "New Books at the Library" column, and even failed to notice Bingham's annual reports. Reasons for this low profile are not hard to find. On the one hand, neither Jessie Bingham nor her board felt the need to expand services their community had grown to expect. On the other, it refused to challenge local values or force its way into the local political discourse. For example, on March 14, 1923, the *News* carried a wire service story entitled "Is Modern Sex Fiction Harmful?" which quoted Dr. Eugene Fisk, who was particularly worried about women in "this age of self-indulgence, of luxury, of the new freedom.... Stories of life that are high-minded, spiritualizing a human passion, create good. The other kind, having a pathological trend, brutalize it and appeal only to the animal sense." Offering a counterpoint was Eleanor Ramos, editor of *Saucy Stories* magazine. "In literature people today are demanding directness, frankness, truth. As editor of a so-called sex magazine, I think of the sex story as one that treats of love from the realistic, rather than the romantic, angle."[67]

The Rhinelander Public Library did not carry the likes of *Saucy Stories*, nor any collection of fiction of the sort it published, which had been filtered out of the pool of possibilities from which it made selections. The library profession ignored titles like these, library officials shunned them, and by then patrons had no expectations that their public library would provide them. In an editorial entitled "Clean Pictures" several years later, the *News* complimented Will Hays, president of Motion Picture Producers and Distributors of America, who promised no pictures that "offend common decency." "At a time when books and plays are becoming more and more emboldened in the presentation of salacious subject matter," the *News* opined, "it is an amazing thing to consider that the 'movies' are almost automatically and voluntarily straightening up."[68] Thus, self-policing was taking place in the motion picture industry and the Rhinelander Public Library; in the latter it was just less obvious.

A NEW REGIME

On March 8, 1926, "Rhinos" (a favorite local self-description even then) voted 1,065 to 802 to adopt a city manager system, in part because the city was broke, and in part because Rhinelander's established families chafed under a socialist government whose luster had by this time worn away. The plan called for an elected five-member city council with supervisory powers over a city manager, who would be responsible for running the city. Initially all existing city boards and commissions were abolished, except for the Board of Education and the library board. In reporting his first budget, City Manager Charles Grau noted that because the library had "other funds" at its "disposal than that raised by tax levy," its budget would be reduced by 40 percent for the coming year. At the December board meeting "the purchasing of new books for the Library and subscribing to periodicals etc. was discussed and the board decided to leave these matters to the Librarian's judgment."[69]

In the fall of 1927, rumors began to circulate that the city would take over the library and abolish the board. Weeks later Jessie Bingham announced her resignation, effective January 1. At a December 12 meeting, the common council heard three resolutions from the library board: first, abolish the thirty-year-old board and transfer library control to the city manager; second, create a three-person advisory committee to the city manager; and third, refuse Bingham's resignation, give her a six-month leave of absence, then ask her to resume her duties. In presenting the resolutions, Board Chairman Steele said trustees believed the library "should be handled by the city manager," and that Bingham's resignation was an opportunity for Grau to make his own selection for the post. In a private letter to Mary Imogene Hazeltine, trustee Mrs. L. A. Leadbetter assured Hazeltine that the board was behind the shift. In January 1928, the council adopted the resolution abolishing the library board and placing the library under the city manager.[70]

Jessie Bingham saw the matter differently than Leadbetter. She told Hazeltine that Grau did not want the library, but because Steele "did not wish them to have a board of which he was not president," he forced the issue. Because of "local influence," she told Hazeltine, Grau was considering as Bingham's replacement Alice Raymond, a former Wisconsin Rapids librarian who ran a Rhinelander boardinghouse. Although Bingham thought it "would not be so bad" if Raymond became interim librarian until the city manager "could engage a Library School graduate," any other course of action was unthinkable. Raymond had not taken WLS courses and was not state certified. "Really, I think it would be a calamity to allow this woman to have the position," Bingham wrote. Shortly thereafter, Grau named Raymond acting librarian.[71]

In April 1928, Hazeltine visited Rhinelander to talk with Grau. She noted that Raymond did not have a state-mandated certificate, and offered to find Rhinelander a temporary replacement until Grau could find a "qualified director." Grau refused; he would stick with Raymond. This worried Hazeltine. She wrote a confidential letter to agents of library book wholesalers Baker & Taylor and the H. R. Huntting Company, reporting that Grau had told her "that he was going to 'shop around,' thinking that he could buy books in the open market where there might be competition. I tried to get across that you could not shop around for books, that they should be purchased through regulation sources." She then told agents to give any order from Rhinelander "first class service" so Grau, unchecked by an inexperienced librarian, would be dissuaded from such a wrongful course of action.[72] So committed was Hazeltine to "best library practices" taught at WLS she was willing to go behind the back of a local government official to check his influence over a public library.

At its October conference, WLA went public: it placed Rhinelander and several other cities on a "most dishonorable" list for employing librarians not certified by the state. Grau reacted quickly. "The action was aimed at cities which had refused to be dictated to by a library association which had no power," he argued. He noted that Raymond had recently completed several WLS courses, and that she would soon apply for a state certificate. And since she had taken over, Grau said, "I don't believe a single patron of the library has any complaint to make over the service received here." Extant records show he was right; RPL patrons seemed quite comfortable with the transition.

Two days later Raymond asked the *WLB* editor to include a notice in the next issue: "Since the resignation of the Library Board last December, the City Manager, having direct charge, has thoroughly repaired the roof and the furnace. The interior has been redecorated and cleaned and presents a very pleasing appearance. . . . The circulation has shown an increase each month since February over the corresponding months last year." *WLB* reprinted it verbatim, adding only that "the improvements are often commented upon and are greatly appreciated by the patrons." Raymond improved library services in other ways. In November 1928, for example, RPL participated in "Good Book Week" for the first time by mounting two exhibits, one displaying adult titles *Booklist* had recommended, the other displaying children's titles that a Milwaukee children's librarian had recommended. Children who read ten from the latter list were given a button inscribed "I read library books."[73]

Although relations between the RPL and the Wisconsin library establishment warmed, the latter did not relinquish a self-assumed responsibility to aggressively promote good reading. It continued to send lists of "good" books. But RPL no longer automatically followed Madison's lead. In a report to the council in 1929, Grau noted that the library had enjoyed its highest January circulation rate since 1910. Two reasons explained this, he said. First, the library was purchasing more new titles; second, "an effort is being made to furnish library patrons with the kind of books they want."[74] Subtext to this comment was that Raymond was willing to stock the popular fiction titles that Wisconsin's professional library community (and WLS alumnae) had been fighting for decades.

Growth did not stop. In October 1929 the library experienced another record monthly circulation. That this happened as entertainment venues from which Rhinelander citizens could choose greatly expanded made the circulation increase even more impressive. In 1929 residents could buy newspapers, periodicals, and popular fiction at local pharmacies, read serialized novels in the *Rhinelander Daily News*, listen to news and entertainment programs on local radio stations (including *Amos 'n' Andy*), and see movies at local theaters. On May 6, 1930, the Majestic hosted Rhinelander's first talkie; six months later Kate McRae opened a rental library in her gift shop.[75] At the beginning of the Great Depression, RPL prospered in this growing culture of fiction presented via print, film, and radio.

But the public library came in for some criticism. "This man Upton Sinclair keeps one book ahead of me," wrote a local citizen to the *News* "Letter Box" in 1930. "And unfortunately for me, the Rhinelander library makes little or no effort to get his books, although the Milwaukee Library stocks them as fast as they come from the press. The reason, I am told, is that Milwaukeeans read Sinclair, but Rhinos do not." The patron was likely referring to RPL collecting priorities on labor issues (to be discussed in more depth in chapter 5) that dated back to 1904.[76] Alice Raymond took note.

In January 1931, RPL exhibited thirty-three paintings by nineteen members of the Madison Art Guild, including *Half Nude*, the *News* reported, "one of the most striking pictures in the exhibit." A month later the library extended its hours to 9:00 P.M. (except Sundays) to accommodate demand, a factor made evident in circulation statistics, which jumped from 37,094 in 1929 to 44,757 in 1930. "This is accountable for several reasons such as better service, addition of many new books, efficient administration, increased interest in the children's department, and to some extent," the *News* said, "the current depression which has brought more people to the library for recreation."[77] The latter was an understatement.

Through it all Raymond continued to promote books and reading (if not exactly the kind of reading that the WLA, WFLC, and *WLB* advocated). When the Depression forced budget cuts, the library reinstituted a rental collection of "the latest popular books." And Raymond continued to listen to her patrons. In a *News* article on murder mysteries at the library, she noted that Upton Sinclair's anti-prohibition *The Wet Parade* (1931) "was added to the library's shelves here at the request of a local minister and a local newspaperman. Strangely enough, these men of different literary tastes both recommend this book." Perhaps Raymond's responsiveness also traces to the previous year's citizen complaint, which demonstrates yet another pressure point in a community-based process of mediating public library book selection. With a collection of 10,594 volumes and circulation of 50,329 (75 percent of which was fiction) in 1931, Rhinelander averaged eleven books per borrower, one above the ALA standard of ten.[78]

Addressing needs created by the Depression continued to guide library acquisitions and activities. "With the Rhinelander Garden Club under way, with the City and Legion sponsoring garden tracts for unemployed families," Raymond noted in a *News* column, "the Rhinelander library can be of service." She then listed gardening books on library shelves. Similarly, the library served as a meeting site for the Garden Club, the Little Theatre Guild, and University of Wisconsin Extension courses. "The increase in circulation," Raymond told Mary Imogene Hazeltine, "is largely due to the centering of outside activities . . . in the library, as well as the unemployment situation." Left unsaid was a common practice of patron use of library rooms during cold months. For many Rhinelander residents the library was warmer than home. A record 1,051 persons used the reading room in December 1931.[79]

On January 30, 1933, Blanche Smith of the WFLC visited the library for its annual review. Smith noticed "an inviting library with pleasant atmosphere but very crowded appearance, due to rather indifferent housekeeping." When Smith recommended that the library clear tables by removing magazine back issues, Raymond protested: "The public missed them when they were taken away." Smith subsequently wrote the city manager that for a town of Rhinelander's size, with an annual circulation of nearly fifty-five thousand, the library needed another full-time employee. In response, the city manager argued that the library had suffered the smallest cut among city departments, and said "the amount set up for book purchases has not been cut at all."[80]

In April 1933, the *News* reported changes at the library, saying, "Rhinelander has grown 'serious minded' during the depression, and in literature has developed a taste for the more profound economic discussions that, in the stock market daze [sic], grew dusty on the library shelves." In particular, socialist Norman Thomas's *America's Way Out: A Program for Democracy* (1931) and *As I See It* (1932) were in high demand. "What kind of people read these books and articles that question the sanity of retaining capitalism any longer?," the *News* asked nervously. "Few of the persons who read them are Socialists; most of them are liberals who have come to doubt the success of 'prosperity' and who seek information on what thinkers believe to be wrong with the present system." Although "requests for serious nonfiction" were growing, the *News* also noted that there was "still a heavy demand for love stories, wild west thrillers, and murder mysteries." When the city manager made another series of cuts to city departments five months later, the *News* protested its effect on the library, saying, "It thus appears that at a time when the people are looking to the library for more service than ever, it has been required to get along on substantially less money."[81]

Blanche Smith's February 1934 annual review noted that the library had been redecorated by federally funded Civil Works Administration (CWA) labor and that a storeroom in the basement had been converted into another community meeting room. To relieve congestion, she suggested that the children's room be placed downstairs in the assembly room. RPL was, like other Wisconsin libraries, coping with growing collections in cramped quarters. On her last night in town, Smith addressed the council. She criticized Rhinelander for giving less support to its library than most similarly sized Wisconsin cities, despite the fact that it was getting more use. And the library needed an additional full-time staff member, she said. The two current employees were working twelve hours a day, five days a week, and often Sundays to mend old books and speedily catalog new ones. Her argument was so forceful, the *News* noted, that the council agreed to give the library an additional $500 for books.[82]

"City Library Needs More Money and More Aid," read a *News* headline the next day. Circulation had more than doubled between 1927 and 1933, it remarked: "These figures are all the more amazing when it is realized that two rental libraries were established in Rhinelander business houses during these years." The city manager advised the council that "within the near future Rhinelander will have to give more consideration to improving its library facilities." The *News* also announced that a cataloger had been temporarily hired with federal relief funds, that federal funds would be used to construct new library sidewalks, and that future plans called for hiring a children's librarian and moving the children's department to the assembly room.[83]

In December 1934 the library hired as new children's librarian Dorothy Whittaker, a 1928 WLS graduate who had experience as a children's librarian in Antigo. A month later the *News* reported forthcoming changes in the library. With the addition of Whittaker, the library extended hours (to Monday–Saturday, 10:00 A.M.–8:30 P.M.), and the children's department (through eighth grade) would be shifted to the assembly room on the lower floor, where it would be open Monday through Friday from three to six, and on Saturdays from ten till six. There Whittaker would conduct a story hour every Saturday morning. The room vacated by the children's department would become a reference room, where reference books would be moved for convenient access, thus relieving some of the pressure on crowded stack shelves. "This will leave the present reading room in the southwest corner for readers only, and will void the noise and confusion attendant to moving about the reference books." What the *News* did not say, however, was that the shift also removed important public meeting space in the Rhinelander community. Fewer people would be visiting the library in the future.[84]

For a while, the changes occurred smoothly. Although it took two months to set up the children's room, Whittaker reported that story hours were well attended. "I remember a session," Whittaker later recalled, "where I had to stand on a table to be heard because it was so crowded." In September 1936 the library learned it merited federal funds to "repair old books" and for "filing, shelf reading, and revision of historical material."[85] But all was not well. That month Blanche Smith again visited the library. "The new children's room is delightful," she said—it had "relieved the congestion" upstairs. At the same time, she noticed that "staff relations" were "somewhat strained." Raymond said that Whittaker was "trying to undermine her." Apparently Whittaker received a salary increase by going directly to the city manager without consulting Raymond. "I do not want to continue under these conditions," Raymond told Smith. Given its personnel problems, Smith worried for the future of the library.[86]

At year's end Raymond submitted an annual report that showed the largest circulation in the library's history. The library owned 11,952 books, and subscribed to fifty periodicals and seven newspapers. Registered borrowers totaled 4,067 (nearly 50 percent of the city's population), circulation totaled 62,031 (fiction accounted for 76 percent of adult circulation and 79 percent of children's). With the rearrangement in the library, reference activity had seen "steady growth . . . with requests being received from study groups, schools, and individuals." And in the children's department, "under the guidance of a trained children's librarian, the boys and girls are encouraged to read the right books." The library was still being used as a meeting room for some groups, including the Tennis Club, the Rhinelander Book Club, and the Junior Literary Club. Because of space limitations, however, the Women's Club had moved its meeting site to City Hall council chambers.[87]

When Blanche Smith visited again in September, she noticed that the relationship between Raymond and Whittaker had deteriorated. Raymond said to her that they worked "quite independently," and that the two had "no open clashes." Smith reported that Raymond "talks of retiring." Whittaker, on the other hand, was more aggressive. She planned to visit parochial grade schools to encourage students to make more use of the library. Smith complimented Whittaker on her initiative, and in subsequent months sent materials and advice to improve children's library collections and outreach. Months later, the *News* began publishing articles about new books available in the children's room.[88]

When Alice Raymond resigned on February 15, 1940, the city manager immediately announced that Whittaker would replace her. "No additional librarians will be employed," however, "except at rush periods."[89] The public hardly noticed. The librarian still reported to the city manager, who reported to the council. The *News* continued to cover library reports, including occasional "New Books" columns. In the summer, Whittaker started a "Young People's Collection" for junior and senior high school students, and located it on the main floor next to the regular adult fiction section. At the end of her first year, Whittaker reported that circulation had again reached "an all-time high."[90]

In May 1940, the *News* reported on the library's most-circulated books in the previous five years. Its three copies of Margaret Mitchell's *Gone with the Wind* had been borrowed an average of once every twelve days since they had been purchased in 1938. Two copies of Hervey Allen's *Anthony Adverse* had been "read with equal record," and one had been withdrawn because it wore out. Other titles that circulated widely in the first five months of 1940 included John Steinbeck's *Grapes of Wrath* (81 times; two copies); Christopher Morley's *Kitty Foyle* (64 times); Rachel Field's *All This and Heaven Too* (59); Daphne Du Maurier's *Rebecca* (53); John Phillips Marquand's *Wickford Point* (50); Kathleen Norris's *Runaway* (48), Charles Nordhoff and James Norman Hall's *Falcons of France* (47); C. S. Forester's *Captain Horatio Hornblower* (45); Richard Llewellyn's *How Green Was My Valley* (37), and Erle Stanley Gardner's *Case of the Stuttering Bishop* (30). Through RPL, the residents of Rhinelander read the same books as millions of other Americans.

In July Whittaker issued a report on magazine circulation, a practice the library had maintained since it opened in 1898. During the first six months of the year magazine circulation (measuring only those checked out and not those read at the library) had increased by 10 percent. Among weeklies, *Time* had circulated 114 times; *Life* had circulated 103 times; and *Saturday Evening Post* had circulated 72 times. *Vogue* (published twice a month) circulated 102 times. The top ten monthlies circulated were *Redbook* (76), *American Magazine* (69), *Good Housekeeping* (67), *Popular Mechanics* (60), *Cosmopolitan* (52), *House and Garden* (50), *House Beautiful* (50), *American Home* (48), *Magazine Digest* (43), and *Reader's Digest* (40). The *Daily News* reported: "Apparently busy people are substituting magazines for books to save time, librarians said." The logic was shallow; book circulation continued to increase and was largely driven by popular fiction. Librarians made no comment on the light use of "information" periodicals like *Atlantic*, *Harper's*, and the *Nation*.[91]

As one of 289 public libraries in Wisconsin, RPL participated in the Victory Book Campaign during World War II. "Principally desired are books containing interesting stories," the *News* noted for the first local drive in January 1942. Such stories, the *News* clearly implied, served an important wartime role. Receiving stations included the library, Red Cross headquarters, and all public and parochial schools. Book Drive Committee members also picked up books at homes if owners called the library. A second Victory Book Campaign followed in 1943 and netted 520 books in Rhinelander.[92]

In October 1943 the library began a "Read and See" project for children. Movies were shown twice each Saturday morning for "all children who have earned their admission ticket by reading library books or attending regular story hours. The purpose of the library movies," Whittaker told the *News*, "is the realistic portrayal of standard children's books to encourage better reading and reading satisfaction as one of the first requisites of today's good American." True to her training, her goal was to connect children to "best reading" books legitimated by the professional library community of which she was a member. A year later eighty-one children read over eight hundred books in the "Beat Japan" project. For each book read, a child got to replace a Japanese flag with a U.S. flag on a map of Pacific islands prominently displayed in the library. The goal was one thousand books, the last of which would replace the Japanese flag over Tokyo.[93] Part of the reason for the "Read and See" project was "an alarming falling off in the use of the Library by children," Whittaker reported to WFLC. "The city superintendent is building up a grade school library and schoolchildren are asked to use the school library. The superintendent cooperates not at all with the public library." WFLC advised Whittaker to visit grade school rooms, attend PTA meetings, and reinstitute a "Parents' Shelf" in the library.[94]

MID-CENTURY CHANGES

In March 1947, the Rhinelander Public Library began a fifteen-minute weekly radio program on local station WOBT, during which Whittaker and her subordinates explained library services and discussed newly arrived titles. Most were *Booklist* recommendations. Whittaker and her colleagues also used the program to promote groups that used the library. For example, the Jack Pine Artists regularly met there and used library art books for inspiration. Although the library no longer had wall space to host exhibits (bookshelves six feet high now lined the walls), Whittaker did interview local artists for the program, and regularly announced where exhibits would be held.[95]

In April 1950, Rhinelander returned to a mayor-alderman system. For the library, that meant a return to a board of trustees. This occurred at the same time that the Wisconsin legislature began supporting library demonstration projects aimed at expanding and equalizing library services for all state residents. Rhinelander had about 45 percent of the population of Oneida County. Three Lakes and Minocqua had small public libraries, but both were largely supported by local women's clubs, not by local taxes. Funded three-year demonstration projects that relied upon bookmobiles to circulate books held by larger public libraries promised to redress some inequities, but county boards of supervisors still had to contribute. In October 1949, the WFLC selected Oneida, Vilas, and Price Counties for a demonstration project. On November 8, the Oneida County Board of Supervisors considered the plan, noted it would cost the county more than $14,000, and by a vote of twenty-one to one rejected the offer.[96]

Two years after Rhinelander switched back to a mayor-alderman model, the mayor finally appointed a library board. On May 13, 1952, he nominated six people, including James Cleary, owner of Cleary's Milk & Ice Cream Company and a director of the Bank of Rhinelander; Don Stefonik, a foreman at the Rhinelander Paper Company and Fourth Ward alderman; Alberta Richards, long-time member of the Rhinelander Women's Club and the Monday Club, whose physician husband was also president of the First National Bank; Frank Maloney, a printer who served as Seventh Ward alderman; Janet Rominsky, a member of the Ladies Guild at Zion Lutheran; and Reinhold Manthey, a machinist at Rhinelander Paper, member and officer in the "Pulp and Sulphite Union" Local 91, secretary of the Ripco Credit Union, and vice president of the Rhinelander Central Labor Council. Unspecified but understood by the mayor, council, and library board, at least one trustee would represent labor, another Protestant faiths, and another Roman Catholics. All the nominees were subsequently confirmed by common council.

As a result of Rhinelander's commitment to labor, the library board's demographic profile looked considerably different than that of its predecessors three decades earlier. That same commitment also separated it from the socio-demographic profiles of the boards of the other three libraries covered in this book, each of which had long before incorporated Catholic representatives, and all of which quickly accepted members with ties to new local organizations like the American Legion, Rotary Club, and chambers of commerce. In Rhinelander, however, library board labor representatives mixed with bank directors, local politicians with local club members, descendants of Rhinelander's Yankee founders with second-generation immigrants.[97] The superintendent of schools served ex officio. In the new board the WFLC saw opportunity; it "might prove to be the difference between the success and failure of the [bookmobile] demonstration that is going to be held there this fall," wrote W. S. Botsford, the WFLC secretary. Botsford worried about Whittaker, however. For some reason, she seemed resistant to him. "Dorothy has become used to the city manager plan," he wrote to colleagues, "and may intend to relegate the new board to a poor position." Botsford decided to attend the first board meeting, scheduled for June 3, 1952.[98]

At the meeting, however, the only board members attending were Manthey, Richards, and Rominsky. Others were absent because of "summer work activities." Botsford and Anne Farrington represented the WFLC, and at Whittaker's invitation the mayor represented the city. With so few present, formal organization was postponed until the next meeting. "Mr. Manthey, a labor man," noted Farrington, "showed keen interest and good judgment in his questions and comments. . . . I believe the greatest hazard will be to keep Mrs. Richards, a personal friend of Mrs. Whittaker and long interested in the library, from developing into a one-woman board." A second board meeting proved no better attended; "it was agreed that election of officers, adoption of the Library Bill of Rights, and appointment of permanent committees be postponed until the full board is present."[99] It was an inauspicious start to a new system of governance for the Rhinelander Public Library.

Not until August 5 did enough board members show up to conduct business. At that meeting trustees voted to participate in the American Heritage Project by becoming one of twenty centers in the state, to request that the A. C. McClurg Company construct a five-day "Combined Book Exhibit" at the library during the same month as bookmobile demonstrations, and to coordinate it all through the "People's Library Committee of the Northern Lakes Area." When WFLC consultant Helen Kremer wrote to McClurg officials, she noted how excited the superintendent of schools was about the potential the book exhibit would have to influence his teachers. Soon thereafter Manthey convinced local unions to endorse the bookmobile project.[100]

October 1952 was a busy month for RPL. Colorful book jacket displays outside the building invited the public to come inside and look at the seven hundred books McClurg had assembled for the Combined Book Exhibit October 13–15. The *News* covered the itinerary of the bookmobile (on loan from the WFLC), and reported how excited people were at its many stops. WFLC official Elizabeth Burr noted that the bookmobiles circulated over five thousand titles that first week. She also reported, "there is more working together as a staff [among Rhinelander librarians] than this consultant would have deemed possible, knowing the underlying clash of personalities and resentments." She especially complimented Kremer for "superb handling of divergent personalities."[101]

By month's end the People's Library Committee was ready to recommend that Vilas and Oneida Counties jointly fund a bookmobile service. To bolster its case, the committee asked principals of schools visited by the bookmobile to write letters of support, and urged citizens of both counties to circulate petitions, write letters, or attend county board meetings. RPL employee Erma Graeber used a library radio program to promote the recommendation. WLFC Secretary Botsford estimated the total cost of the service would be four thousand dollars; Oneida County would be asked to contribute two-thirds, Vilas County would be asked to pay for one-third. The Oneida County Board of Supervisors met October 28 to consider the proposal, and although fifty people representing county women's clubs, PTAs, church services, 4-H clubs, civic groups, and social, patriotic, labor, and fraternal organizations crowded the room, the board rejected the request. "It acted soundly," judged the *News*. "The schools are the centers of educational and cultural interest in rural Oneida County, and any activity associated with these interests should be a part of the school program."[102]

But Erma Graeber would not accept defeat. She immediately contacted Rhinelander's city councilmen and members of the Oneida County Board of Supervisors, trying to persuade them to change their minds. Complaints about "lobbying" soon reached WFLC officials. On November 21, Helen Kremer wrote to the school superintendent (an RPL ex officio board member): "If your librarians have been 'lobbying,' it seems to us that they are only doing what all the librarians in the state are trying to do, —arrive at a plan that will provide the 'best library service to the greatest number at the least possible cost.'" But Graeber's intensity angered too many. The library board met on December 2, noted the opposition of the County Board of Supervisors, and concluded that "this project should be taken over by the People's Library Committee."

Shortly thereafter the council protested against "lobbying" by unnamed city employees. On December 10, 1952, Graeber resigned. "My ideas of library service apparently do not meet the approval of others," she told the *News*. Five days later she addressed the Rhinelander Rotary Club to give her side of the story. The *News* merely noted that she had addressed the club; the *Wisconsin Library Bulletin*, however, carried her speech in its entirety, and complimented her for "courage undaunted." Graeber continued to agitate for a regional library system with Rhinelander at its center.[103]

Without much success, however. The initiative languished. On November 3, 1953, Helen Kremer made a "surprise" visit to Rhinelander. She knew the library board would meet that evening, and Dorothy Whittaker discouraged her from attending. "You wouldn't be interested in coming," Whittaker said. Kremer also noticed that a part of the National Book Week exhibit in the library lobby was labeled "Catholic bookshelf." When she told Whittaker that such a practice might lead to requests for similar displays by other religious groups, "the advice was not wanted or approved." (Perhaps Kremer was unaware of the unwritten rule that at least one trustee had to be Catholic.) In private conversation with Kremer, children's librarian Mrs. H. D. Sansburn gave "a full report on the 'terrible state' of things and her own nervousness as a result of the constant plaguing" by Whittaker. "She stated she had very much wanted to attend our summer workshop, but had been told she definitely would not be able to go and get 'any of those Commission ideas.'" Obviously Whittaker resented efforts from outside forces to control what she wanted (or saw possible) for her library. "It is to be doubted if much can be done in the situation in Rhinelander," Kremer concluded, "until a new board and/or librarian takes over."[104]

In 1956, 8,750 people lived in Rhinelander; 90 percent were born in the United States; 80 percent of the families owned their own homes. The city was served by one radio station (WOBT), two theaters with a total seating capacity of 1,300, a drive-in theater large enough to accommodate five hundred cars (over seven thousand were registered in Oneida County), three bowling alleys, four tennis courts, and a nine-hole golf course. Four hotels and eight motels offered rooms for visitors and tourists, many of whom were attracted in the summer by Rhinelander's recreational advantages; Oneida County housed three hundred resorts and campgrounds capable of accommodating twenty-five thousand visitors. Within a twelve-mile radius of the town center, Oneida County had 232 lakes, eleven trout streams, and two rivers. While there, tourists spent about $3 million annually. Local industries employed 3,200; many were unionized. One newspaper (circulation 4,200) informed its citizens; 5,038 phones enabled them to communicate quickly. One hospital affiliated with the Catholic Church admitted 3,630 patients in 1955, and eighteen churches addressed Rhinelander's spiritual needs.[105]

Rhinelander also hosted a variety of benevolent and fraternal organizations, including the Eagles, Odd Fellows, Knights of Columbus, Masons, Woodmen of the World, Sons of Norway, and the Women's Catholic Order of Foresters. Patriotic organizations included chapters of the American Legion, American Red Cross, Boy Scouts, and Veterans of Foreign Wars. Welfare organizations included the Service League and the League of Catholic Women (on May 2, the RPL board recognized Mrs. Alan Pradt as its newest "representative of the League of Catholic Women on the Library Board"). Business was represented by the Rhinelander Chamber of Commerce, the Junior Chamber of Commerce, the Business & Professional Women's Club, the Better Resorts Association, and the Oneida County Tavern Keepers Association. Labor claimed locals of the "Carpenters & Joiners," the "International Association of Letter Carriers," the "Municipal Employees Union," the "Oneida County Employees Union," "Papermakers" (Local No. 66), and the "Plywood Box & Door Workers Union." Records indicate that none of these organizations held meetings in the public library. Eleven schools (five elementary, one senior high, one junior high, one vocational, and three parochial) addressed Rhinelander's educational needs. In July 1956 the city and county approved a new Union High School District that included the city and seven surrounding towns. The new high school was scheduled to open in 1957; its library would accommodate one hundred students, one thousand books, and one professional librarian. Two small conference rooms "where a teacher may take a group of students to work so as not to distract other students who are in the library" would be attached.[106]

It was in this milieu that the Rhinelander Public Library existed. In 1956 it held 20,545 books (2.3 per capita, below the ALA standard of 3.0), subscribed to ninety-six newspapers and periodicals, and had 3,120 registered borrowers (36 percent of Rhinelander's citizens, below the ALA standard of 45 percent). That year it circulated 54,212 books, or 6.2 per capita (below the ALA standard of 9.0). Adults accounted for 59 percent of circulation; juveniles accounted for 41 percent. Like libraries elsewhere, RPL no longer reported how much of its circulation was fiction. The library employed three librarians. Every summer it ran a reading program for children; every Saturday morning during the school term it hosted story hours. On

October 27, 1956, Superintendent of Schools C. A. Vig assessed the state of education in Oneida County, and—despite its performance when compared to other public libraries in the nation and state—pronounced RPL an "asset" for children. "Rhinelander can be very proud of its library; its staff is very cooperative, friendly, and efficient in serving the needs of all ages of our youth. Young people find it a good place to improve themselves and enjoy its pleasant surroundings." At the library, he said, "our young people have a source of the best in reading material. More of the world's knowledge and experience is found behind these four walls than in any spot in our community."[107]

CHAPTER FIVE

Literature Suitable for a Small Public Library

Main Street Public Library Collections

T he cultural politics of public libraries are written in the collections they acquire. To evaluate those politics, I created a database of the entire inventory of the four midwestern libraries described in this book, based on bibliographic information systematically entered into accessions books through 1970. As previous chapters show, by 1901 the Main Street public library had become a local institution of cultural authority meeting a particular set of expectations and needs. For example, all had sets of encyclopedias, several dictionaries, and a variety of handbooks. For current information, all subscribed to a variety of middle-class general interest periodicals, local newspapers, and at least one state or regional newspaper.[1] All also provided access to canonical Western literature—often in the form of compendiums like Library of the World's Best Literature series.

Developing book collections, however, was a community endeavor requiring compromise between three groups who in unobtrusive ways mediated decisions about what kinds of books they wanted on library shelves. One group existed outside the community: the library profession (and its many literary establishment allies) used its self-assumed power to recommend against certain titles and for others through a growing number of collection guides and periodicals. The other two were local groups. One consisted of trustees representing local community leaders who used their influence to select, project, and on rare occasions enforce a set of community cultural and literary values.[2] The other consisted of library patrons who used their power to choose from the pool of possibilities made available to them. This group exercised significant influence on the contours of collections, primarily because its members were the source of the circulation rates against which public libraries were routinely measured for community value—but used those libraries voluntarily. Always this community influence on public library collections was a balancing act, and because the three groups influencing collections routinely compromised quietly, seldom did the mediation process result in public battles. Instead it took the form of rules, regulations, and service conventions—like rental collections—that evolved into sets of expectations. Some were common to all four libraries, some were unique to each. This chapter analyzes these collections against a larger world of print culture.

TURN-OF-THE-CENTURY COLLECTIONS

Pioneering work has already been done on one Main Street library. In *Reading on the Middle Border,* Christine Pawley compares an Osage Library Association catalog of 1876 with the contents of the Sage Library in 1893. Fiction accounted for 42 percent in the former, 48 percent in the latter, history 44 percent in the former, 46 percent in the latter. Most surprisingly, however, science accounted for 10 percent in the former, 5 percent in the latter; and of the latter, one-third had been inherited from the former. This would suggest that Sage Library selectors did not place high value on providing up-to-date scientific information, and Pawley's accompanying analysis of circulation records demonstrates that patrons used the library for scientific information very slightly.

Pawley also used extant circulation records for the years 1890–1895 and matched them against census records and a database she compiled from the Sage Library's accessions books to discern who read what when. For this five-year period she discovered that two-thirds of the library's users were female, nearly 60 percent were between the ages of ten and thirty, and the vast majority came from Osage's socially well-positioned citizens. Nearly two-thirds were either Methodist or Congregationalist; Catholics and Lutherans accounted for less than 5 percent. At the same time, however, her research revealed not only heavy use by several Osage citizens who did not fit this profile (including Scandinavian immigrants, working-class Lutherans and Catholics, and widows living with their children), but also a reading population of old people who frequently read stories written for youth, youth who read stories written for adults, men who read stories written for women (and vice versa), and family members who read the same stories together and individually. Although the Sage

Library acquired collections largely to please a user group whose reading interests frequently differed from publishers' and authors' perceptions of targeted audiences, patrons outside that user group who were equally independent in their reading choices were never turned away from Sage Library collections.

And what Sage Library readers wanted most between 1890 and 1895 were Christian success stories written by authors generally ignored by the literary establishment. For these kinds of stories—directed to "middle-class, American-born Protestants"—Sage Library readers were "the ideal audience." Christian success story authors, "with their nativist leanings, held up as an ideal the independent farmers, merchants, and craftworkers who formed the bulk of Osage's population" and Sage Library's users. "This literature was anachronistic," Pawley notes, "but from the perspective of Osage's Protestant middle class, it had real meaning."[3] For residents of Osage, fiction helped bind groups into community-based reading networks. And like the public libraries in Sauk Centre, Rhinelander, and Lexington in 1900, the Sage Library enabled greatly expanded access to these stories. As a result, in an age when the American culture of print witnessed an expansion of mass-market newspapers, magazines, and books, the stories local public libraries provided became essential to more readers of all classes, ethnicities, and ages, and both genders.

Pawley's analysis of Sage Library circulation records also identifies its twenty most popular titles between 1890 and 1895. Of that twenty the Charles H. Moore Library had eight, the Bryant Library had nine, and Rhinelander Public Library had seven. All three owned four titles in common with the Sage Library: George Eliot's *Daniel Deronda* (1883), Lew Wallace's *Ben-Hur* (1880), Charles King's *The Colonel's Daughter* (1883), and F. H. Burnett's *Little Lord Fauntleroy* (1886). Three titles by A. D. T. Whitney were on the Sage Library's list of most popular titles: *Sights and Insights* (1876), *Faith Gartney's Girlhood* (1865), and *Odd or Even?* (1880); each was owned by at least two of the other three libraries. Five other titles on the list were owned by at least one of the other libraries.[4]

E. P. Roe's *An Original Belle* (1885) ranked second on the Sage Library list of most-popular books. The Moore Library owned a copy, and, although the Bryant Library did not, E. P. Roe was represented in its collections by nine other titles. Rhinelander meanwhile had no titles by Roe in its collection. *A Brave Lady* (1870) by "Miss Mulock" (a pseudonym for Dinah Maria

Mulock Craik) ranked fourth on the Sage Library list. Rhinelander possessed a copy, but the Moore Library did not. It did, however, own nine other Mulock titles. The Bryant Library owned three. Bertha M. Clay's *For Another's Sin* (1886) ranked fifth on the Sage Library list. None of the other three libraries owned Clay titles. *Airy, Fairy, Lillian* (1882) by "the Duchess" (Margaret Wolfe Hungerford) ranked sixth on the list. Although neither the Moore Library nor the Bryant Library owned that title, the Moore Library owned two Duchess titles, and the Bryant Library owned five; Rhinelander Public Library (RPL) owned none. Finally, Susan Warner, author of the best-selling mid-century novel *The Wide, Wide World* (1854), had three titles on the Sage Library most-popular list: *Diana* (1877), *Queechy* (1852), and *The Letter of Credit* (1882). The Moore Library had no Warner titles except *Wych Hazel* (1876). The Bryant Library did have *Wide, Wide World*, as well as *Queechy*. Rhinelander owned *The Wide, Wide World*, but had no other Warner books in its collection.

Pawley also identifies twenty authors most popular in the Sage Library collection between 1890 and 1895. Almost all were represented in the other three libraries, but there are some surprises. As one might expect, Sir Walter Scott, Charles Dickens, and William Dean Howells are well represented, but "Pansy" (pseudonym for Isabella Alden), ranked first with Sage Library patrons, had only three titles in the Rhinelander collection, one in the Moore Library, and none in the Bryant Library. Miss Mulock, ranked second in the Sage Library, was represented in RPL and the Moore Library by six titles, but the Bryant Library owned none of her books. On the other hand, third-ranking E. P. Roe was not represented in RPL, while the Moore Library carried thirteen of his titles and the Bryant Library owned nine. Ninth-ranking Oliver Optic was well represented in the other three libraries (RPL owned four, the Moore Library owned sixteen, and the Bryant Library owned twenty-one), while Harriet Beecher Stowe, eighth on Sage Library list, and represented by sixteen titles in the Bryant Library collection, was represented in the Moore Library by just three titles and in RPL by none.

Another way to analyze collections is to compare holdings for controversial books. On February 1, 1901, for example, the *Washington Post* published a list of fifty-four books a Boston Public Library (BPL) "Fiction Committee" had banned from its shelves.[5] On the list were Edith Wharton's *Touchstone* (1900), Henry James's *The Two Magics* (1898), Jules Verne's *An*

Antarctic Mystery (1900), and Robert Herrick's *Love's Dilemmas* (1898). Some popular authors had several titles on the list, including Maria Louise Pool, with *Friendship and Folly* (1898), *Golden Stream* (1898), and *Sand 'n' Bushes* (1899); Gertrude Atherton, with *Californians* (1908), *Senator North* (1900), and *A Daughter of the Vine* (1899); and Amelia Barr, with *Was It Right to Forgive* (1899) and *Trinity Bells* (1899). Of the fifty-four titles BPL banned in 1901, thirty-five were absent from the collections of all four libraries studied in this book.[6]

Holdings of the remaining nineteen titles, however, show differences. At least three of the four libraries shared ownership of five titles: E. N. Westcott's *David Harum* (1898), Winston Churchill's *The Celebrity* (1898), Amelia Barr's *Trinity Bells*, R. W. Chambers's *The Conspirators* (1900), and Molly Seawell's *The Loves of Lady Arabella* (1898). The Sage Library actually owned three copies each of the first three of these. Two of the four libraries shared ownership of three titles: Paul Leicester Ford's *Tattle-Tales of Cupid* (1898), Egerton Castle's *"Young April"* (1899), and Jesse Lynch Williams's *Adventures of a Freshman* (1899). When matched against the BPL list, the Moore Library had six titles, RPL had ten, and the Sage Library and the Bryant Library had eight each. Thus, while Sinclair Lewis was preparing for college in Sauk Centre in 1901 he had access to eight titles in his public library that had been banned in the larger, older, and ostensibly more cosmopolitan Boston.

Although not on the Boston list, Mark Twain's *Huckleberry Finn* had been controversial from the day it was published in 1885. For example, the public library in Concord, Massachusetts, banned it as "trash and suitable only for the slums." This attitude had staying power. The Des Moines Public Library "sequestered" *Huckleberry Finn* and *Tom Sawyer* in 1900. "Who can estimate the evil that may come from one book with wrong tendencies in the hands of our boys and girls?," the Des Moines library director wrote in *Public Libraries* (to which the Sage Library subscribed).[7] Although popular, *Huckleberry Finn* was not cited in the 1893 ALA catalog. It did, however, make the 1904 edition. In 1902, the Sage Library had two copies (and two more copies of *Tom Sawyer*), and RPL had one; the Moore Library received a gift copy a year later. The Bryant Library did not acquire a copy until 1914 (nearly thirty years after it was published).

What to conclude from this? First, while these four turn-of-the-century Main Street libraries seemed to agree with the BPL Fiction Committee on thirty-five of fifty-four titles it had rejected in 1901 (65 percent), citizens of Sauk Centre, Osage, Rhinelander, and Lexington nonetheless had varied access to the remaining nineteen (35 percent). Second, the four collections had ample supplies of popular authors being read by millions across the nation, but each community also had particular favorites in multiple copies, and particular authors not favored at all. Although community leaders sitting on book selection committees were not trained in librarianship, they had access to guides like *Current Literature, Review of Reviews, Literary Digest,* and the ALA catalog. They acquired authors with whom they felt comfortable and avoided authors with whom they were not comfortable, and each category varied from community to community with exceptions noted in previous chapters. Local newspapers published no patron complaints about what their public libraries stocked, or failed to stock. At the same time, neither newspapers nor board minutes for these libraries give evidence of efforts to remove titles already acquired.

1901–1917

In the spring of 1907 the trustees of the Bryant Library tried an experiment. Although trustees had already published their annual request for "citizens to send in lists of books they wish to have . . . placed in the library," in May they indicated a desire "to have the public pass [judgment] upon the nature of the books purchased." To accomplish this they asked six "well known citizens" to "take some of the books recently purchased, read them critically and write their estimate" in the *Herald.* The May 9 issue of the *Herald* carried two reviews. In the first, local physician J. M. McMasters reviewed William Jordan's *Self Control: Its Kingship and Majesty* (1905), which had been donated to the library by the local Methodist minister. McMasters very much liked the book, but even more the gesture of the man who donated it. "The thanks of the community are due to the reverend gentleman whose good sense, excellent judgment and liberality have placed this book on the shelves of our public library; it is an offering that will bloom perennially, and bear fruit, long after the author and donor are gathered to their fathers." *Self Control* stayed on Bryant Library shelves until 1941. In the second review, Louise M. Oehler (wife of the Congregationalist minister) reviewed Sarah Greene's *Vesty of the Basins* (1892), a novel about Maine's coastal people. Although Oehler regarded as "too irreverent" some characters who gave a "wrong impression of the author's position over against [sic] sacred and religious things," overall the book's value lay "in the simplicity and fidelity of the author's descriptions of the people, events and places." *Vesty* stayed on Bryant Library shelves until 1936.[8]

A month later the *Herald* published Oehler's husband's review of Robert Hichens's *The Garden of Allah* (1904), a romance that focuses on a courtship between a "renegade Trappist monk" and "a devout Roman Catholic who is also an English noblewoman." Oehler pronounced the book "sincere," but because it was "at times too suggestive," the book "should not be given out indiscriminately." Although the author ultimately solved the problem between his protagonists (the monk returned to the cloister; the woman remained unmarried), Oehler "would have found another solution." Despite this tepid review, *Garden of Allah* remained on Bryant Library shelves until 1936. A week later the paper published another review by McMasters, this one on Elizabeth Miller's novel *Saul of Tarsus* (1906). "This book condemns itself in the first chapter by investing this demigod . . . with an insignificant personality," the doctor argued, "and having offered this affront to all admirers of true Christian manhood, it drops him completely and proceeds with a commonplace tale of love (mostly illicit)." McMasters ranked the book with "the stories of Zola or Ouida."[9] Since the Bryant Library had no books by either Zola or Ouida, perhaps McMasters's judgment should have been final. Despite his condemnation, however, *Saul of Tarsus* remained on the library's shelves until 1945.

The following week *Herald* editor Charles Hendryx reviewed *The Northerner* (1904), a Civil War romance by Nora Davis. "A woman—a real sensible, womanly woman—ought to know better than to foist upon a long suffering public as poor an imitation as is this alleged literary effort." Although Hendryx concluded that *The Northerner* would not "soil any reader's morals," still it was "one of the many fourth rate novels" that will "cut little figure in the literary world." The Bryant Library kept the book until 1936. The final review was submitted by Mrs. C. C. Tobey, a Gradatim Club member and Congregationalist, who analyzed Clarence R. Burleigh's *Raymond Benson at Krampton* (1907), a story of college life in a New England town. "It is such a story as almost any boy could write, being a monotonous recounting of athletic games, football and baseball predominating."

Tobey reassured her readers that although "no harm would accrue from the reading," it was a "weak book." Bryant librarians pulled Burleigh's book in 1914.

Thus ended the series. All reviewers were leading members of Sauk Centre's social and civic life, all spoke to the influence of books on human behavior and community morals, all compared contents they analyzed against their own value system (which they regarded as absolute). Although *Herald* readers knew clearly where these titles ranked in the reviewers' hierarchy of reading, none were pulled from the shelves. Carefully avoiding judgment, the Minnesota Library Association's *Library News and Notes* concluded that the review experiment constituted "some interesting reading." For unknown reasons, however, the experiment stopped with Tobey's review. In future months the *Herald* instead ran lists of recently acquired library books; none were reviewed.[10]

Sometimes signals from other cultural agencies were unequivocal, however. When the Massachusetts Supreme Court declared Elinor Glyn's best-selling *Three Weeks* (1908) "obscene" in 1909, none of the four libraries studied in this book owned a copy. When the New York Society for the Suppression of Vice brought cases against David Graham Phillips's *Susan Lenox: Her Fall and Rise* (1917) in the century's second decade, none held this title.[11] Nor did the library profession equivocate. To the "menacing tide" of books clamored for by the masses, ALA President Arthur Bostwick said in 1908 that the librarian should respond firmly: "Thus far shalt thou go and no farther." In a *Library Journal* symposium entitled "What Shall the Libraries Do About Bad Books?," librarians described how they treated "doubtful fiction." Some sequestered those titles on separate shelves, then monitored patrons who perused their contents or tried to check them out. Others kept these titles in locked bookcases (called the "Inferno" in library jargon of the day), and forced patrons to ask for them.[12]

"Bad books" were not the only printed materials causing library professionals concern. In "Magazines and Morals," Lutie Stearns told *Wisconsin Library Bulletin* readers in 1911 that "the popular magazine depends almost wholly upon news-stand circulation, for its readers belong to what has come to be called, among the craft, the 'shifty' class." Especially perplexing was a *Cosmopolitan* story "which for outspoken and daring sensualism has never had a rival in public print." Magazines carrying such stories, she argued, "should be barred from library tables." Stearns also told of a local "unthinking librarian" who had cut out the frontispiece of a heroine in a "daringly sensual" *Cosmopolitan* story and pasted it upon the front cover to draw attention to it—"this in the face . . . of the general warning" by the Wisconsin Library Association "against the noxious influence of this same periodical."[13] Among the four libraries studied here, only the Moore Library subscribed to *Cosmopolitan*.

Sixteen months later, in April 1913, WLB published *Booklist* editor Elva Bascom's article, "Selection of Fiction." "The great mass of readers think of the library solely as a source of entertainment," Bascom wrote, "and their most frequent and constant demand is for a good novel." But in 1912 *Booklist* reviewed only 170 of the 1,000 novels published. Bascom worried about "saccharine slush" like Florence Barclay's *The Rosary* (1910), "machine-made affairs" like the Harold Bindloss stories, and novels "dealing attractively with gambling, speculating, bribing, double-dealing, and kindred unethical or immoral actions" like Ernest W. Hornung's "gentleman-burglar stories," Katherine Thurston's *The Gambler* (1905), and George R. Chester's *Young Wallingford* (1910). She also detested authors who "deliberately misrepresented historical factions and characters" like Emerson Hough, and hated immoral attitudes on display in Maurice H. Hewlett's Sanchia series and in Robert W. Chambers's recent stories. "We are all agreed," she said, that those novels "in which a man or woman sins and flourishes unrepentant are not proper candidates for the open shelves of our libraries." Although the "well balanced reader can get no harm from these stories," she worried about "the adult or boy or girl" with "an immature mind."[14]

Although *The Rosary* will be addressed later, among other titles that Bascom listed RPL had three by Bindloss, two of Thurston's *The Gambler*, five by Hough, two by Hewlett, and four by Chambers; only Hornung and Chester were missing. The Bryant Library had fourteen Bindloss books, four by Hough, five by Hewlett, eleven by Chambers, and none by Thurston, Hornung, or Chester. The Sage Library had thirty-seven Bindloss titles, twelve by Hough, two by Hewlett, twenty-eight by Chambers, and one by Hornung. It also had seven titles by Thurston (although not *The Gambler*), but none by Chester. The Moore Library had seven Bindloss titles, five by Hough, one by Hewlett, and two by Chambers, but none by Hornung, Thurston, or Chester. That the record is so mixed demonstrates the extent to which the mediated process of public library book selection was unique to each community. It also disproves Elva Bascom's claim that "all" were agreed about what constituted "saccharine slush" or threatened "an immature mind."

In the summer of 1912, the Bryant Library began a popular fiction rental service. Patrons paid five cents per week, and when rental income for a title equaled the book's cost, the book was placed on open shelving. By mid-July, "some sixty-odd works of light fiction" were available, including Gene Stratton Porter's *The Harvester* (1912) and *At the Foot of the Rainbow* (1907), Florence Barclay's *The Rosary* and *The Following of the Star* (1911), Irvin Bacheller's *Keeping Up with Lizzie* (1911), Helen R. Martin's *The Fighting Doctor* (1912), Meredith Nicholson's *A Hoosier Chronicle* (1912) and *The Lords of the High Decision* (1909), Corra Harris's *The Circuit Rider's Wife* (1910) and *Recording Angel* (1912), Kathleen Norris's *Mother* (1911), Zane Grey's *Riders of the Purple Sage* (1913), Booth Tarkington's *The Guest of Quesnay* (1908), Zona Gale's *Romance Island* (1906), Frederick Palmer's *Over the Pass* (1912), Anne Douglas Sedgwick's *Tante* (1911), Norman Duncan's *The Measure of a Man* (1911), Grace Richmond's *The Twenty-fourth of June* (1914), and Richard Harding Davis's *White Mice* (1909).

Analyzing this list against titles cited in *Booklist* reveals significant differences between the collecting practices of the four libraries studied in this book and recommendations coming from library professionals and literary luminaries. Although *The Harvester, Tante*, and *A Hoosier Chronicle* all made best-seller lists, *Booklist* did not review *Tante* and thought *Harvester* "sentimental to a degree." Except for its "mixed metaphors and other crudities of style," *Booklist* suggested that readers would like *Rosary* "for its sincere religious feeling, high moral tone, and abounding sentiment" and *A Hoosier Chronicle* because it was a "fairly successful and always readable attempt at a serious study of political and social life in Indiana."

Booklist also had opinions on other books in the Bryant Library rental collection. *Keeping Up with Lizzie* was "a slight story based on a very good idea, but ineffectively and inartistically developed." Of *Fighting Doctor*, *Booklist* said: "Slight and sentimental." Of *The Guest of Quesnay* it declared: "Not wholly convincing, but has much of the charm of Tarkington's earlier stories and some delightful minor characters." *White Mice*, it judged, was a "light, lively tale of average interest." On the other hand, *Booklist* praised *The Circuit Rider's Wife* ("a keen and unfailing humor relieves the pathos of a record that is probably in most respects true to facts"), *At the Foot of the Rainbow* ("similar ... to the author's 'Freckles,' but better done in every way"), *Over the Pass* ("two unique, well drawn characters and a breezy style give this book individuality and interest"), *The Measure of a Man* ("the tone of this book is sincere, optimistic and, without obvious preaching, has a strong religious undercurrent"), and *Twenty-fourth of June* ("will be liked by young girls").[15] By not including reviews of *Riders of the Purple Sage*, *Romance Island*, *Tante*, and *Mother*, *Booklist* recommended against acquisition by public libraries. Generally *Booklist* ignored authors identified with the "sentimental school," like Kathleen Norris and Gene Stratton Porter. Despite *Booklist*'s efforts to critique or ignore popular fiction, however, enough Bryant Library patrons showed preference for these kinds of novels that within months the rental collection generated twenty-five dollars.[16]

Looking for consistency in the collections of the other three libraries is difficult. That RPL had ten of the titles in the Bryant Library rental collection might be explained by guidance it received from publications like *Booklist*, but at the same time the Moore Library (with no trained librarian and no *Booklist* subscriptions or ALA catalogs) had seven. The Sage Library had twelve, and for nine held two copies. Except for the Bryant Library, Zona Gale's *Romance Island*, Florence Barclay's *Under the Mulberry Tree*, and Helen Martin's *The Fighting Doctor* were held by none of the libraries. But even these comparisons are somewhat deceptive, since the long-standing popularity of certain authors and titles forced acquisition later. While only the Bryant Library and Sage Library had copies of *Riders of the Purple Sage* in 1912, within ten years the other two acquired multiple copies, probably because of popular demand, perhaps because the library profession had by then lowered its resistance.

Analysis of contested titles is another way to compare collections. Many reviewers found Kate Chopin's novel *The Awakening* (1899) offensive. Dealing with a woman's spiritual, intellectual, and sexual "awakening," it was listed in none of the early ALA catalogs. The St. Louis Public Library immediately banned it upon publication. Theodore Dreiser's *Sister Carrie* was originally printed by Doubleday in 1900, but when the publisher's wife objected to its contents the publisher suppressed it immediately. Although a 1907 second edition received wider circulation, *Sister Carrie* was still banned in many places through mid-century. In 1915 birth control advocate Margaret Sanger issued *Family Limitation*, a pamphlet the New York Society for the Suppression of Vice immediately got a New York court order to declare "contrary not only to the law of the state, but to the law of God." Sanger was subsequently jailed for writing it, her husband for distributing it. *Family Limitation* made no list of recommended titles for a public library.[17]

With all the attention these three titles merited, selectors for the four studied libraries undoubtedly knew of their existence. Before 1960, none acquired a copy of *The Awakening*. Theodore Dreiser's *Sister Carrie* did slightly better. ALA catalogs ignored it until the 1926 edition; Wilson catalogs cited it in 1915, single-starred it in 1950, double-starred it in 1960. The Bryant Library did not acquire a copy until 1927, just after the novel was cited in the 1926 edition of the ALA catalog. Rhinelander did not purchase its first copy until 1963. Neither the Sage Library nor the Moore Library acquired a copy before 1970. And just like Kate Chopin's *The Awakening*, Margaret Sanger's *Family Limitations* was never cited in any ALA or Wilson catalog, and none of the four libraries acquired a copy.

Women's suffrage was an issue that public libraries in the Midwest could not ignore, although many tried. In June 1912, *Michigan Librarian* published Helen M. Thomas's "Selected Bibliography of Woman Suffrage." "The intention has been to bring forward some of the questions at issue," Thomas said, "both for and against, in general and in particular, here and elsewhere."[18] Checking the 135 books she cited against the Main Street Public Library Database reveals no matches. Missing were any titles by suffrage notables like Anna Howard Shaw and Lucy Stone. In 1907 the Sage Library acquired two copies of the first volume of what eventually became a six-volume *History of Woman Suffrage*, edited by Elizabeth Cady Stanton, Susan B. Anthony, and Matilda Joslyn Gage. Four volumes had been published by 1912. Thomas also listed E. Sylvia Pankhurst's *The Suffragette* (1911) and Belle Squire's *Woman Movement in America* (1911), both recommended by *Book Review Digest* (the *Digest* called the latter a "moving picture of the phases of suffrage history"). No Main Street library held copies of either.

Major women's organizations like the National American Woman's Suffrage Association and the National Society for Women's Suffrage (based in London, England) do not show up in the database as publishers or authors. Nor does the database contain any book published before 1920 with the phrase "woman's suffrage" in the title (a similar search of Library of Congress holdings turned up eighty-six). However, several authors in the bibliography are represented in Main Street collections: Marie Corelli for *Barabbas* (1894), *Thelma* (1895), and *God's Good Man* (1904), but not *Woman,—or Suffragette* (1907); and John Stuart Mill for *On Liberty* (1859) and *Principles of Political Economy* (1848), but not for *Subjection of Women* (1869) and *Suffrage for Women* (1871). Thomas also listed a 1911 debate handbook entitled *Selected Articles on Woman Suffrage* (1910), but none of the libraries obtained it.

Librarians and trustees may have assumed that patrons could obtain current information on "woman suffrage" (as it was then commonly called) from newspapers and magazines to which they subscribed. At the same time, however, based upon the paucity of book titles on women's suffrage acquired by the four libraries before women were given the right to vote in 1920, one is hard-pressed to conclude that they seriously attempted to inform their communities on this significant issue. Given the involvement of the many women's club members in local suffrage activities who had also helped establish the libraries, this phenomenon is even more surprising.

The "labor question" also preoccupied Americans during the first decades of the twentieth century. In the four Heartland communities discussed here, only Rhinelander had an industrialized population sufficient to justify a sizeable collection of labor materials. That RPL was aware of this was obvious. In 1909 Ada McCarthy highlighted Robert Hunter's *Socialists at Work* (1908) in her monthly newspaper column—"an interesting and strong depiction of the achievements of socialism and social reform in the parliaments and in art and literature." A year later she profiled John Graham Brooks's *The Social Unrest: Studies in Labor and Socialist Movements* (1907). "Nowhere else, so far as we are aware, can the reader gain so quickly a comprehension of the ideas and aspirations of the struggling classes. Mr. Brooks has studied their ideas and aspirations with a sympathy rare among the privileged classes."[19]

Several Heartland public libraries modeled responses to "the labor question" that Ada McCarthy could have emulated. In November 1911, for example, the recently elected Socialist Party mayor of Two Harbors, Minnesota, just north of Duluth, complained. "There appears to be a dearth of books on sociology and political economy in our public library." The library was committed to acquiring books "by impartial students of social questions," the librarian responded, then reported it had books by "such noted out and out Socialists as [Karl] Marx, [John] Spargo, [Reginald Wright] Kauffman, and the group of Fabian socialists, not to mention novels by [Edward] Bellamy, Jack London, and Upton Sinclair. In direct opposition to these we have [William H.] Mallock's 'Critical Examination of Socialism' and [W. Lawler] Wilson's 'The Menace of Socialism.'"[20]

Rhinelander was exposed to similar pressures. On March 8, 1912, the *Rhinelander Herald* reported on a lecture by Ralph Korngold of Milwaukee entitled "Socialists at Work," an event attended by a "large audience." "Socialism is the sword of Damocles which is hanging above the head of Capitalist Society," the paper reported Korngold having said. "By giving up a little the exploiters of labor hope to be allowed to keep much." But Korngold was preaching to a choir. His audience consisted largely of working-class people employed in local mills, self-taught through networks embedded in local organizations and imagined communities bound by printed products like *Appeal to Reason* (a socialist paper that in 1913 had a circulation of 750,000).[21] Many were recent immigrants who had brought with them ideologies disseminated by printed materials. In the column immediately to the left of the *Herald* report on Korngold's speech was an article on "New Books at the Library," featuring titles on gardening and listing new works of fiction and nonfiction. Most were annotations that matched *Booklist* entries. The library never subscribed to *Appeal to Reason*.[22]

If its primary responsibility was to inform, the public library of 1912 had an obligation to provide material on labor—and especially labor unrest—beyond magazines and newspapers. Some suspected that librarians were not meeting this responsibility. In 1915, for example, one witness at a U.S. Commission on Industrial Relations hearing in Washington DC argued that librarians in Carnegie-donated buildings did not acquire materials critical of the philanthropist.[23] To evaluate how well the Main Street public libraries did, collections were matched against titles issued by the Charles Kerr Publishing Company of Chicago (largest publisher of socialist literature in the United States during the Progressive Era),[24] the first seven volumes of *Booklist* (1905–1912) for titles it recommended on "Labor and Laboring Classes," "Social Problems," and "Socialism," and the first four editions of the ALA catalog (which covered books published through 1921) under the DDC numbers 331 ("Capital and Labor") and 335 ("Socialism").

In addition to its periodical, the *International Socialist Review* (started in 1900, but never subscribed to by the four libraries), the Kerr Publishing Company also issued inexpensive editions of staple texts like Marx's *Das Kapital* (1867), Karl Kautsky's *The Class Struggle* (1910), George Plechanoff's *Anarchism and Socialism* (1909), and Karl Liebknecht's *Militarism* (1917). It published six titles by Algie Simons, including *Packingtown* (1899), *Single Tax versus Socialism* (1899), *Anarchism and Socialism* (1901), *Economic Foundations of Art* (1903), *Compensation* (1904), and *Labor Politics* (1904). Mary Marcy's *Out of the Dump* (1909) and *Shop Talk on Economics* (1911) sold especially well. And in its Pocket Library of Socialism series Kerr published May Wood Simons's *Woman and the Social Problem* (1903), Kautsky's *The Social Revolution* (1903), William Liebknecht's *No Compromise—No Political Trading* (1903), Friedrich Engels's *Socialism, Utopian and Scientific* (1901), *Origins of the Family, Private Property and the State* (1902), and *Landmarks of Scientific Socialism* (1907), Marx's *Wage-Labor and Capital* (1902), and Marx and Engels's *The Communist Manifesto* (1848). Of these titles, Rhinelander acquired Engels's *Landmarks of Scientific Socialism* in 1909. However, not until 1955 did RPL acquire *Communist Manifesto*. The Bryant Library obtained *Das Kapital* in 1899 and Jean Jaurès's *Studies in Socialism* in 1907 (neither published by Kerr), but before 1970 the Moore and Sage Libraries held no works by Marx or Engels.

Of titles cited above, *Das Kapital* was listed in the first and second editions of the ALA catalog, Engels's *Socialism, Utopian and Scientific* in the second edition, *Communist Manifesto* and Liebknecht's *Militarism* in the fourth. In its first seven volumes, *Booklist* identified under "Labor and the Laboring Classes," "Social Problems," and "Socialism" such works as William H. Beveridge's *Unemployment* (1909), Andrew Carnegie's *Problems of Today* (1908), John R. Commons's *Trade Unionism and Labor Problems* (1905), Hutchins Hapgood's *Spirit of Labor* (1907), Reginald Wright Kauffman's *What Is Socialism?* (1910), Scott Nearing's *Social Adjustment* (1911), John Spargo's *The Socialists: Who They Are and What They Stand For* (1906), and W. Lawler Wilson's *Menace of Socialism* (1908). Of the thirty-one titles *Booklist* recommended for all public libraries under "Labor and Laboring Classes," the thirteen titles recommended under "Social Problems," and the twenty-four titles recommended under "Socialism," the four Heartland libraries owned none.[25]

Analyzing the collections for contested titles and works on controversial subjects like woman's suffrage and labor unrest again reveals mixed

results. For whatever reasons, all four Main Street libraries avoided controversial titles endorsed by professional collection guides. They often
chose the popular fiction that library leaders regularly belittled, while
they frequently ignored titles recommended by library professionals on
controversial subjects that challenged dominant myths of American exceptionalism, egalitarianism, and consensus. Thus, on some subjects the
four libraries deliberately chose not to "inform" their patrons, who, if the
absence of either public protest or private complaints to trustees is an
indication, seemed little concerned.

Finally, my database shows that these Main Street public libraries did
not provide the ethnic press publications subscribed to by many European
immigrants who moved into their communities between 1890 and 1917.[26]
Fiction continued to account for 65–75 percent of each library's circulation and it was this fiction, read by immigrants, which helped assimilate
them into the local culture and connect them to national cultures through
shared reading. If patrons carped about ethnically biased library collections to friends or family, they never brought these complaints to local
library officials or the press. By 1917, patrons had evolved a set of reading
habits and borrowing practices clearly reflected in the kinds of collections
the Heartland's small public libraries assembled for their use.

1917–1929

All four Main Street libraries described in this book subscribed to periodicals, paying for most, though were some donated. In his 1920 edition
of *The Library Primer*, John Cotton Dana listed thirty-one periodicals
recommended for "a small library," and starred those "suggested for first
purchase."[27] Among them were middle-class staples like *Harper's, Ladies
Home Journal, Scribner's, Good Housekeeping, Literary Digest, National
Geographic,* and *Youth's Companion.* In her 1918 annual report, Jesse Bingham listed RPL periodicals that included all of Dana's starred titles except
Popular Science Monthly (instead, the library subscribed to *Popular Mechanics*). On Dana's list but not Rhinelander's were periodicals like *Industrial Management,* the *Nation,* the *New Republic,* and several educational
periodicals like *School and Society, Elementary School Journal,* and *School
Life.* It is possible that the school system carried the latter, but it is surprising that the library did not carry *Industrial Management.* That it had

neither the *Nation* nor the *New Republic*—both viewing the world from the political left—should not be surprising, given the conservative nature of the RPL board.

Periodicals in the Moore Library—led by a board and librarian largely unconnected to Michigan's library profession—were quite different. While the library did subscribe to six titles on Dana's list (*Harper's, Ladies' Home Journal, Scribner's, Literary Digest,* and *Popular Science Monthly*), it also included *Cosmopolitan,* which many librarians considered objectionable. Nonetheless, summer tourists patronizing the Moore Library probably welcomed this periodical as standard fare, and found no problem with its contents. Like their book collections, the periodicals to which these four libraries subscribed showed similarities and differences—connecting patrons to national networks of information, while also reflecting each community's unique hierarchy of reading and local culture.

Books still consumed the majority of collection budgets. On the nation's most celebrated 1920s censorship cases, Main Street libraries were mute. For example, when the New York Society for the Suppression of Vice sued publishers of James Cabell's *Jurgen* (1919)—described by the *New York Tribune* as a "nasty . . . barroom story refurbished for the boudoir"—the novel became famous. No Main Street library obtained a copy, however. Similarly, when a Boston rental library owner was fined for circulating Robert Keable's *Simon Called Peter* in 1922, none of the four bought that book either. In 1927, a Chicagoan who had recently moved from a small Iowa town, "where blue laws, censorship, prohibition, the klan and fundamentalism are taken for granted," told the *Chicago Tribune* that she was surprised not to find copies of Voltaire's works at the Chicago Public Library. Like Chicago, no Main Street library had any works by Voltaire, including *Candide.*

Other controversial titles published between 1917 and 1929 fared no better. In 1928, Radclyffe Hall published *The Well of Loneliness,* a novel describing homosexual impulses that plagued its autobiographical heroine. In December 1928, New York police seized eight hundred copies and arrested a local bookseller because, a local magistrate said, the novel "idealized and extolled" perversion and would "debauch public morals" and "deprave and corrupt minds," especially of "the weaker members of society." On April 29, 1929, a three-judge panel overturned a lower court opinion.

Publishers immediately began an ad campaign, and within a year sold over one hundred thousand copies. Not until 1945 did the Bryant Library obtain a copy; none of the others ever acquired it.[28]

Popular fiction—especially series fiction for youth—continued to perplex the nation's professional library community. The Heartland was no exception. In June 1921, the *Bulletin of the Iowa Library Commission* castigated "some libraries" for "making the mistake of advertising their new fiction" in local newspapers. "The desire to attract people to the library is legitimate," the author argued, "but to attempt to do so with new fiction as bait is like tempting a sick person to eat food which will make him sicker and also increase the percentage of sickness in the town." In the issue following, another author explained why the ALA did not endorse serial fiction for boys and girls. "The fact that, after he had mastered the first book" of the series "he can sail through several volumes without mental effort, is exactly what makes the reading of series delightful to the child, and here is the greatest danger, for the child slips easily into the rut of easy reading." As a result, the author concluded, "librarians have adopted the general rule that any series that runs to more than four volumes is unsafe."[29]

These sentiments became a constant in professional literature. But some in small-town America found the drumbeat grating, and perceived it as an effort by distant experts to control local institutions. In 1922, for example, the *Mitchell County Press* wrote: "When we were small, every time a boy went wrong or failed to amount to anything, the blame was laid to the 'dime novel,' and to be caught reading one of the awful things called for nothing short of punishment." Nonsense, the *Press* explained. Sure, the literature was exaggerated, but the hero was always depicted with "an impeccable sense of honor. He was the sort of man who is true to a friend or a promise through all sorts of awful trials." Rather than "start a new demand for a more rigid censorship," the *Press* said, adults needed to show more confidence in America's youth. "Most of our young folks have enough sophistication nowadays so that a pretty hard [picture or book] would be required to give them a new angle."[30]

But the library profession pressed on, convinced that its position was best for library patrons. In 1926, ALA polled thirty-six thousand children in thirty-four cities to identify their favorite book; 98 percent named a book by Edward Stratemeyer, creator of fiction series like the Rover Boys, Tom Swift, and the Hardy Boys. In June 1927, the *WLB* reprinted "Not Recommended for Circulation," a list of series fiction for youth that Mary Root had originally compiled for *Maryland Library Notes*. Months later *LN&N* published Root's article "as a warning." Root's bibliography listed sixty-one separate series, including all books by Horatio Alger (121 titles in print), Martha Finley (the Elsie Dinsmore series), Harry Castleman (60 titles), Oliver Optic (140 titles), Edward Ellis (10 titles), and Edward Stratemeyer (112 titles).[31]

One iteration of the list made it into a 1929 issue of the *Wilson Bulletin* (later known as *Wilson Library Bulletin*), to which Ernest Ayres, proprietor of a Boise, Idaho, bookstore took great exception. "Why worry about censorship, so long as we have librarians?," he asked. "True, these worthy arbiters of our literary pabulum cannot hale an author into court for offenses against their esthetic preferences, but they can—and do—exercise a most rigid censorship over what the dear public shall—and shall not—read. The mere fact that the aforesaid dear public pays all the bills appears to be a negligible factor in the situation." He specifically mentioned authors like Alger, Castleman, Ellis, Finley, Optic, and Laura Lee Hope. "Is it the place of librarians, holding a position as trustee of public funds, to tell men and women who enjoyed those books when they were young, that their children shall not be allowed to read the same titles?"[32]

How did Main Street public libraries fare against Root's list? All four libraries in this study held Alger titles, which totaled seventy-four in my database. Most were included in original collections, but as they wore out they were regularly replaced, one as late as 1967. Castleman did not fare as well; only two titles appear under his name. Oliver Optic, on the other hand, merited 132 books across the four collections. Edward Ellis was represented 58 times, primarily with titles from his Launch Boys series. Martha Finley's name shows up 85 times, primarily for her Elsie Dinsmore titles. Laura Lee Hope fared equally as well; her Bobbsey Twins were represented in the four collections seventy times.

These numbers are not evenly represented in all libraries. For example, in the RPL collection (run by a professionally trained librarian since 1902), Alger was only represented twice. *Frank Fowler* was acquired in 1900, as was *The Errand Boy*. Edward Ellis had three titles in the collection, including *Adrift in the Wilds*, *Lost in the Rockies*, and *The Young Scout*, all acquired in 1900. Oliver Optic was represented with four separate titles, all of which were acquired in 1898. Martha Finley had one title (*Elsie on the Hudson*), acquired in 1898. Six Bobbsey Twin books show up in accessions books, but all were acquired in 1933 (which suggests that they were donated during Alice Raymond's tenure). From the acquisition records, it appears that Rhinelander did not purchase these series titles in large numbers (none after 1902), and thus they were not available to local patrons, who, if they wanted them, would have had to obtain them at local newsstands and drug stores, or by mail.

The other three libraries embraced series fiction, however. The Sage Library had thirty-six Alger books, twelve by Ellis, eighty-one by Optic, twenty-four by Finley, and twenty-five Bobbsey Twins books. At the Moore Library, patrons could find twenty-one Alger books, thirty-three by Ellis, twenty-six by Optic, thirty-seven by Finley, and forty Bobbsey Twins books. In Sauk Centre, Bryant Library patrons could chose from thirteen Algers books, seventeen by Ellis, twenty-one by Optic, thirty-four by Stratemeyer, and nineteen by Finley, but surprisingly no Bobbsey Twins books. Thus, the three Main Street libraries in which library directors and their trustees had limited or no professional training were not taking their cues from the nation's library community, and tended to agree with Ernest Ayres's opinion of series fiction.

Other authorities also tried to influence what people should not read. In May 1927, the Vatican launched a campaign against what it considered immoral literature. By this time American Catholicism had begun to lose its immigrant orientation and more Catholics assumed leadership roles in local establishment cultures. Among the titles American Catholics attacked were Percy Marks's *The Plastic Age* (1924), Theodore Dreiser's *An American Tragedy* (1925), Warwick Deeping's *Doomsday* (1927), and Sinclair Lewis's *Elmer Gantry* (1927).[33] Their attacks may have had local influence. The Moore Library eventually acquired the Marks and Lewis books, but not until 1936 and 1938 respectively. Sage Library had Deeping and Lewis, both acquired the year they were published. The Rhinelander Public Library acquired copies of Marks, Dreiser, and Deeping in the years they were published, but did not acquire *Elmer Gantry* until 1934. The Bryant Library was the most liberal of the group. It acquired copies of Marks, Dreiser, Deeping, and multiple copies of Lewis the same year they were published.

Because Sauk Centre was Lewis's hometown, it is not surprising that the Bryant Library acquired three copies of *Elmer Gantry* in 1927, and regularly replaced them as they wore out. But the book was not accepted in "the Paris of Stearns County" without protest. When Lewis published it, the Rev. Cecil S. Sparkes of the Congregational church—which had been Lewis's father's congregation—gave a sermon in which he called the novel "an inartistic piece of sensationalism . . . decidedly lewd from cover to cover." By that time the Bryant Library had four copies, all of which were in constant circulation.[34]

In 1929 most public libraries would have agreed with a motto that the ALA had adopted in 1879—"the best reading for the greatest number at the least cost." But rhetoric did not always match reality, even for "the least cost." From 1919 to 1928 Emanuel Haldeman-Julius sold one hundred million books in his Little Blue Books series. His Girard, Kansas, printing plant was the largest mail-order house in the world, supplying self-help works for autodidacts at very low cost, making them easily available, sizing them to fit in a pocket, and placing them in easily identified light-blue covers. Besides the mail-order house, Haldeman-Julius also established sixty-three Little Blue Book shops in the early 1920s, including shops in Detroit, Milwaukee, Chicago, and Minneapolis.[35] If they wanted, librarians and library officials from Sauk Centre, Osage, Rhinelander, and Lexington could have perused the shelves of these bookshops when they visited their nearest big city. "The Haldeman-Julius hip-pocket library has a fine picked list of the best things men have thought and written," Carl Sandburg wrote. "It is a brick-layer's hope, the mucker's dream, the wop's wonder of an education." Letters from readers and reports from Little Blue Book shops indicate, historian Dale Herder notes, that readers were fairly young, mostly male, and generally middle-brow in their literary tastes. Four subject classifications, Haldeman-Julius argued, addressed 90 percent of the nation's nonfiction reading interests—"Sex and Love"; "Self-Improvement"; "Freethought and Skepticism"; and "Fun and Laughter."[36]

Under the first subject classification he published *What Every Married Woman Should Know* (100,000 sold annually), *What Every Married Man Should Know* (100,000), *Woman's Sexual Life* (75,000), *The Physiology of Sex Life* (65,000), *Modern Aspects of Birth Control* (70,000), *Prostitution in the Modern World* (130,000), Boccaccio's *Illicit Love* (80,000), Gauthier's *One of Cleopatra's Nights* (60,000), Gorki's *26 Men and a Girl* (60,000), and de Maupassant's *A French Prostitute's Sacrifice* (60,000). All, Herder says, were "reliable and factually based." Several were written by medical authorities and pioneer sex researchers like Havelock Ellis, Margaret Sanger, and William J. Fielding.[37] Although sales figures demonstrate demand, no Main Street library held any of these titles.

For his Self-Improvement series Haldeman-Julius published *How to Improve Your Conversation* (75,000 sold annually), *How to Improve Your Vocabulary* (75,000), *Hints on Etiquette* (70,000), *How to Write Letters* (50,000), and *How to Fight Nervous Troubles* (40,000). Again, no Main Street library had any of these titles. In his Freethought and Skepticism series he published *Reasons for Doubting the Bible* (30,000), *Forgery of the Old Testament* (30,000), and *The Myth of the Resurrection* (30,000). None appeared in the four Heartland libraries.

To assess the impact of Haldeman-Julius publications, in 1974 and 1975 Herder invited readers of the *American Rationalist* and *Progressive World* to comment on their use of Little Blue Books between 1919 and 1951. A Minneapolis man with an eighth-grade education wrote: "The Little Blue Books opened my mind. From them it taught me that there are two sides to every coin. Now I say, 'Thinking brains are better than praying lips.'" A dentist from Milwaukee said: "Haldeman-Julius was my greatest 'eye-opener.'" A retired fireman from Detroit wrote: "I ordered Little Blue Books regularly from the time that Haldeman-Julius started publishing until he died. His little books were wonderful. They covered everything that anyone would want if they thirsted for knowledge."[38]

That the Little Blue Books met such an enthusiastic response between 1919 and 1951, that they were read by millions during those decades, that so many people testified to their value in their lives, that they accomplished for their readers (according to their own words) many of the things that library rhetoric claims as an institutional imperative, and that so few Haldeman-Julius publications show up in Main Street collections shows both a significant disconnect and the power of a professional discourse. Although some titles Haldeman-Julius reprinted are cited in the ALA catalogs, Haldeman-Julius publications are not. Neither do they appear in *Booklist* or the bibliographic guides published by the H. W. Wilson Company. To measure impact by sales figures alone, Haldeman-Julius was addressing an obvious information need in the areas of sex, self-improvement, skepticism, and humor. Yet Main Street public libraries ignored his publications.

There were no copies of *Jurgen*, *Simon Called Peter*, or *Well of Loneliness* in Main Street public libraries before 1929. There was a mixed response at those libraries to titles like *The Plastic Age, An American Tragedy*, and *Elmer Gantry*, books being contested by self-assumed moral authorities like the Vatican and Boston's Watch and Ward Society. The libraries owned no titles at all published by Emanuel Haldeman-Julius. Given the libraries' history through 1929, this should not be surprising. For each community a set of forces continued to operate within a process, by then decades old, that unobtrusively helped mediate a set of cultural and literary standards. These standards were reflected in decisions about what to include in public library collections and what not to include. If literary critics and academic experts were not uniform in forceful praise of controversial titles like *Well of Loneliness*, then local library officials were not about to order them without patron demand. If literary critics and academic experts sent mixed signals—as with *Elmer Gantry*—local library officials either selected or did not select based upon compelling needs unique to each community. Sometimes they justified their decisions by referencing the critical acclaim of high-culture authorities. Sometimes it was simple patron demand, as scores of Sauk Centre citizens fully expected the Bryant Library to carry multiple copies of *Elmer Gantry* despite strong protest from local clergy.

Sometimes local officials defied literary critics, academic experts, and library professionals, and willingly catered to strong local patron demand by stocking large amounts of series fiction, in part because local leaders had read the series and popular fiction condemned by library professionals and judged themselves to have suffered no harm, in part because those officials knew that the circulation rate was a measure of their institution's value to the community and that without series and popular fiction that rate would decrease dramatically. On the other side of the circulation desk in this mediation process stood the patrons, who by 1929 knew what kind of reading they could expect from the public library, and with the power of numbers they demanded it. Gradually both came to agree on the collection's parameters.

At the same time, however, patrons knew what kind of reading *not* to expect from their public library. That included contested titles like *The Well of Loneliness* and *Simon Called Peter*, for which they apparently made no demand. That even included a set of highly popular works issued by an unconventional publisher whose titles were seldom reviewed in *Booklist* or cited in ALA catalogs.[39] By 1929 the bias against nonestablishment publishers was already systemic, and citizens who over the decades developed habits of public library use had already evolved an expectation that such titles would not be there. If they wanted titles by Haldeman-Julius, the citizens in Sauk Centre, Osage, Rhinelander, and Lexington recognized that they had to buy their own. And so they did.

Other kinds of titles were treated differently by individual communities. In 1929 Moore Library patrons could find plenty of Bobbsey Twins books, but Bryant Library patrons could not. In Sauk Centre, Bryant Library users could find plenty of Horatio Alger books, but Rhinelander Public Library users could find none. At RPL, patrons could check out a copy of *An American Tragedy*, but at the Sage Library none was available. The Sage Library had Deeping's *Doomsday*, while the Moore Library did not. Titles absent from public library collections reflect community cultural and literary values mediated through time and by several groups. The results are as unique as the communities in which they were negotiated.

1929–1945

Between 1929 and 1945, the people running Main Street libraries continued their attempts to meet patron reading interests within broadly defined cultural and literary boundaries. In each community local leaders defined community standards, but increasingly found themselves mediating these standards with outside influences. Sometimes the national government rendered strong opinions. On March 18, 1930, for example, the *Sauk Centre Herald* reported a U.S. Senate debate over censoring foreign books. Utah's Reed Smoot had brought several such books to the Senate chamber, the *Herald* reported, including Anatole France's *Rabelais* (1929), *Kama Sutra*, Honore de Balzac's *Droll Tales* (1929), Giacomo Casanova's *Memoirs* (1925), D. H. Lawrence's *Lady Chatterley's Lover* (1930), and Frank Harris's *My Life and Loves* (1922). "These books will be admitted over my dead body," Smoot told his colleagues. If local citizens had checked Smoot's list against holdings of the four libraries in this study, they would have found none on the shelves. With one exception (Sage Library acquired *Lady Chatterley's Lover* in 1959), none were added in the next four decades.

Sometimes pressure came from local officials. In April 1939, Stearns County was home to a drive to eliminate "indecent literature—books and magazines on the news stand," the *Herald* reported. Two Catholic priests urged locals "to work in their own communities toward the elimination of such reading material."[40] Main Streeters left no record of any complaint against the Bryant Library for making "indecent literature" available. That no record of protests against the other three libraries can be found suggests that the collections had no material to which these self-appointed moral authorities objected.

Sometimes board members and librarians had to mediate their selections with "higher" reading tastes advocated by the nation's literary establishment and a supporting cast of library professionals whose collection guides were grounded on establishment opinion. Sometimes board members and librarians also had to mediate their selections with emerging middle-brow reading tastes evident in Book-of-the-Month Club selections. Sometimes the former merged with the latter. An analysis of Main Street library holdings for four particular titles will illustrate. All books received literary acclaim, and several were very controversial when published.

Zora Neale Hurston's *Their Eyes Were Watching God* was not so much controversial in the U.S. public library community as ignored. Although the book was critically acclaimed, it was not a best-seller, nor did it even generate much attention when published in 1937. *Their Eyes Were Watching God* recounts the life of an African American woman who found contentment, triumphs over sexism and poverty, and married three times before finding a man as concerned with her happiness as with his own. Although her novel was cited in the 1941, 1950, and 1960 editions of *Fiction Catalog*, among the four libraries studied here, all serving almost entirely white communities, only the Bryant Library acquired a copy in 1938, and that was as a gift.

John Steinbeck's *Grapes of Wrath* (1939), on the other hand, was highly popular, but met scattered opposition in public libraries across the country immediately after it was published. The East St. Louis Public Library burned copies because of the vulgar words it contained, and other public libraries in Missouri, Oklahoma, and California (including Steinbeck's home town, Salinas) banned it from their shelves.[41] Despite the controversy, however, the ALA 1943 catalog cited it, and the 1941 *Fiction Catalog* gave it a double star, a ranking it retained in the 1950 and 1960 editions. The Sage and Bryant Libraries bought copies shortly after it was published; the Rhinelander and Moore Libraries acquired copies a year later. In subsequent decades all regularly replaced copies when old ones wore out or disappeared from shelves.

Richard Wright's boyhood experiences in public libraries are well documented in *Black Boy*. While working in Memphis in the 1920s he subverted Jim Crow laws by forging a note to the public librarian: "Dear Madam: Will you please let this nigger boy have some books by H. L. Mencken?" His novel *Native Son* (1940), which addressed the problems of growing up in an urban ghetto, was a Book-of-the-Month Club selection and in the early 1940s outsold even Steinbeck's *Grapes of Wrath*, which won the 1940 Pulitzer Prize for Fiction. *Native Son* merited a single star in the 1941 *Fiction Catalog*, and double star in the 1950 and 1960 editions. The Bryant and Rhinelander Libraries purchased copies in 1940; the Moore Library was given a copy two years later. The Sage Library still had not acquired a copy by 1970.

Lillian Smith's novel *Strange Fruit* (1944) addressed interracial marriage, abortion, and lynching. After it was published, the U.S. Post Office refused to pass any copies through the mail. *Strange Fruit* was also banned in Boston.[42] The novel was cited in the 1952 ALA catalog supplement; *Fiction Catalog* gave it a single star in 1950, and a double star in 1960. The Bryant and Rhinelander Libraries purchased copies the year it was published. RPL purchased a second copy three years later. The Moore and Sage Libraries, however, still did not have a copy in their collections in 1970.

Thus, for these novels that received literary acclaim and were supported by the serialized collection development guides published for library professionals, the four libraries show mixed responses. By 1945 the Bryant Library had all four titles, and RPL three of four. Both libraries were run by trained professionals who made the selection decisions. Of the four titles, the Sage Library owned only *Grapes of Wrath*. Given its track record on popular fiction over the years, this may seem surprising. At the same time, however, all three titles dealt with issues of race. That Osage, Iowa, was an overwhelmingly white community may help to explain its relative indifference to these three books, which likely were not being requested by local patrons. That the Moore Library acquired copies of *Grapes of Wrath* and *Native Son* was probably a combination of local summer tourist demand and, in the case of the latter, BOMC status.

Sometimes board members and librarians who mediated patron demand dealt with outside influences by ignoring them. Always at the ready with advice were state library associations. For example, in a 1933 *Wisconsin Library Bulletin* article, author "M. K. R." not only listed reasons why public libraries—specifically small public libraries—ought to reject certain novels ("sophisticated novels dealing with corrupt and unwholesome phases of society"; those depicting "brutal realism," manifesting an "improbable and unconvincing plot," or "dealing with sex in a manner offensive to certain readers"), she also identified several transgressing authors, including Eleanor Hallowell Abbott, Bess Streeter Aldrich, and Jean Webster. At the time, Abbott had four titles on RPL shelves, eight at the Bryant Library, ten at the Sage Library, and seven at the Morris Library. Aldrich was represented by five books at RPL, nineteen at both the Bryant and Sage Libraries, and seven at the Moore Library. Webster was represented by fourteen books at RPL, thirteen at the Bryant Library, twenty-four at the Sage Library, and five at the Moore Library.[43]

Between 1929 and 1945 the library profession's drumbeat against series fiction continued. The Little Golden Books series began publication in 1942, and before the end of the decade sold three hundred million low-cost children's books—including *Poky Little Puppy*—at thousands of retail outlets. Library professionals shunned the series by refusing to review them in conventional bibliographic guides like *Horn Book*. Nonetheless, except for the Moore Library, all Main Street libraries in this study had copies of *Poky Little Puppy* by 1944. An *Iowa Library Quarterly* article that year, entitled "Discarding: What and How, or How to Weed a Book," included "A Partial List of Series Not Circulated by Standard Libraries." The list seemed hardly partial: it named 125 series, including books by Horatio Alger, Oliver Optic, Mary J. Holmes, Edward Stratemeyer, and Laura Lee Hope.[44] As demonstrated previously, most of these authors were well represented in Main Street libraries.

In 1930, the Stratemeyer syndicate created Nancy Drew, a wildly popular series authored by the pseudonymous Carolyn Keene. Millions of girls read these books. At a 1993 University of Iowa Nancy Drew conference, one participant recalled: "A shy, bookish child growing up in the 1950s family with lots of rules and little money, I longed to be Nancy, with her confidence, wealth, independence, loving friends, indulging parents." Another reported: "I grew up in Roseville, Minnesota, and went to the Ramsey County Library, and every time I walked in I walked right up to the front desk and said, 'Where are your Nancy Drew books?' And the librarian would look at me with disgust and say, 'We don't have *those* here.'"[45] Two Main Street libraries agreed with Ramsey County Library policy. Before

1970, RPL and the Bryant Library had no Nancy Drew books. Although the Sage Library eventually acquired forty-two titles before 1970, none appeared on its shelves before 1945.[46] Only the Moore Library acquired any Nancy Drew books before 1945. That year, three books—this first of an eventual collection of seventy-three—were available for readers.[47]

Main Street library holdings of the Hardy Boys series (another Stratemeyer creation, this one for adolescent males) showed differences with holdings of the Nancy Drew series titles. The Rhinelander Public Library carried no titles by pseudonymous author F. W. Dixon before 1970, while the Bryant Library held eight, all acquired during Bernice Finnegan's tenure. The Moore Library, however, had eighty-five titles in the series (ten acquired before 1945). But champion in the group was the Sage Library, which listed ninety-eight Hardy Boys titles in its accessions books (seven acquired before 1945). Thus, while those running RPL were consistent in stocking no Stratemeyer series, those running the Bryant Library broke ranks by acquiring the Hardy Boys series. The Sage and Moore Libraries were consistent: they owned scores in both series.

In a 1940 editorial entitled "Keep Libraries Free," the *Rhinelander News* endorsed the ALA's recently passed Library Bill of Rights. "Libraries must be universal," the *News* argued. "If every group could get the books thrown out of the libraries which it thinks bad, there would be no more libraries worth the name."[48] In part the editorial was reacting to 1930s Nazi book-burning activities so heavily criticized in the United States. But the irony here is that many of the most widely demanded titles in RPL and other Main Street libraries had consistently and persistently been condemned by Heartland state library commissions, state library associations, and their mouthpieces, state library journals. All professed to know the difference between "good" and "bad" reading; all showed little hesitation to advocate for the former, and to disparage the latter. That the four libraries in this study often ignored their advice shows not only resistance to outside pressures, but also the power of local communities to define "best reading" for themselves. As analysis of Main Street collections demonstrates—both for holdings of contested titles that merited literary acclaim and for popular fiction that met professional condemnation—between 1929 and 1945 librarians and their boards diligently and routinely worked with local patrons who drove circulation rates to evolve a discernibly unique community definition of "best reading." The process was highly democratic and, because it seldom sparked public comment, largely invisible.

1945–1956

The years 1945–1956 provide many opportunities to analyze Main Street collections from a variety of perspectives. In 1946, for example, Benjamin Spock published *The Common Sense Book of Baby and Child Care*, which in subsequent decades became the second-best-selling title in history after the Bible. Curiously, no Main Street library bought a copy after it was published. Similarly, for years the professional children's library community was apprehensive about Laura Ingalls Wilder, whose books had been popular since the 1930s.[49] But the availability of Wilder books in Main Street libraries was inconsistent, another indication that Heartland librarians did not always follow recommendations from the professional library community. The Bryant Library had three Wilder books in its collection through 1970, all purchased before 1943; *Little House on the Prairie* was not among them. On the other hand the Sage Library had nineteen Wilder books, including five copies of *Little House on the Prairie*. RPL had thirteen Wilder books by 1954, but not until that year did it acquire *Little House on the Prairie*. Not until 1944 did the Moore Library acquire eight different Wilder titles (including *Little House on the Prairie*); thereafter these were regularly replaced. In part, RPL and the Sage Library look good because they acquired an eight-volume Wilder collection that Harper published in 1954, just after ALA began offering a Laura Ingalls Wilder Medal.[50]

Other patterns emerge from analysis of the four libraries' collections in light of censorship incidents across the nation. Some of that censorship focused on paperbacks and comic books, some stemmed from anticommunist crusades of the McCarthy era, and both were amplified by local concerns about sex, violence, and juvenile delinquency. Local groups crafting censorship campaigns were largely directed by outside forces. That all four communities in this study were aware of censorship is obvious from local newspaper coverage and organizational activities. Yet despite the fact that attitudes toward censorship had shifted in postwar America (with large numbers of the public now against it in principle) and despite the fact that many leaders in the library profession persistently fought it, a careful reading of local newspapers published during these years suggests that censorship activities did not publicly affect Main Street libraries. At no time did local newspapers carry any stories about individuals or organizations questioning library books, periodicals, or other print or nonprint materials; at no time did they carry a story of local librarians bravely resisting attempts to censor by local groups or organizations. At the same time, however, consensus is hard to find. Because each of the four communities addressed these issues in unique ways, so did each of the public libraries serving them.

In early October 1946, the Rhinelander Women's Club hosted a program entitled "Are Today's Books Objectionable?" One member described complaints made against recently published books, and suggested ways to curb the sale of indecent literature. The county nurse advocated alternatives to censorship, especially the need to recommend good books to youth. After further discussion the club polled its members: Should good books be promoted? Should legal action be taken against objectionable books? Or should the situation be left as it was? A majority voted to promote "better books."[51] Two months later a Rhinelander Service League replicated the program. One program attendee noted that highly controversial titles like Betty Smith's *A Tree Grows in Brooklyn* (1943) and Kathleen Winsor's *Forever Amber* (1944) had been read "as widely as the Bible." (All four libraries in this study had *A Tree Grows in Brooklyn*, some in duplicate. Only the Bryant and Rhinelander Libraries, however, had *Forever Amber.*) Another attending reminded all there that "censorship is a matter of taste." Others sidestepped the issue by recommending that good literature be read to children from an early age.[52]

Comic book reading particularly concerned parents. "Children have been forbidden to read comic books of any kind," one author told *Wisconsin Library Bulletin* readers in 1946. "This attitude on our part has made the forbidden fruit all the more delectable." The solution? If librarians, educators, and parents "quietly but persistently put good juvenile reading matter in the paths of the children, the menace of the comic book would die a natural death."[53] But the *Rhinelander Daily News* thought differently. It reported that 95 percent of young adults surveyed in Dayton, Ohio, read comic books. "Obviously, the same proportions of Dayton's younger generation are not and will not turn into juvenile delinquents. It seems to us, on the basis of these figures and other clear evidence, that comic books do not make young criminals by themselves, and blanket condemnation of them is quite unjustified."[54]

While the *News* would not condemn comics, it felt differently about "pocket books." An April 1950 editorial listed some of "the highly inflammatory subjects with which certain of these publications deal." Once the *News* brought attention to "the sale of unsavory literature" (paperbacks) in Rhinelander, women's organizations approached local merchants. Results were immediate: "the books were cleaned out or were less prominently displayed." The local district attorney went a step further, however. He wrote to distributors of these "objectionable" publications, and cited two Wisconsin statutes that he argued gave his office power to prosecute if they refused to cooperate. Subsequently, complaints about paperbacks disappeared from *News* pages.[55]

In April 1951, Professor John R. Barton of the University of Wisconsin spoke to the Rhinelander Women's Club. "Even as the schools and churches are dependent on a community and a community on them," he said, "so does a library help to make a community even as a community makes a library." Sociological forces within the community, he argued, "determine the capacities of its library," and he largely attributed to local middle classes whatever successes local libraries experienced. "Not only must the materials and services of a community be pointed toward the individual, but the individual must be pointed toward the community in terms of community standards, ideals, and values." Unknowingly, Barton had just explained why in Rhinelander copies of the *Police Gazette* were hidden under a buggy seat in the 1920s, and why copies of *Crime Detective* were secreted in Rhinelander garages in the 1950s.[56]

John R. Barton and Franklin E. Rector had just completed a study of the "social and educational resources" of Wisconsin public libraries. Part of that study surveyed all public libraries in the state to discern "if there had been any objections to any reading matter in the library, and if so, to state the title or type of material and reason for the objections." Responses were suspect: 10 percent chose not to answer and 52 percent said they had received no objections. Of the remaining 38 percent who did cite objections, 25 percent identified "frankness and profanity" as the reason for objections, 2 percent cited "religious or political propaganda, including matters such as Fascism, Nazism, and Communism." Another 3 percent fit a category that Barton and Rector labeled a "library censorship," materials most often characterized by the response that "that kind of material is not allowed to get on the shelves."[57]

Although the label "library censorship" was somewhat hyperbolic, Barton had stumbled onto a professional practice without recognizing its apparatus. The systems set in place decades before to winnow public library acquisition possibilities to a manageable pool privileged some titles, suppressed others. This explains why no Nancy Drew book was ever featured on the Rhinelander Public Library WBOT radio program, why Rhinelander's young men would not find Hardy Boys mysteries on the library shelves, and why authors like Mickey Spillane, James T. Farrell, and John D. MacDonald seldom found their way into its collections. At the same time, "community" explains why so few objected. The formations of librarians' professional discourse had made the statement "not censorship but selection" a part of the "library faith" and effectively masked the systemic biases built into this ostensibly neutral filtering system.

In 1939 Pocket Books introduced a second paperback revolution when it sold 1.5 million books marketed originally in hardbound editions. By mid-century ten major publishers had sold nearly three hundred million paperbacks, mostly through one hundred thousand newsstands and drugstores in the United States. To maximize sales, publishers created alluring covers and crafted provocative blurbs, then displayed them on racks with covers facing out to attract passersby. As hardbound volumes, the titles occasioned little public reaction. As paperbacks, however, they met a strong response. Some people argued that such literature affected the nation's moral standards, some argued that paperbacks led to increased juvenile delinquency, and some argued that they were evidence of a communist plot to take over the country. Some argued all three.

Several groups addressed this issue, among which was the National Organization for Decent Literature (NODL), a Catholic group that in 1938 emerged from the Legion of Decency, established in 1934 to monitor sex and violence in movies. NODL was organized to conduct "a systematic campaign in all dioceses of the United States against the publication and sale of lewd magazine and brochure literature."[58] By the early 1950s NODL was turning its attention to paperbacks and comic books. Lists of "Magazines Disapproved"—which included "Pocket-Size Books"—began to appear in the *Priest*, a NODL monthly started in 1944 and sent routinely to parishes across the country. Many priests simply turned these lists over to parish organizations, which then screened display racks at local drugstores and newsstands for offending titles. In Detroit, the Archdiocesan Council of Catholic Women, the Detroit Council of Church Women, and the Detroit Council of Churches united for a local campaign. In St. Paul, Minnesota, an Organization for Decent Literature emerged from efforts by local Catholics to police local stores.[59]

Reactions to these pressures took several forms in local politics. Some cities established censorship boards. In Lansing, Michigan, the city council used licensing power to control local merchants. Any license could be revoked for "cause," which included the sale, distribution, rental, or loan of any book "containing obscene language or obscene prints, pictures, figures or descriptions, manifestly intending to corrupt the morals of youth." In St. Cloud, Minnesota, the council created a review board to screen for printed material considered "obscene, immoral, lewd," or "suggestively obscene, immoral or lewd; or [that] ridicules any person or persons by reason of race, creed, or color; or advocates Un-American, or subversive activities." Between 1950 and 1953 the board condemned over three hundred paperbacks. Similar ordinances passed in the Minnesota towns of Eveleth, Faribault, Foley, Hibbing, Northfield, Virginia, Brainerd, and Morris.

In May 1952, the Sauk Centre mayor called for a "halt" to the sale of "indecent literature" in his town. Thirty-three people attended a meeting in June and heard Mrs. Emma Bard, who had spearheaded the St. Cloud NODL campaign three years earlier. "What is in some of the comic and pocket books on sale throughout the country is terrible!," she said. "Some of the books, available to anyone, describe in detail crime; some mock law; some mock religion, God, Jesus; encourage dope addiction; marital infidelity; and other moral-less practices." She recommended a "ban list" like St. Cloud's. To address the issue in Sauk Centre, the mayor appointed a "Citizens Advisory Committee" drawn from local civic, social, and church groups. Within a month members took Bard's "ban list" into local stores, checked it against inventory, and brought to merchants' attention anything that matched. Because the *Herald* subsequently carried no stories of resistance, compliance among local merchants was probably uniform. Certainly the Bryant Library was not under suspicion. On the one hand, many of its board members were owners and managers of the stores being screened or members of organizations and churches pressing the campaign; on the other, the professional selection system that Lewis Olds used already filtered these kinds of materials out of the universe from which he made library selections.[60]

Efforts in Rhinelander took similar form. In December 1952, a NODL committee of sixty women in a "Decency Crusade" screened Rhinelander's thirty newsstands weekly to "check off the books that are named in a monthly list issued by the national organization." When committee members found matches, they requested "that no such books be offered for sale." Merchants who complied by "cooperating 100 per cent" were given plaques that they could display in store windows for ninety days; they were also acknowledged in the newspaper. One NODL official explained that comic books and pocket books were "the biggest offenders because they are aimed at youth." Results were not surprising. "Without exception," the committee noted, "Rhinelander merchants have shown themselves to be very cooperative to the suggestions of the Decency Crusade workers."[61] As in the case of the Bryant Library, those running RPL had nothing to worry about. The filtering guides Whittaker used to put books on her shelves generally did not cite the kinds of materials being pulled from Rhinelander's newsstands and drugstores.

An analysis of 370 "condemned" titles listed in eleven issues of the *Priest* between January 1952, and January 1953, matched against *Booklist* recommendations and Main Street collections will illustrate the influence these censorship campaigns had. Each semimonthly *Booklist* reviewed twenty-five adult fiction titles, or six hundred per year. Of the 370 books that the *Priest* considered objectionable, *Booklist* cites only seven in its volume 47 (September 1950–August 1951), that period during which most of the 370 were published. Thus, if Main Street librarians looked to *Booklist* for guidance, less than 2 percent of the titles NODL condemned were listed. Of those seven titles, only one showed up at a Main Street library—the Sage Library acquired a copy of Thomas Raddall's *The Nymph and the Lamp* (1950) the year it was published (but before NODL listed it).[62]

The list of 370 "condemned" titles included not only most of the works of Mickey Spillane—*I, The Jury* (1947), *One Lonely Night* (1951), and *Vengeance Is Mine* (1950), but also selected works by Erskine Caldwell—*God's Little Acre* (1933), *Tobacco Road* (1932), *Episode in Palmetto* (1950), and *A Place Called Estherville* (1949); John MacDonald's *Murder for the Bride*

(1951) and *The Brass Cupcake* (1950); James T. Farrell's *Bernard Clare* (1946), *Gas House McGinty* (1933), and *A Hell of a Good Time* (1948); John O'Hara's *Butterfield 8* (1935), *Hope of Heaven* (1938), and *Appointment in Samarra* (1934), John Steinbeck's *To a God Unknown* (1933); William Faulkner's *Wild Palms* (1939), *Pylon* (1935), *Sanctuary* (1931), and *Soldier's Pay* (1926); and Kathleen Winsor's *Forever Amber* (1944) and *Star Money* (1950). Of the 370 books, 328 of them (88 percent) were held by none of the four libraries in this study. Of the forty-two owned by one or more of those libraries, twenty-six were in only one library (thus, 96 percent of the titles the *Priest* listed were not in three of four libraries); none of these forty-two were in all four libraries. That the libraries themselves were very selective is obvious. Many other books by authors of NODL-condemned titles—James T. Farrell, John O'Hara, Erskine Caldwell, John Steinbeck, John MacDonald, and William Faulkner, for example—were well represented in the collections.

Of the list of condemned titles held by a total of one library each, RPL had the most. In 1936 it acquired a Knopf hardbound edition of Carl Van Vechten's *Nigger Heaven* (1926), which Avon later published as a paperback in 1951. In 1948 it acquired a Lippincott hardbound edition of Pat Frank's *An Affair of State* (1948), which Bantam later issued as a paperback in 1950. In 1956 it purchased a Random House hardbound edition of John O'Hara's *A Rage to Live* (1949), which Bantam had released as a paperback in 1951. RPL had also acquired a hardbound edition of Max J. Exner's *The Sexual Side of Marriage* published by Eugenics in 1938 (Pocket Books issued a paperback edition in 1948) and in 1949 bought a hardbound edition of Bucklin Moon's *Without Magnolias* (1949), which Pocket Books issued later in 1949. In 1946 RPL acquired a copy of James T. Farrell's *Bernard Clare*, which New American Library issued as a paperback in 1951, but not his *Judgment Day* (1935), which World Publishing issued as a paperback in 1944 (the Bryant Library acquired it in 1946).

RPL also acquired a hardbound edition of Ann Petry's *Country Place* (1947), which New American Library issued as a paperback in 1950. In 1946 it purchased Erskine Caldwell's *A House in the Uplands* (New American Library issued it in paperback in 1946), but did not purchase Caldwell's *This Very Earth* (1948) or *Tragic Ground* (1944), both of which were also issued by New American Library. (Sage bought *This Very Earth* in 1948.) In 1946 RPL bought a Vanguard hardbound edition of Caroline Slade's *Lilly Crackell* (1943), which New American Library released as a paperback in 1950. It also purchased Kathleen Winsor's *Star Money* as an Appleton hardbound edition in 1950, the same year New American Library released it as a paperback. RPL owned Nelson Algren's *Man with the Golden Arm* (1949)—in 1956 it purchased a Doubleday hardbound edition published in 1949 (New American Library had issued a paperback edition in 1950). Of the four libraries, RPL was the only one to acquire Ben Ames Williams's *It's a Free Country* (1945), a Houghton hardbound edition that came out six years before Popular Library released it as a paperback in 1951. Except for the condemned *It's a Free Country*, Williams was a very popular author in Main Street libraries. The Moore Library had six of his titles, the Sage Library owned fourteen, the Bryant Library owned eight, and RPL owned eighteen. Many were duplicates.

Like RPL, the Bryant Library owned Boccaccio's *Tales from the Decameron*. In 1946 the Bryant Library acquired a Garden City Books hardbound edition originally published in 1930; RPL bought a Book League of America hardbound edition in 1956. The two libraries also owned two copies each of Kathleen Winsor's *Forever Amber*. Both initially purchased the Macmillan hardbound edition in 1945, the year the book came out. Each purchased an additional copy a year later, four years before New American Library brought out the paperback edition that NODL condemned. The Bryant Library purchased a Random House hardbound edition of Budd Schulberg's *What Makes Sammy Run* (1941), which Bantam brought out in paperback in 1945, and in 1944 it purchased a Duell hardbound edition of Rosamond Marshall's *Kitty* (1943), which Pocket Books issued in paperback three years later. It did not acquire Marshall's *Celeste* (1949), which the Sage Library added in 1949, the same year Dell issued it as a paperback. In 1947 the Bryant Library did acquire a Dutton hardbound edition of Natalie Scott's *The Story of Mrs. Murphy* (1947), which Pocket Books issued two years later as a paperback; in 1943 the Bryant Library also acquired a Sun Dial hardbound edition of Thorne Smith's *Turnabout*, published originally in 1931; Pocket Books reissued it as a paperback in 1947. In 1946 the Bryant Library acquired a copy of James T. Farrell's *The Judgment Day* (1935), which World Publishing had issued in 1944. In 1946 it acquired a Vanguard hardbound edition of Willard Motley's *Knock on Any Door* (New American Library reissued it in 1950), and in 1946 it acquired a Creative hardbound edition of George Henderson's *Jule, Alabama Boy in Harlem*, which Avon reissued as a paperback in 1946. The Bryant Library added its hardbound edition of Faulkner's *Sanctuary* in 1931. New American Library issued a *Sanctuary* paperback in 1950. The Bryant Library bought a Farrar, Rinehart hardbound edition of Philip Wylie's *Night unto the Night* (1944) in 1944. New American Library later issued a paperback in 1950.

In 1959 the Sage Library acquired a Grove Press hardbound edition of D. H. Lawrence's *Lady Chatterley's Lover*, originally issued in 1928, and reissued as a paperback by New American Library in 1946. Similarly, the Sage Library was the only one of the four libraries to acquire Erskine Caldwell's *This Very Earth*; it purchased a hardbound edition in 1948, the same year New American Library issued a paperback. In 1950 it acquired a 1949 New Directions hardbound edition of Paul Bowles's *The Sheltering Sky* (1949), which New American Library issued as a paperback in 1950. In 1949 the Sage Library acquired a Random House hardbound of Irwin Shaw's *The Young Lions* (1948), which New American Library issued as a paperback in 1948.[63]

The only condemned title that the Moore Library held that was not owned by the other libraries was Gordon Merrick's *The Strumpet Wind* (1947). Popular Library issued it as a paperback in 1952; Moore acquired a copy in 1953. Like the Sage Library, however, the Moore Library owned James M. Cain's *The Postman Always Rings Twice* (1934). The Moore Library purchased its hardbound edition in 1938; the Sage Library got its hardbound edition in 1950, three years after Pocket Books came out with a paperback. Three of the four libraries owned Christopher Morley's *Kitty Foyle* (1939). Lippincott published the original hardbound edition in 1939, and within the year the Moore, Bryant, and Rhinelander Libraries all had copies on their shelves. RPL was the only library to acquire a paperback edition when Signet issued it in 1950.

What does all this suggest about Main Street public library collecting practices? People in charge either agreed with or were intimidated by local NODL committees. Since boards at each had at least one Catholic, agreement was more likely than intimidation. In those few instances where libraries held condemned titles, mostly the libraries had purchased hardbound editions before the reissued paperbacks became controversial and subject to NODL condemnation. That librarians subsequently refused to buy the cheaper paperbacks should not be surprising. The library profession identified with a publishing establishment that privileged hardbound editions over the paperbacks that newsstands and drugstores sold largely to working-class readers.[64] Their propensity for privileging hard-bound editions gave them another reason to say "that kind of material is not allowed to get on the shelves." That RPL had the highest number of condemned titles should not surprise. It was directed by a professional trained to access literary establishment reviews supporting her selection decisions. She had also been socialized into a profession in which intellectual freedom advocacy and censorship opposition became professional imperatives. At the same time, however, having only 4 percent of the 370 titles condemned by NODL suggests that "selection, not censorship" was not her acquisitions modus operandi, but that community influence played a much larger role in collection decisions.

In the midst of Wisconsin Senator Joseph McCarthy's anticommunist crusade, the *New York Times* broke a story on June 22, 1953, that the U.S. Department of State had banned more than forty authors and several hundred books from U.S. libraries abroad between February 19 and June 21. Included were authors Howard Fast, Dashiell Hammett, William Z. Foster, Anna Louise Strong, and Lillian Hellmann. Although this may have frightened Heartland citizens, it could not have surprised them. For years local newspapers had been carrying stories about communist "fronts." On December 12, 1946, for example, the *Jeffersonian* ran an editorial decrying "intellectual drifters" who as "dupes" of "known Communists" were a "threat to freedom that is difficult to measure."[65] The *Rhinelander Daily News* reprinted the *Times* story on June 23, and on July 6 published an editorial saying, "The people of this country have too long endured the creeping threat of censorship over what they should be allowed to say or print or read or, by inference, think." But the remarks of the *News* were focused primarily on the censorship of political speech; the *News* made no comment on the work of the local NODL committee or the American Legion.[66]

Like NODL campaigns, McCarthyist pressures affected the four libraries. On occasion library officials offered tepid rejoinders. For example, in his August 1955 *Sauk Centre Herald* column, Lewis Olds encouraged citizens to read Henry Steele Commager's *Freedom, Loyalty, Dissent* (1954) because Commager "looks at recent phenomena such as loyalty purges, the irresponsible smearing of individuals, the wholesale labeling of organizations as 'subversive,' and presents the issues at stake more clearly than ever before."[67] At its January 5, 1955, meeting, the RPL board discussed a patron complaint that Lorraine and Jerrold Beim's *Sasha and the Samovar*

(1944) was "subversive in content." At the time the library had nine Beim titles, and had acquired *Sasha* the same year it was published. After reviewing "objectionable" passages, the board unanimously decided "that the accusation was entirely untrue, unfounded and unfair."[68] These two examples, however, were the exception rather than the rule. For the most part Main Street library officials remained mute.

Analysis of authors of overseas banned books represented in Main Street collections reveals that none were removed (although some may have gone to an "Inferno"), and neither board minutes nor local newspaper coverage indicate that anyone ever objected to titles by any of the authors. Among the mysteries Dashiell Hammett penned that the State Department found objectionable were *The Dain Curse* (1929), *The Glass Key* (1931), *The Maltese Falcon* (1930), and *The Thin Man* (1934). Howard Fast's books were represented in even larger numbers, and included *Citizen Tom Paine* (1943), *Freedom Road* (1944), *The American* (1946), *The Selected Works of Tom Paine* (1945), *Patrick Henry and the Frigate's Keel* (1945), *The Last Frontier* (1941), and *The Unvanquished* (1944).

RPL bought *The Thin Man* in 1934 and *Citizen Tom Paine* in 1943. Both were still in its collections in 1953. The Bryant Library had all four Hammett titles, and Fast's *The American*, *Citizen Tom Paine*, *Freedom Road*, and *Patrick Henry and the Frigate's Keel*, all acquired between 1942 and 1947. It also acquired Lillian Hellman's *The Children's Hour* (1934) in 1935, and kept it in the collection. The Sage Library held *The Dain Curse*, *The Maltese Falcon*, and *The Glass Key*. All were acquired in the early 1930s. Its Fast collection included *Freedom Road* and *The Unvanquished*. The Moore Library had no titles by Hammett in its collections.[69]

Analyzed against political and cultural censorship by local, state, and federal authorities (elected and self-appointed) between 1945 and 1956, the collections of the four libraries show as much consistency in their inconsistencies as did society at large. Patterns inherited from previous generations continued (acquisition of popular fiction and some hardbound editions acclaimed by the literary establishment). Pressing print culture trends, such as paperbacks and comics, were resisted (even though many new paperback titles simply reprinted hardbound editions already in collections). In some communities, local authorities protested the censorship of political speech, but said nothing about the suppression of other forms of speech (such as paperbacks and comic books). Most communities said nothing at all, but followed the lead of others. That there was no instance of censorship of public library materials reported in local newspapers strongly suggests that by 1956 librarians and trustees at the four libraries in this study knew very well what was acceptable and defensible in their collections.

The universe from which Main Street librarians and trustees identified acquisitions possibilities had over the years been subtly yet carefully defined by service traditions that effectively accommodated and mediated patron demand, community standards, and the literary establishment's recommendations championed by library professionals in their printed guides. Although librarians and trustees argued with veracity that at mid-century they pursued a policy of "selection, not censorship," their collecting practices clearly demonstrate that local conditions—and not a national standard—gave primary definition to that phrase. The contours of public library collections they relinquished to subsequent generations did not differ substantially from those they inherited. By 1956, Main Street public libraries had become familiar and safe institutions with a diminishing amount of public space that found quiet yet unique niches among other cultural institutions in their small-town Heartland communities.

Agent of Social Harmony

L ast year some members of the Iowa Library Association were promoting the passage of the Library Services bill (S. 1452), which proposed to match Federal with State funds for the promotion and benefit of libraries," Sage Library trustee W. L. Calloway wrote to his congressman January 25, 1952. "I expressed my opposition to the bill at the time as one more step in the attempt of the Federal government to gain control of our educational institutions." It was, he said, another example of "the big stick." Calloway had been on the board since 1943, and in 1945 was its president. He was owner of Calloway Lumber, a Republican, and Congregationalist. Because he worried that federal interventions would force the library to relinquish some of its independence, he requested of his congressman to "let me know the present status of the bill."[1]

For decades the ALA had been lobbying the federal government for funding to extend library services to all U.S. citizens. In 1956, they were successful. The next year President Dwight Eisenhower signed the Library Services Act (LSA), which made it to his desk primarily because librarians in southern states convinced their legislators (many of whom held crucial committee chairs) that the legislation would not curtail states' rights because state library agencies would determine how funds were distributed.[2] Many bought bookmobiles that traversed remote areas previously little served by public libraries. The bookmobiles—often managed directly by a state library agency, sometimes by a newly structured county or regional library system—were stocked with titles cited in *Fiction Catalog, Public Library Catalog*, and *Children's Catalog*. Calloway was right to be concerned about the Sage Library losing some of its independence, but his concern about who held "the big stick" was misplaced. He feared the federal government, but it was his state library agency—run by library professionals who prioritized how these funds were allocated—that wielded this new power. Each of the four communities discussed in this book met this power (or what Dorothy Whittaker called "those Commission ideas") in different ways and at different times.[3]

On November 28, 1956, the Sage Library board heard a State Library official discuss the recently passed Library Services Act. "She told how much Iowa was entitled to and presented three plans which had been worked out for the use of such funds in Iowa. A copy of these plans is to be sent to the Board for further consideration." Change was in the air; Calloway was still on the board, but if he had objections, board minutes do not record them.[4] Six months later, the board voted to "grant free use of the library to rural residents" and "participate in the Travelling Library Service being funded through the Library Services Act." In August 1957 the new librarian found space for the eight hundred books the service would be sending. On January 1, 1962, the Sage Library joined a federation of sixty-five libraries (eventually known as the North Iowa Library Extension). At the same time, the county levied a tax that enabled any Mitchell County resident to withdraw books from any public library within the county. In June the board received $1,000 of the $2,500 allocated by the federal government for Mitchell County.[5] In 1995 the Sage Library moved into a new and larger building. The old building was renovated in 1997 and now serves as Osage City Hall and home to the Osage Chamber of Commerce.

In 1950, by then one of 432 Iowa public libraries, the Sage Library had 14,336 volumes to serve a population of 3,436 (4.2 per capita), and a circulation of 22,594 (6.6 per capita). In 2008, as one of 559 Iowa public libraries, the Osage Public Library (it changed names in 1995) had 35,230 volumes to serve a population of 3,451 (10.2 per capita) and a circulation of 109,031 (31.6 per capita). Although the latter includes media like DVDs and videocassettes, printed fiction still accounted for 25 percent of total adult circulation. Nearly all books circulated to juveniles were fiction.

Rhinelander had similar experiences. In November 1956, WFLC consultant Ione Nelson addressed the Rhinelander chapter of the American Association of University Women about the LSA. Nelson told her audience that the WFLC would likely use those funds for bookmobile services to remote parts of the state, including its northern region. After her speech, one woman told Nelson: "Thank God, bookmobile service and regional library development is rearing its head again." Another told her that most people in rural areas believed that the Rhinelander Public Library "was a closed corporation and that area service would rectify this." Ironically, Nelson's talk took place in the RPL children's room. In May 1959 the WFLC brokered an agreement between the City of Rhinelander and Oneida, Florence, Forest, Langlade, and Vilas Counties to locate a regional library service with headquarters in Wausau that would be funded in part by LSA dollars; RPL would provide reference services.[6]

Dorothy Whittaker stayed as library director at RPL until 1971. Although she accepted the inevitable, she preferred a separate regional library reference service with a full-time male director. Men are "much easier and more pleasant to work with," she told a WFLC representative in 1961. As of this writing, the Rhinelander District Library still occupies its original Carnegie building (albeit expanded and renovated in 1985), and is part of the Wisconsin Valley Library Service encompassing seven counties in North Central Wisconsin—one of seventeen library systems in Wisconsin.[7] In 1950, by then one of 294 Wisconsin public libraries, RPL had 17,542 volumes to serve a population of 8,774 (2 per capita), and a circulation of 52,365 (6 per capita). In 2008, as one of 458 Wisconsin public libraries, the Rhinelander District Library had 80,000 volumes to serve a population of 7,687 (10.4 per capita) and a circulation of 79,854 (10.4 per capita).

For a while federal funds for libraries distributed through state library agencies did not affect the Moore Library. After fifty years of service Florence Walther retired in 1961. Once she left, the board took a more active role in Moore Library matters. In subsequent years the library moved many bookshelves to improve patron access. The collection was finally cataloged in the 1970s, and the back shed made into a permanent room. In 1971 the library affiliated with the St. Clair County Library System (later the Blue Water Library Federation), and thus gave its patrons interlibrary loan access to books from other libraries. In August 1977 the library made the State Register of Historic Sites. In the 1980s the board voted to renovate the second floor and open it to patron use. An open house held during National Library Week in April 1984 commemorated the accomplishments. When the Blue Water Library Federation dissolved in 1996, the Moore Library moved to the White Pine Cooperative.

In 1950, then one of 515 Michigan public libraries, the Moore Library had 7,265 volumes to serve a population of 594 (12.2 per capita), and a circulation of 4,577 (7.7 per capita). In 2008, as one of 658 Michigan public library systems, the library had 14,929 volumes to serve a population of 1,046 (14.3

per capita) and a circulation of 24,206 (23 per capita). Fiction (including videos) accounted for 85 percent of adult circulation, 84 percent of juvenile circulation. An appropriations increase enabled the Moore Library to add hours of opening from twenty-one per week in 2005 to forty in 2008.

At the end of the 1980s Sauk Centre expended much energy debating whether to save the cupola atop the library. On one side were Bryant Library board members and the newly formed Sauk Centre Historical Society; on the other side was the city council, which argued that costs for the project had not been included in the original estimates for remodeling and expanding the library. Because the council would not budge, the board, the Historical Society, and private citizens raised the necessary funds. To that the council had no objection. Plans for expansion continued. In July 1990, however, the council voted to make the Bryant Library part of the Great River Regional Library System. In response, five board members resigned to protest what they considered a loss of local control. Still the council pressed on. Because cost estimates for remodeling, expanding, and making the Carnegie building accessible to physically disabled people came to over one million dollars, some suggested in the late 1990s that Sauk Centre raze the structure and move the Bryant Library into another building. A second bid came in at $600,000, however, and by 1998 the library had added two new wings and provided space in the lower level for the Historical Society.[8]

In 1950, then one of 257 Minnesota public libraries, the Bryant Library had 16,005 volumes to serve a population of 3,140 (5.1 per capita) and a circulation of 29,133 (9.3 per capita). Fiction accounted for 64 percent of adult circulation, 56 percent of juvenile circulation. In 2008, as one of 359 Minnesota public libraries, it had 31,726 volumes to serve a population of 3,930 (8.1 per capita) and a circulation of 81,301 (20.7 per capita).

Analyzing just the circulation statistics for all four libraries against the introduction of newer forms of information and communications technologies over time (silent films in the 1900s, radio in the 1920s, sound films in the 1930s, television in the 1950s, and computers at the end of the twentieth century) shows that these technologies had little or no long-term effect on total patron use. Despite predictions by evangelists of information technology in the early 1980s that the American public library would not survive the century, these four rural Heartland public libraries were busier in 2008 than they had been middle of the twentieth century.

Through their books, periodicals, and programming (like theme-based women's club meetings and Children's Book Week) these libraries connected local populations to outside worlds and facilitated the imagined communities that reading common texts—whether popular fiction, literary fiction, or informational nonfiction—provided. Main Street public libraries certainly were repositories for the literary establishment that dominated the intellectual world, but they were also active agents in reading cultures that looked to middle-brow and other forms of popular fiction for imagination and information. The books and periodicals these libraries had in their collections largely reinforced dominant myths of American exceptionalism, egalitarianism, and consensus. Had they mostly challenged these myths, the libraries probably would not have survived the twentieth century.[9]

In all cases these public libraries grew out of institutions that Yankee founders replicated from social libraries they knew in New England. None was started by pioneer sodbusters; none of the founders associated themselves with organizations run by local socialists, populists, or members of the Grange or the Knights of Labor. Nor did these libraries emerge as a result of popular pressure. Instead, they emerged from a proliferating group of voluntary agencies in the late nineteenth century with a desire to mold and police morality in their local communities. All four libraries were established by Protestants (especially Congregationalists) who had a tradition of using print in certain ways that were replicated in the libraries they organized. Only over time did library boards include Roman Catholics and Lutherans, but never Jews or confirmed atheists in the period covered by this book. They generally believed that the growth their communities experienced in the late nineteenth century was an affirmation of the rightness of progress, and that the new public library was tangible evidence.[10]

Over time the influence of specific lodges, church groups, and women's clubs to which trustees belonged waxed and waned, but one constant remained. Before 1956 these four libraries were part of one of the few civic institutions where women were allowed to lead and encouraged to participate. That more women than men used the library may explain this; that the former functioned as caregivers for children much more than the latter probably also explains why story hours and summer reading programs were so important to Main Street public libraries.

In the public libraries studied here, community leaders (a small-town bourgeoisie largely consisting of middle-class professionals like lawyers, teachers, and clergy, who functioned as mediators to the outside world and served as local carriers of culture) and a substantial but ever-changing fraction of the local citizenry (whose own perceptions of class were often muted by a sense of unity and stability that their small town embodied) combined to create local hegemonies. A part of these hegemonic practices was evident in local public library services they crafted into a set of expectations that subsequent generations not only embraced but also supported. And as these expectations became layers of tradition, the traditions automatically imposed limits on what those running public libraries were willing to assume or not to assume as community priorities and responsibilities. Certainly the provision of stories contained in printed texts was one tradition, but in the first half of the twentieth century preserving these printed stories held a higher priority than providing public space for community meetings, and as these stories cumulated into larger collections, the libraries chose to sacrifice meeting space to preserve the texts. And for the most part, their patrons seemed to agree with this priority. Between 1876 and 1956 local newspapers reported no resistance.

At the same time, however, a hierarchy of reading defined by a national literary establishment that made clear and deliberate distinctions between high culture and popular reading texts before 1950 was decidedly flattened by the leadership and local patrons of these public libraries. In part this exercise of local power looks like cultural democracy at work, perhaps in part even an act of defiance against outside influences. But whatever it was, it had carefully defined limits. Although Main Street collections provided some opportunities to challenge the race, class, and gender biases manifest in the everyday lives of local citizens who used them, patrons generally preferred reading materials that offered dependable pleasures, and from these texts they appropriated in ways that tended to reinforce values and reaffirm the convictions about life that they had inherited from previous generations.

But it was not always so. For all these years, these four libraries reached substantial fractions of citizens in their community in profound ways difficult to discern because they have generally worked quietly, and enabled their users to appropriate freely without interference except for the general parameters the traditions of services and collections have imposed. By 1956, public library use in the four communities had been in many ways habitualized and ritualized, for people of different ages and both genders. To some extent, public library users were trained by experience to use their public libraries in different ways at different times in their lives, sometimes as place, sometimes as source of information, most often as a source of reading materials. Sometimes, however, they were all three. On occasion they fed the dreams of young people like Sinclair Lewis by expanding on the official knowledge that local compulsory educational institutions controlled so tightly.[11] At the same time, however, the historical record does not demonstrate that these public libraries contributed in meaningful ways to check declining trends such as population and job loss in small-town America. Nor does it appear that these Main Street libraries functioned as important information institutions to address local economic problems.

Physically, most of these libraries looked alike. Even today Americans can recognize a Carnegie public library, upon whose steps thousands of children strapped their roller skates in the 1930s and on whose lawns they twirled hula hoops in the 1950s. Adorning their walls and helping to create imagined communities unifying Americans across the country were patriotic prints like Emanuel Leutze's *Washington Crossing the Delaware*, busts of Shakespeare and Lincoln, and textual facsimiles of the Declaration of Independence and the U.S. Constitution and its Bill of Rights. As places, these four libraries functioned as destination sites local citizens used to model appropriate social behaviors, manifest civic participation, and celebrate citizenship. Figuratively through the materials they supplied, and literally through the public space they provided, these public libraries brought together close friends, families and acquaintances, and provided a safe place to assimilate strangers and newcomers into the community. To an extent public libraries were places to see and be seen, and primarily sites of self-presentation rather than confrontation. Mostly they were benign agents in local socialization activities, primarily reinforcing local definitions of normalcy rather than challenging patterns related to age, ethnicity, gender, and class. In these four communities the public library was one site where people became aware of their interconnections and formed interdependencies. The ritual of public library use helped habituate local citizens into the local culture and at the same time celebrate reading and literacy. Just as the Sunday morning church bells gave voice to communal bonds that symbolized the small town, so did the public library with its traditions and services. To some extent, in the minds of community citizens the local public library was fact, symbol, and myth.

Although these four libraries are located in the Midwest, one is hard-pressed to identify particular characteristics they manifested before the middle of the twentieth century that would specifically label them as regional. Each town had a Main Street which in small-town America constituted what literary historian Richard Lingeman calls the "main artery through which the lifeblood of the town flowed"; cultural geographer Richard Francaviglia calls it "primarily a social environment."[12] Admittedly, the communities into which library trustees imagined themselves were for the most part local. As local people, these trustees identified largely with local problems, values, rules, and patterns of behavior. Because of that identification, they generally held the community's trust, for good and ill, as they built their civic institutions.

To some extent Main Street reflected regional cultures, but its public library was more an occupant on Main Street than a contributor to the regional culture that Main Street fostered and replicated. Local public libraries did generally carry their local and one major state newspaper, on occasion a state periodical, and often the works of local authors and famous native sons and daughters who had moved away. But for the most part the libraries were not asked by local communities to be regionally distinctive; rather, within limits, they were expected to homogenize local culture and accommodate and reinforce local, state, and national values. By refusing to stock foreign-language titles, for example, they did very little to assimilate foreigners unless the immigrants first learned English. And for all four communities, race as an issue seemed unimportant because the people local citizens saw on Main Street and the world they constructed around them were almost all white.

On Main Street, public libraries were less ambiguous space, not as affected by ethnicity, race, class, gender and age as the street itself was. On occasion the question of where to locate libraries became negotiation points for arranging Main Street, but always they were a positive element to be featured, not hidden. Some space within the library building was segregated (children's rooms, for example) but for the most part patrons of all classes and both genders were free to wander about inside. And although over time these buildings provided community space for thousands of meetings and encounters of all kinds, the vast majority of these were firmly grounded on approved middle-class activities, tastes, and values.

While professionalism certainly improved library administration, service, and efficiency over the decades, researchers of the history of librarianship have largely ignored two of the most important services that Main Street public libraries provided for most of the twentieth century. First, analysis of "library as place" has been largely absent from their research agendas, even though—as this book demonstrates—libraries regularly served as important public spaces for the kinds of meetings and informal gatherings that knit communities together.

An even greater failing has been lack of attention to the multiple roles that reading plays in everyday life, especially the popular fiction that drove circulation rates in public libraries across the country. When Louise Rosenblatt argued in *Literature as Exploration* (1938) that fiction of any kind has the potential to spark imagination and inform in many ways, the professional library community largely ignored her conclusions.[13] Instead, researchers assumed that nonfiction had the primary power to facilitate "reading for information." After World War I the purpose of most reading research in librarianship was aimed at reducing the reading of fiction and increasing the reading of nonfiction. When Douglas Waples and Ralph Tyler stated in *What People Want to Read About* (1931) that "for women of limited schooling to overcome their indifference to political and economic problems would do more to improve the condition of American society at large than for men to take more interest in art," and when Pierce Butler argued in *An Introduction to Library Science* (1933) that "the complacent American toleration of the feminization of its culture" was evident in women's novel reading and that the library had an obligation to develop public enlightenment with better reading and to provide reliable information to help attain the democratic ideal, they overlooked the possibility that library patrons (most of whom were women) were not indifferent to "political and economic problems" simply because they read fiction.

Because positivist researchers like Waples and Tyler assumed that printed books had single meanings that led to predictable "satisfactions," they could not discern that for "women of limited schooling," members of different social classes, and people of different races, ages, and ethnicities the definition of politics and the economic circumstances in which (as individuals and groups) they found themselves were being addressed in many ways by the popular fiction they were reading.[14]

Similarly, efforts to identify a library philosophy and articulate a library purpose and mission have been limited largely because they take a top-down, "user in the life of the library" approach rather than a bottom-up, "library in the life of the user" approach. The former mostly ignores patron influence on library practices, but the latter allocates a degree of power to patrons who by their own volition use the library, and thus makes that influence essential to understanding the public library's community roles. For example, highly cited library scholar Jesse Shera says the library's basic mission "is to maximize the social utility of graphic records," clearly a top-down perspective. Similarly, Charles B. Osburn argues the that "function" of the library "is the stewardship of the social transcript." Patrick Williams's *The American Public Library and the Problem of Purpose* (1988) calls for a return to "purpose" built on a narrow definition of "education." Because of this top-down thinking he does not consider that people engage different kinds of texts (including fiction delivered via print and other media) for multiple reasons in different ways at different times in their lives. Similarly, when former ALA president Michael Gorman argues in *The Enduring Library* (2003) that the three "pillars of librarianship"—collection development, reference work, and cataloging—ground the library's fundamental mission, users play little role in his explanation of why the library endures.[15]

These observations are not entirely wrong, but because they take a "user in the life of the library" approach they fail to evaluate the purposes, functions, and missions the public library fulfills as public space. In addition, because that "user in the life of the library" approach generally leads them to overlook fiction (print and otherwise)—which to this day accounts for the vast majority of circulation in all public libraries—they fail to adequately account for the power its stories have to inform, foster ideas, construct community, develop a sense of discovery, inspire, and offer encouragement. Over the years the well-organized Main Street public libraries covered in this book made possible the mission that John Wight, Edward Everett, and George Ticknor foresaw for them in the middle of the nineteenth century by providing information services and defining what "graphic records" and what parts of the "social transcript" they wanted to pass on to subsequent generations. (Except for the Moore Library, all had the Library of the World's Best Literature series on their shelves in the early twentieth century). At the same time, however, they did so much more.

The clear differences between these four Main Street public libraries help identify each community's uniquely negotiated cultural center. As stated previously, the cultural politics of a library are written in its collections. What gets placed there is the result of a mediated process—sometimes open, sometimes hidden—that involves a number of influences, including an understanding of the library's history and a perception of its future. What David Welky finds for the culture of print in the Great Depression applies equally to these four libraries between 1876 and 1956. Mainstream print culture's "ability to preserve the comfortable messages of yesteryear while absorbing the lessons of the present was vital," he says, and "made the cultural center a continual work in progress. . . . This combination made culture exciting—a seemingly forward-looking thing capable of crystallizing, solving, or explaining away our problems—without making it so exciting that it became frightening or disconnected from old realities."[16] Main Street public libraries enabled their communities to shift that center over the decades. By helping to define and determine the cultural centers of their local communities, they constituted themselves as reading spaces and meeting places essential to preserving the social order. They also helped minimize a sense of threat, fear, and separation. Sometimes that meant not buying materials on controversial topics like socialism and women's right to vote.

Throughout the first half of the twentieth century, whenever the library profession tried to press limitations on the provision of fiction these Main Street public libraries consistently and successfully resisted, albeit not uniformly. Something in the local culture explains the differences. Some "good" books took a long time for public libraries to acquire, and some never made it into collections. Perhaps because of belated approval of *Sister Carrie* (1900) in library collection guides, the Bryant Library did not obtain a copy until 1927 and RPL not until 1963; the Sage and Moore Libraries still did not have copies in 1970. And while all four libraries purchased copies of Steinbeck's controversial *Grapes of Wrath* within a year of publication, only the Bryant Library (1899) had a copy of Marx's *Das Kapital* in 1970.

In 1905 the four public libraries all owned copies of George Eliot's *Daniel Deronda*, Lew Wallace's *Ben-Hur*, and F. H. Burnett's *Little Lord Fauntleroy*, but Harriet Beecher Stowe—Sage Library's eighth most popular author in 1895 and represented on Bryant Library shelves with sixteen titles—had only three titles on Moore Library shelves, and none on RPL shelves. In 1935, the Moore Library owned twenty-one titles by Horatio Alger, twenty-six by Oliver Optic, and forty Bobbsey Twins titles; the Sage Library had similar numbers. The Bryant Library, on the other hand, had plenty of books by Alger and Optic, but no Bobbsey Twins. RPL had only two Alger titles, four by Optic, and six Bobbsey Twins books (all of which appear to have been donated during the Great Depression). Similarly, scores of Nancy Drew mysteries found their way onto Sage and Moore Library shelves by 1956, but none appeared on the shelves of RPL and the Bryant Library. RPL also refused to stock Hardy Boy mysteries; by 1970 the Bryant Library had eight of these, the Moore had eighty-five, and the Sage Library had ninety-eight. And in the politically charged McCarthy era, none of the four appear to have pulled any titles on U.S. Department of State lists of banned books.

Analyzing seventy-nine titles that Alice Payne Hackett identifies in *Fifty Years of Best Sellers, 1895–1945* against Main Street collections reveals striking consistencies.[17] Some of these titles have been discussed previously, including Florence Barclay's *The Rosary*, Gene Stratton Porter's *The Harvester*, Sinclair Lewis's *Main Street* and *Elmer Gantry*, Kathleen Winsor's *Forever Amber*, and Lillian Smith's *Strange Fruit*. Holdings for all libraries range from a low of 72 percent for the Moore Library to a high of 90 percent for the Bryant Library. Of the best-selling titles missing for all libraries, however, the majority of these were nonfiction. Seventeen of the twenty-two titles on Hackett's list and not in the Moore Library were nonfiction; five of the eight on the list that were not in the Bryant Library were nonfiction. Although all the libraries quickly acquired copies of Emily Post's *Etiquette* (1924) and Dale Carnegie's *How to Win Friends and Influence People* (1937), none owned a copy of Henry Adams's bestselling *The Education of Henry Adams* (1919), or Lin Yutang's *The Importance of Living* (1938). Only the Sage Library owned a copy of Lulu Hunt Peters's *Diet and Health* (1925). This suggests that each of the four libraries privileged fiction in its acquisitions policies. This impression is strengthened by the fact that almost all best-selling titles purchased in multiple copies were fiction.

Little in the primary source data screened for this study indicates that any of these communities established and supported their public libraries primarily to keep their local citizens informed so that political democracy could function. Admittedly, some of this occurred in connection with the reading rooms frequented by retired men, the story hours visited by grade-schoolers, the term papers researched at the library by high school students on weekday evenings and Saturdays, and the reports constructed there by women's club members. But rarely in the history of these libraries did anything "learned" in these information-seeking practices show up later in public discourse on controversial political issues. Because local controversies covered in newspapers seldom cited library resources or programs, one also has to conclude that Main Street public libraries did not make many contributions to the critical debates about sewer systems and street paving in the local public sphere. First and foremost, then, they were not "arsenals of democracy" in the traditional sense of that phrase. Neither were they essential civic institutions of social control. Rather, all four communities established libraries primarily as reading institutions for the dissemination of "good" books, and "good" was largely defined by those who demanded and selected these books.

If the "library faith" was fact, this study should have shown that the small-town public library was a locally supported civic institution that over the years—and especially after the ALA passed a Library Bill of Rights in 1939—resisted attempts to censor and at the same time provided information (sometimes controversial) that was essential for an informed citizenry. "Books and reading matter selected for purchase from the public funds should be chosen because of the value and interest to people of the community," declared the 1939 version of Library Bill of Rights Principle 1, "and in no case should the selection be influenced by the race or nationality or the political or religious views of the writers." Principle 2 read: "As far as available materials permits, all sides of questions on which differences of opinion exist should be represented fairly and adequately in the books and other reading matter purchased for public use." But the history told here in this book shows that this is not how these four communities developed and used their collections. Rather, analyzed from a "library in the life of the user" perspective, it is clear that the Main Street public libraries became local agents—physical and figurative—through which their community's citizens—elite and common—accomplished two tasks essential for local harmony. First, they provided public space to demonstrate and teach social behaviors and responsibilities acceptable to the community. Second, they provided literary space through collections and services that offered models for successful living, solving problems, and achieving an orderly life at the same time that they mediated in peaceful ways a set of ever-shifting cultural values constantly influenced by interior and exterior forces. Sinclair Lewis disliked the social harmony and behavioral conformity he saw in his hometown (so did his character Carol Kennicott), and could only appreciate the public library he wrote into *Main Street* for the potential its collections had to transport him to other places. "To the Bryant Library, Sauk Centre," he inscribed on a gift copy of one book he sent home in 1937, "with love and lively memories of the days when its books were my greatest adventures."

The purpose and mission of the Main Street public libraries studied here were not primarily to supplement formal education, to pursue a policy of "not censorship, but selection," or to provide information considered essential for the marketplace or the politics of democracy. Those were secondary goals, and because the library was an institution that local citizens did not have to patronize, these goals were regularly and necessarily compromised, despite professional rhetoric. Their actual primary purpose and mission—as crafted over the generations by local leaders and users—was to foster the kinds of social harmony that community spaces and stories, experienced and shared, provide.

Notes

INTRODUCTION

1. See, for example, Deanna Marcum, *Good Books in a Country Home: The Public Library as a Cultural Force in Hagerstown, Maryland, 1878–1920* (Westport, CT: Greenwood Press, 1994); and Ronald E. Bergquist, "'It Could Have Been Bigger, But Its Residents Like It as It Is': Small Town Libraries in Moore County, North Carolina" (PhD diss., University of North Carolina at Chapel Hill, 2006).

2. My original study included the Morris Public Library of Morris, Illinois, but because analysis of its history proved so similar to that of Sage Library, it was not included in this book. For coverage of Morris, see "'An Established Institution': The Morris Public Library of Morris, Illinois, 1913–1953," *Journal of Illinois History* 13 (Winter 2010).

3. Sinclair Lewis, *Main Street* (New York: New American Library, 1961), quotes taken from pp. 128, 129, and 257. Can the connections between William Cullen Bryant's poem "Thanatopisis," Lewis's use of the Bryant Library as a youth, and the women's club Lewis named the "Thanatopsis Society" in *Main Street* be coincidental?

4. About the "library faith," see also Oliver Garceau, *The Public Library in the Political Process* (New York: Columbia University Press, 1949), 50–51.

5. See Leonard S. Marcus, *Minders of Make-Believe: Idealists, Entrepreneurs, and the Shaping of American Children's Literature* (Boston: Houghton Mifflin, 2008), 32–70; and Jacalyn Eddy, *Bookwomen: Creating an Empire in Children's Book Publishing, 1919–1939* (Madison: University of Wisconsin Press, 2006), 30–48.

6. See the author's "The American Public Library: Construction of a Community Reading institution," in *A History of the Book in America, Volume 4: Print in Motion; The Expansion of Publishing and Reading in the United States, 1880–1940*, ed. Carl F. Kaestle and Janice A. Radway (Chapel Hill: University of North Carolina Press, 2009), 431–51; and his "The Structure of Librarianship: Essay on an Information Profession," *Canadian Journal of Library and Information Studies* 24 (April 1999): 17–37.

7. ALA began publishing *Booklist* as a monthly in 1905; it has served public library professionals ever since. Other ALA selection guides used for this study include: U.S. Bureau of Education, *Catalog of "A.L.A." Library: 5,000 Volumes for a Popular Library Selected by the American Library Association* (Washington, DC: Government Printing Office, 1893); Melvil Dewey, ed., *A.L.A. Catalog: 8,000 Volumes for a Public Library, with Notes* (Washington, DC: Government Printing Office, 1904); Elva L. Bascom, ed., *A.L.A. Catalog, 1904–1911. Class List: 3,000 Titles for a Popular Library with Notes and Indexes* (Chicago: American Library Association, 1912); *A.L.A. Catalog, 1912–1921: An*

Annotated List of 4,000 Books (Chicago: American Library Association, 1926); Marion Horton, ed., *A.L.A. Catalog, 1926–1931: An Annotated List of Approximately 3,000 Titles* (Chicago: American Library Association, 1933); Marion Horton, ed., *A.L.A. Catalog, 1937–1941: An Annotated List of Approximately 4,000 Titles* (Chicago: American Library Association, 1943); and Florence Boochever, ed., *A.L.A. Catalog, 1942–1949: An Annotated List of Approximately 4,500 Titles* (Chicago: American Library Association, 1952). Wilson Company guides used for this study include: *English Prose Fiction: A Selected List of About 800 Titles Cataloged by Author and Title with Annotations* (Minneapolis: H. W. Wilson, 1908); *Fiction Catalog: A Selected List of about 350 Novels, Cataloged by Author and Title with Annotations* (Minneapolis: H. W. Wilson, 1909); *Standard Catalog Series: Fiction Catalog: A Selected List of About 2,000 titles Cataloged by Author and Title with Annotations* (Minneapolis: H. W. Wilson, 1913); Corinne Bacon, comp., *Standard Catalog for Public Libraries: Fiction Section*, 2nd rev. ed. (New York: H. W. Wilson, 1931); Minnie Earl Sears et al., comps., *Standard Catalog for Public Libraries, 1934 Edition: An Annotated List of 11,700 Titles with a Full Analytical Index* (New York: H. W. Wilson, 1934); Dorothy E. Cook and Dorothy H. West, comps., *Standard Catalog for Public Libraries, 1949 Edition: An Annotated List of 12,000 Titles with Full Analytical Index* (New York: H. W. Wilson, 1949); Dorothy H. West and Estelle A. Fidell, comps., *Standard Catalog for Public Libraries, 4th Edition, 1958: A Classified & Annotated List of 7,610 Non-Fiction Books Recommended for Public & College Libraries, with a Full Analytical Index* (New York: H. W. Wilson, 1959); Dorothy E. Cook and Isabel Stevenson Monro, comps., *Fiction Catalog, 1941 Edition: A Subject, Author, and Title List of 5,050 Works of Fiction in the English Language* (New York: H. W. Wilson, 1942); Dorothy E. Cook and Estelle A. Fidell, comps., *Fiction Catalog, 1950 Edition: A Subject, Author, and Title List of 3,400 Works of Fiction in the English Language with Annotations* (New York: H. W. Wilson, 1951); and Estelle A. Fidell and Esther V. Flory, comps., *Fiction Catalog, Seventh Edition, 1960: A List of 4,097 Works of Fiction in the English Language with Annotations* (New York: H. W. Wilson, 1961).

8. Lester Asheim, "Not Censorship, but Selection," *Wilson Library Bulletin* 28 (September 1953): 63–67.

9. The phrases "user in the life of the library" and "library in the life of the user" are not my inventions. See Douglas L. Zweizig, "Predicting Amount of Library Use: An Empirical Study of the Public Library in the Life of the Adult Public" (PhD diss., Syracuse University, 1973).

10. See Robert Darnton, "What is the History of Books?" in *Reading in America: Literature and Social History*, ed. Cathy N. Davidson (Baltimore: Johns Hopkins University Press, 1989), 27–52; and Michel de Certeau, *The Practice of Everyday Life* (Berkeley: University of California Press, 1984). Like "library in the life of the user," the idea of finding middle ground between "market" and "resistance" models in the social history of reading did not originate with me. See Christine Pawley, "Beyond Market

Models and Resistance: Organizations as a Middle Layer in the History of Reading," *Library Quarterly* 79 (January 2009): 73–93.

11. Janice Radway, *Reading the Romance: Women, Patriarchy, and Popular Literature* (Chapel Hill: University of North Carolina Press, 1991).

12. Benedict Anderson, *Imagined Communities: Reflections on the Origin and Spread of Nationalism* (New York: Verso, 1983). More recently, François Furstenberg refers to printed works read in common by people not geographically connected as "civic texts." See François Furstenberg, *In the Name of the Father: Washington's Legacy, Slavery, and the Making of a Nation* (New York: Penguin, 2006), 20–21.

13. Elizabeth Long, *Book Clubs: Women and the Uses of Reading in Everyday Life* (Chicago: University of Chicago Press, 2003). Quotes taken from page 9.

14. Stephen Greenblatt, *Renaissance Self-Fashioning: From More to Shakespeare* (Chicago: University of Chicago Press, 1980); Barbara Sicherman, "Sense and Sensibility: A Case Study of Women's Reading in Late-Victorian America," in Davidson, *Reading in America*, pp. 201–25; and Gordon Hutner, *What America Read: Taste, Class, and the Novel, 1920–1960* (Chapel Hill: University of North Carolina Press, 2009), 45.

15. Jurgen Habermas, *The Structural Transformation of the Public Sphere: An Inquiry into a Category of Bourgeois Society* (Cambridge: MIT Press, 1989).

16. John E. Buschman and Gloria J. Leckie, *The Library as Place: History, Community, and Culture* (Westport, CT: Libraries Unlimited, 2007). See especially Julia A. Hersberger, Lou Sua, and Adam L. Murray, "The Fruit and Root of the Community: The Greensboro Carnegie Negro Library, 1904–1964," 79–99. See also Redmond Kathleen Molz and Phyllis Dain, *Civic Space/Cyberspace: The American Public Library in the Information Age* (Cambridge: MIT Press, 1999), which also addresses "library as place" issues, but mostly from an "information access" perspective. D. W. Davies's *Public Libraries as Cultural and Social Centers: The Origin of the Concept* (Metuchen, NJ: Scarecrow Press, 1974) is useful, but largely manifests a "user in the life of the library" perspective. For other examples of works that explore the role of place in American history, see James A. Secord, *Victorian Sensation: The Extraordinary Publication, Reception, and Secret Authorship of Vestiges of the Natural History of Creation* (Chicago: University of Chicago Press, 2001); and David Henkin, *The Postal Age: The Emergence of Modern Communications in Nineteenth Century America* (Chicago: University of Chicago Press, 2006).

17. Jeffrey Alexander, *The Civil Sphere* (New York: Oxford University Press, 2006). Quotations from pp. 75–76 and 78–79. Other historians have made similar points. "Socioliterary experience," argue Ronald J. and Mary Saracino Zboray, often occurs in "dense networks of kin, friends, and neighbors, deeply imbuing it with social relations and implicating it in them." See Ronald J. Zboray and Mary S. Zboray, *Everyday Ideas: Socioliterary Experience among Antebellum New Englanders* (Knoxville: University of Tennessee Press, 2006), xviii.

18. "Main Street" has a rich historical literature. See, for example, Lewis E. Atherton, *Main Street on the Middle Border* (Bloomington: Indiana University Press, 1954); Richard V. Francaviglia, *Main Street Revisited: Time, Space, and Image Building in Small-Town America* (Iowa City: University of Iowa Press, 1996); and Richard O. Davies, *Main Street Blues: The Decline of Small-Town America* (Columbus: Ohio State University Press, 1998). For good summary pieces on Midwest history, see James H. Madison, ed., *Heartland: Comparative Histories of the Midwestern States* (Bloomington: Indiana University Press, 1988); and Andrew R. L. Cayton and Susan E. Gray, eds., *The Identity of the American Midwest: Essays on Regional History* (Bloomington: Indiana University Press, 2001), especially Cayton's essay, "The Anti-Region: Place and Identity in the History of the American Midwest," pp. 140–59.

19. Resistance to this idea in library and information studies has a long history. Two of the more recent studies to make this case are Patrick Williams, *The Public Library and the Problem of Purpose* (Westport, CT: Greenwood Press, 1988); and Juris Dilevko and Candice F. C. Magowan, *Readers' Advisory Service in North American Public Libraries, 1870–2005* (Jefferson, NC: McFarland & Company, 2007). On the other hand, see Stephen Krashen, *The Power of Reading: Insights from the Research* (Portsmouth, NH: Heinemann, 2004), and especially his "Anything But Reading," *Knowledge Quest* 37 (May–June 2009): 18–25. "Both the popular media and professional literature are filled with suggestions on how to improve reading," he notes in the latter, "but the one approach that always works is rarely mentioned: provide readers with a supply of interesting and comprehensible books."

20. For background information on American library history before 1880, see Kenneth E. Carpenter, "Libraries," in *A History of the Book in America, Volume 3: The Industrial Book, 1840-1880*, ed. Scott E. Casper, Jeffrey D. Groves, Stephen W. Nissenbaum, and Michael Winship (Chapel Hill: University of North Carolina Press, 2007), 303–18.

21. For background information on the Boston Public Library, see W. M. Whitehill, *Boston Public Library: A Centennial History, 1854–1954* (Cambridge: Harvard University Press, 1956). For background information on the public library movement, see Jesse H. Shera, *Foundations of the Public Library: The Origins of the Public Library Movement in New England, 1629–1855* (Chicago: University of Chicago Press, 1949); and Sidney H. Ditzion, *Arsenals of a Democratic Culture: A Social History of the American Public Library Movement in New England and the Middle States from 1850 to 1900* (Chicago: American Library Association, 1947).

ONE. PRIDE OF A CENTURY

1. For background information in Minnesota history, see Annette Atkins, "Minnesota: Left of Center and Out of Place," in *Heartland: Comparative Histories of the Midwestern States*, James H. Madison, ed. (Bloomington: Indiana University Press),

9–31. For background information on the history of Sauk Centre, see Ivy Louise Hildenbrand, *Sauk Centre: The Story of a Frontier Town, The First 50 Years, 1855–1905* (Sauk Centre: Sauk Centre Historical Society, 1993); Rosalind Gilbert, *Our Century: Revisiting Sauk Centre in the 20th Century* (Sauk Centre: Sauk Centre Herald, 2000); and *A Historical Sketch of Sauk Centre* (Sauk Centre: First State Bank of Sauk Centre, 1954). See also 60th anniversary edition of *Sauk Centre Herald* (hereafter cited as *SCH*), 7/7/1928.

2. Information taken from Hildebrand, *Sauk Centre*, chapter 1; William Bell Mitchell, *A History of Stearns County*, vol. 1 (Chicago: H. B. Cooper Jr., 1915), 171; *SCH*, 1/17/1929; 5/23/1946; 5/20/1948. See also Kathleen Conzen, "Peasant Pioneers: Generational Successors Among German Farmers in Frontier Minnesota," in *Countryside in the Age of Capitalist Transformation: Essays in the Social History of Rural America*, ed. Steven Hahn and Jonathan Prude (Chapel Hill: University of North Carolina Press, 1985), 259–92; Henry Johnson, *Other Side of Main Street: A History Teacher from Sauk Centre* (New York: Columbia University Press, 1943), 3, 6–7, 31; and Ben Du Bois, *History of Sauk Centre*, Wisconsin Historical Society (hereafter WHS) Pamphlet Collection, p. 7. See also *SCH*, 11/4/1915, a special issue devoted to the history of Sauk Centre.

3. *SCH*, 11/19/1868. "Books were not plentiful in the early days of Sauk Centre," recalled pioneer Florence Graber. "But Reading Clubs were formed, and they had a sort of circulating library by exchanging their reading material with each other." See also recollections of Samuel Bjone, Nellie Wakefield, and Florence Graber, bound into *History of Sauk Centre*, no date, p. 5, Bryant Library Archives (hereafter cited as BLA). See also Helen B. Baker, "Bryant Library Started Friday, Nov. 13, 1869," *SCH*, 7/7/1928. Other Minnesota communities were also establishing library associations at this time. The earliest appears to have been Northfield in 1856. See Theodore C. Blegen, *Grass Roots History* (Minneapolis: University of Minnesota Press, 1947), 182–86.

4. See *Lowell (MA) Daily Citizen and News*, 6/1/1872, for news item on Bryant's gift to Cummington.

5. Original articles of incorporation in BLA. See also L. T. Story, "Cheap Homes in the Sauk Valley," 1879, Sauk Centre Area Historical Society, Sauk Centre, MN (hereafter SCAHS), p. 4.

6. Minutes, 2/9/1880, BLA. See also *SCH*, 6/7/1928; 11/15/1951.

7. See Minutes, 5/7/1880; 5/10/1880; 5/12/1880; 5/26/1880, BLA; *SCH*, 1/31/1935; letter, L. T. Storey to S. M. Bruce, 4/22/1880, copy found in SCAHS.

8. Minutes, 5/25/1880, BLA.

9. Minutes, 3/26/1881; 5/28/1881; 2/27/1883; 5/8/1883, BLA; *SCH*, 4/11/1881; 3/1/1883; 5/20/1883. That these authors were popular in late-nineteenth-century midwestern public libraries was not unusual. Mary J. Holmes's obituary read: "Such is the demand for her novels at the public libraries that it has often been necessary to keep twenty or more sets on the shelves." See *Chicago Daily Tribune*, 10/7/1907.

10. Minutes, 3/1/1884, BLA; *SCH*, 3/4/1886; 3/25/1886; 5/27/1886; 8/5/1886. Soliciting se-lection recommendations from the public before spending library money became common practice every spring. See, for example, *SCH*, 5/5/1887; 3/24/1892.

11. See Mark Shorer, *Sinclair Lewis: An American Life* (New York: McGraw Hill, 1961), 4–10; Johnson, *Other Side of Main Street*, 59; *SCH*, 9/9/1886; *SCH*, 1/17/1889; *Avalanche*, 3/4/1889. See also "Retrospective," *SCH*, 8/8/1895; and 3/1/1956 for memoir concern-ing status of Main Street in 1895. Wooden sidewalks were not replaced with ce-ment sidewalks until the summer of 1898. See *SCH*, 8/10/1898. See also 10/31/1901 for turn-of-the-century summary of Sauk Centre.

12. See *SCH*, 3/25/1888, 3/29/1888; 4/12/1888; 5/17/1888; 8/23/88; Minutes, 3/1/1888; 5/7/1888, BLA. See also Hildebrand, *Sauk Centre*, 61; Johnson, *The Other Side of Main Street*, 77–83; and Marilyn Brinkman, *Bringing Home the Cows: Family Dairy Farming in Stearns County, 1853–1986* (St. Cloud, MN: Stearns County Historical Society, 1988), 6. For a summary of the Protestant press between 1880 and 1940, see William Vance Trollinger, Jr., "An Outpouring of 'Faithful' Words: Protestant Publishing in the United States," in *A History of the Book In America, Vol. 4: Print in Motion: The Expansion of Publishing and Reading in the United States, 1880–1940*, ed. Carl F. Kaestle and Janice A. Radway (Chapel Hill: University of North Carolina Press, 2009), 359–77.

13. By the turn of the century the federal government had authorized a distribution system for government documents, justifying the system as evidence of meeting its obligation to keep citizens informed. Not coincidentally, however, politicians were pleased when local public libraries routinely recognized this largesse as "gift" in local newspapers. For background information on government docu-ments distribution, see Charles A. Seavey and Caroline F. Sloat, "The Govern-ment as Publisher," in Kaestle and Radway, 260–75. See also Oz Frankel, *States of Inquiry: Social Investigations and Print Culture in Nineteenth Century Britain and the United States* (Baltimore: Johns Hopkins University Press, 2006).

14. *SCH*, 3/21/1889; 6/13/1889; 6/20/1889; 7/4/1889; 5/14/1891; *Avalanche*, 5/16/1889; 6/20/1889; Johnson, *The Other Side of Main Street*, 77–83; Minutes, 2/27/1891, BLA.

15. *SCH*, 8/27/1891; 9/10/1891; 9/17/1891; 9/24/1891; 11/5/1891; 11/12/1891; 12/10/1891; 2/4/1892; 2/25/1892; 8/25/1892; 9/1/1892; 4/20/1893; 1/26/1893; 4/27/1893; Minutes, 5/2/1892; 5/1/1893, BLA.

16. Minutes, 4/12/1894, BLA. Not all connections between the Bryant Library and the Chicago World's Fair were as positive. Board member A. H. Pettit, who had said he was going to the World's Fair in August, never returned to Sauk Centre after a Min-neapolis firm for whom he was loaning money found in the interim that he had de-faulted on his accounts by $40,000. See *New York Times*, 9/30/1893 (hereafter *NYT*).

17. *SCH*, 5/11/1893; 5/18/1893; 9/28/1893; Minutes, 12/29/1893; 3/8/1894; 3/29/1900, BLA. For evidence of purchasing practices, see binder titled "Invoices" in BLA. For a discussion of the origins of the ALA catalog, see Wayne A. Wiegand, "Catalog of 'A.L.A. Library' (1893): Origins of a Genre," in *For the Good of the Order: Essays in*

Honor of Edward G. Holley, ed. Delmas Williams, et al. (Greenwich, CT: JAI Press, 1994), 237–54.

18. *SCH*, 7/5/1894.

19. See Minutes, 6/12/1894; 6/28/1894, BLA; *SCH*, 6/14/1894; 6/21/1894; 6/28/1894; 7/5/1894; 10/24/1895. See *SCH*, 4/24/1902 for story on the Gradatim Club. Throughout the country in the late nineteenth century, middle-class women used print to connect with each other locally, regionally, and nationally in numerous ways. For an extended discussion of this phenomenon, see Anne Ruggles Gere, *Intimate Practices: Literacy and Cultural Work in U.S. Women's Clubs, 1880–1920* (Urbana: University of Illinois Press, 1997). Bryant librarians were routinely invited to become Gradatim members.

20. Minutes, 3/17/1898, BLA; *SCH*, 3/31/1898; 4/21/1898; 5/11/1899. See also Shorer, *Sinclair Lewis*, 16–18.

21. Minutes, 9/17/1896; 1/21/1897; 3/25/1897; 11/11/1897; 3/10/1898; BLA; *SCH*, 1/21/1896. See also Johnson, *The Other Side of Main Street*, 73; and Shorer, *Sinclair Lewis*, 15–16, 24–25. His first wife claims Sinclair "did most of his reading in the public library" before leaving Sauk Centre in 1905. See Grace Hegger Lewis, "When Lewis Walked down Main Street," *NYT*, 7/3/1960. Such a loyal patron was he that on one occasion in 1903, Lewis wrote in his diary that he'd "had charge of the reading room tonight." See Diary entry, 6/9/1903, Sinclair Lewis Papers, Beinecke Rare Books & Manuscripts Library, Yale University, New Haven, Connecticut (hereafter cited as Lewis Mss.), Box 59.

22. *SCH*, 12/8/1898; 1/5/1898; 3/23/1898; 5/11/1899; 8/10/1899; 11/2/1899. See also Minutes, 10/19/1899, BLA.

23. The *SCH* discusses these libraries in a 1/24/1924 article, which also announced that supervision of the traveling library collections had passed to the State Board of Education in 1919.

24. *SCH*, 12/13/1900; 3/26/1901; 5/2/1901; 5/9/1901; 5/23/1901; 4/10/1902; 4/17/1902.

25. *SCH*, 5/30/1901; 7/25/1901; 11/28/1901; 3/27/1902; 11/24/1902. See also Diary entries for 1/24/1900 and 3/30/1901, Lewis Mss., Box 59.

26. Minutes, 12/18/1902, BLA; Letter, Cooper to Bertram, 12/17/1902, Reel 28, Carnegie Corporation Papers (hereafter cited as CCP). None of the other libraries covered in this book ever purchased a copy of *A Little Grey Sheep*, which circulated so well in Sauk Centre that the Bryant Library purchased a second copy a year later.

27. All of this correspondence is in Reel 28, CCP. See Hogan to Morris, 1/13/1903; Harris to Carnegie, 1/17/1903; Hogan to Bertram, 1/22/1903; Bertram to Hogan, 1/26/1903; Hogan to Bertram, 1/31/1903; Bertram to Hogan, 1/12/1903; Hogan to Bertram, 2/20/1903. See also Minutes, 2/17/1903, BLA; and Sauk Centre City Council Resolution, 2/1/1903, copy in Reel 28, CCP. Board member E. J. Lewis had also kept his son Harry informed while the latter was in college. See Diary entries for 1/31/1903 and 2/21/1903, Lewis Mss., Box 59.

28. *SCH*, 2/19/1903; *Avalanche*, 2/19/1903.

29. *SCH*, 2/26/1903; 3/19/1903; 4/2/1903; *Avalanche*, 2/26/1903; Minutes, 2/21/1903, BLA. See also Hogan to Bertram, 2/28/1903, Reel 28, CCP. On February 21, 1903, the library board also authorized that a building key be issued to the superintendent of schools so school officials could use the library during hours it was normally closed. See Minutes, 11/16/1911, BLA.

30. Minutes, 6/4/1903; 6/13/1903; 6/27/1903; 8/25/1903; 9/23/1903, BLA; *SCH*, 6/11/1903; 8/20/1903; 9/24/1903; 10/16/1903; 12/17/1903; 12/24/1903; 12/31/03. For a copy of the Bryant Library notice for bids, see *American Architect and Building News*, June 6, 1903, 12.

31. Letter, Hogan to Carnegie, [n.d.]; Bertram to Hogan, 1/26/1904, Reel 28, CCP; *SCH*, 1/28/1904; 2/4/1904; 10/6/1904.

32. *Library News & Notes*, no. 1 (December 1904): 8 (hereafter *LN&N*); *SCH*, 11/17/1904. The Bryant Library was one of eighty-three Minnesota Carnegie libraries erected between 1899 and 1917. On November 17, 1904, the board was already receiving complaints about the absence of a children's room. See Minutes, 11/17/1904, BLA.

33. For information on Lewis and the Bryant Library, see Shorer, *Sinclair Lewis*, 102, 286–88.

34. Sprague to Carnegie, 4/27/1906; Bertram to Sprague, 5/3/1906; Sprague to Bertram, 5/18/1906; Bertram to Sprague, 6/13/1906; Sprague to Bertram, 7/6/1906; 8/8/1906; Bertram to Sprague, 9/1/1906; Sprague to Bertram, 9/17/1906; Sprague to Franks (Carnegie's cashier), 1/22/1906; Reel 28, CCP; Minutes, Ladies Musical Club, 4/30/1906, BLA; *SCH*, 5/31/1906; 9/20/1906; *LN&N* no. 9 (December 1906): 38.

35. Minutes, 7/18/1907; 3/22/1909; 2/15/1912, BLA; Minutes, 3/22/1909, Ladies Musical Club, BLA; *SCH*, 7/25/1907; 2/20/1908; 3/19/1908; 11/4/1908; 3/4/1909; *LN&N* 3 (September 1912): 180; *LN&N* 3 (December 1912): 186.

36. Minutes, 1/16/1913, BLA; *SCH*, 2/13/1913; *LN&N* 4 (March 1913): 36. While residents of the Home School had Bryant borrowing privileges, local citizens initially resisted and in 1921 specifically forbade integrating them into their public schools. See *SCH*, 6/27/1928.

37. *SCH*, 9/25/1913; 10/2/1913. Actual agreement struck between school officials and the Bryant Library board is dated 10/29/1913 and can be found in Minutes, BPL Archives. Subsequent updated agreement dated 1/19/1922 also in Minutes, BLA. See also *LN&N* 4 (December 1913): 73. In subsequent years, teachers increasingly took responsibility for Saturday story hour. See, for example, *SCH*, 11/22/1923.

38. Mitchell, *A History of Stearns County*, vol. 2, 715–16; *SCH*, 6/7/1928. See also Vance Bourjaily, "'Red Lewis' Town Is Kinder to Him Than He Was to It," *Smithsonian*, 16 (December 1985), 51. See also Minutes, 5/18/1916, BLA; Shorer, *Sinclair Lewis*, 234; *SCH*, 6/18/1916; and *LN&N* 5 (September 1916): 39.

39. *SCH*, 4/2/1914; 5/14/1914.

40. Minutes, 3/21/1918, BLA; *SCH*, 4/4/1918; *Boston Evening Transcript*, 8/25/1917. Elsewhere in Minnesota, librarians treated "suggestive" fiction like *Beyond* differently.

One librarian noted that she kept the "least objectionable" on a special shelf, the "most objectionable" locked up and available "only to those who do not seem to be asking for them just from curiosity." See *Library Journal* (hereafter *LJ*) 47 (November 1, 1922): 907–11; *LN&N* 6 (June 1920): 100.

41. *SCH*, 1/6/1921; 3/31/1921.

42. *SCH*, 7/21/1921; Minutes, 10/5/1922, BLA. See also Shorer, *Sinclair Lewis*, 273–74. See *SCH*, 8/11/1921; 9/15/1921; 9/15/1921; *LN&N* 6 (December 1921): 196. See also *Kansas City Star*, 8/31/1921; *Grand Forks (ND) Herald*, 10/13/1921; and *Montgomery (AL) Advertiser*, 10/16/1921, for evidence of the popularity of *Main Street*.

43. *SCH*, 7/6/1922; 3/27/1924; *LN&N* 8 (June 1925), 24–25; *St. Paul (MN) Dispatch*, 6/10/1926; *Minneapolis Journal*, quoted in *SCH*, 2/10/1927. Warner Brothers turned *Main Street* into a movie, which played Sauk Centre in 1923. The *Herald* gave it a perfunctory review. See *SCH*, 7/12/1923. On February 13, 1923, Lewis wrote his father that his subsequent book, *Babbitt*, was the only novel that had made Hugh Walpole's and William Lyons Phelps's best-of-1922 lists. "You might be interested to look that up in the library," he suggested to his father. See Diary entry, 2/13/1923, Lewis Mss., Box 51.

44. *SCH*, 3/28/1929; 5/23/1929; 6/6/1929; 10/3/1929; Minutes, 2/19/1931, BLA.

45. *SCH*, 11/17/1932; 4/27/1933; 10/26/1933; 12/14/1933; 1/11/1934; Minutes, 11/16/1932; 12/19/1933, BLA.

46. Minutes, 1/25/1934; 2/15/1934, BLA. See also *SCH*, 2/22/1934.

47. *SCH*, 3/22/1934; 8/16/1934; 8/30/1934; 12/20/1934; Minutes, 3/22/1934; 4/19/1934; 7/31/1934; 8/8/1934, BLA.

48. Minutes, 9/2/1934; 10/19/1934, BLA; *SCH*, 10/18/1934; 11/8/1934.

49. *SCH*, 12/13/1934; 1/17/1935; 1/24/1935.

50. For evidence of this process, see Minutes, 7/17/1930, BLA. See also *SCH*, 3/21/1935; 4/18/1935; 6/13/1935.

51. *SCH*, 4/25/1935; 5/30/1935; 6/20/1935; 8/15/1935; 9/19/1935; 9/26/1935; Minutes, 5/16/1935, BLA; *LN&N* 11 (September 1935): 108–9, 120.

52. *SCH*, 10/24/1935; 11/7/1935. Phone conversation with Richard Hedin, August 12, 2008.

53. *SCH*, 4/16/1936; Minutes, 9/18/1936, BLA. Biographical data on Philip Steiner gleaned from pages of *SCH*.

54. *SCH*, 7/2/1936; 8/27/1936; 11/19/1936; Minutes, 8/27/1936, BLA.

55. Minutes, 1/21/1937, BLA; *SCH*, 1/14/1937; 5/5/1937; 9/2/1937; 9/16/1927; 10/21/1937; 3/24/1938.

56. *SCH*, 11/25/1937. After this date, Lewis routinely donated a copy of every book he published. See also Minutes, 2/17/1938, BLA. Finnegan repeated this story in an interview with St. Cloud radio station KFAM. See *SCH*, 8/25/1938.

57. *SCH*, 11/10/1938; 11/24/1938; 12/22/1938. Phone conversation with Richard Hedin, August 12, 2008.

58. *SCH*, 2/23/1939; 3/16/1939; 3/23/1939; 10/12/1939; 4/11/1940.

59. *SCH*, 2/29/1940; 3/14/1940.

60. *SCH*, 8/29/1940; 9/19/1940; 10/3/1940; 11/7/1940; 11/21/1940; 12/5/1940.

61. *SCH*, 1/23/1941; 1/30/1941.

62. *SCH*, 3/13/1941. See also 4/17/1941. In an editorial dated November 19, 1947, the *Herald* again noted that Sauk Centre had "lost some of its geographic remoteness since the days of Carol Kennicott, and become closer physically to goings-on in Minneapolis, Chicago, New York and Washington through motor car, airplane, and radio." Remarkably, the *Herald* did not acknowledge that Bryant Library books borrowed and read by Sauk Centre citizens over previous generations had been accomplishing much the same thing.

63. Phone conversation with Richard Hedin, August 12, 2008.

64. *SCH*, 6/26/1941; 8/14/1941. In October, the board adopted a bylaw making it mandatory for the Bryant librarian to be state certified as a high school teacher. See document dated October 15, 1941, Minute Book, BLA.

65. *SCH*, 10/30/1941; 11/27/1941; 1/8/1942; 1/15/1942; 3/26/1942; 4/23/1942; 7/22/1942. See also Minutes, 1/15/1942, BLA. For a discussion of American public libraries and World War II, see Patti Clayton Becker, *Books and Libraries in American Society during World War II: Weapons in the War of Ideas* (New York: Routledge, 2005). See also Brett Spencer, "Preparing for an Air Attack: Libraries and American Air Raid Defense during World War II," *Libraries & The Cultural Record* 43, no. 2 (2008): 125–49.

66. *SCH*, 8/13/1942; 11/26/1942; 2/11/1943.

67. *SCH*, 4/29/1943.

68. *SCH*, 6/10/1943; 8/18/1943; 9/16/1943; 5/18/1944; 6/1/1944; Minutes, 5/18/1944, BPL Archives.

69. *SCH*, 10/21/1943; Minutes, 11/18/1943, BLA. For discussions of westerns and their readers, see John G. Cawelti, *The Six-Gun Mystique* (Bowling Green, OH: Bowling Green State University Press, 1984); and Jane Tompkins, *West of Everything: Inner Life of Westerns* (New York: Oxford University Press, 1992).

70. *SCH*, 9/2/1943; 3/23/1944; 8/3/1944; 8/17/1944; 11/9/1944; Minutes, 4/20/1944, BLA.

71. Minutes, 9/19/1945; 11/15/1945, BLA. The *Sauk Center Herald* gave no biographical details for Hoidahl when it announced her appointment or resignation.

72. *SCH*, 4/25/1946; 5/29/1947. Biographical data on board members gleaned from *SCH*. See also *SCH*, 10/7/1948; 6/1/1950.

73. *SCH*, 10/24/1946; 11/21/1946; 12/19/1946; Minutes, 2/20/1947, BLA.

74. *SCH*, 5/1/1947; 5/15/1947; 6/5/1947; 8/21/1947; Minutes, 9/27/1947; 1/5/1948, BLA.

75. Minutes, 1/6/48; 1/15/1948, BLA; SCH, 1/15/1948; 1/22/1948.

76. *SCH*, 4/29/1948; 5/13/1948; 6/24/1948. Before 1970 none of the other three libraries covered in this book acquired a copy of *Streetcar Named Desire*.

77. *SCH*, 7/22/1948; 10/7/1948. Olds ultimately got his degree in August 1951. See *SCH*, 8/2/1951.

78. *SCH*, 11/13/1948; 12/23/1948; Minutes, 11/18/1948; 12/16/1948, BLA.

79. *SCH*, 1/6/1949; 1/13/1949; 2/17/1949; 5/12/1949.

80. *SCH*, 6/30/1949; 8/25/1949; 9/8/1949; 10/27/1949; 11/10/1949; 12/15/1949; Minutes, 10/20/1949, BLA.

81. Minutes, 1/19/1950, BLA; *SCH*, 2/2/1950; 3/1/1950; 4/20/1950; 5/4/1950; 5/18/1950; 8/17/1950.

82. *SCH*, 9/21/1950; 10/2/1950; 10/9/1950; 11/1/1950; 12/28/1950.

83. *SCH*, 1/25/1951; 2/1/1951; 3/1/1951; 5/31/1951.

84. *SCH*, 4/26/1951; 5/25/1951; 8/30/1951; 9/20/1951.

85. *SCH*, 11/2/1953; 11/12/1953; 4/29/1954; 6/3/1954.

86. *SCH*, 11/11/1954; 3/3/1955; 6/16/1955; 8/4/1955; 8/18/1955.

TWO. A CREDIT TO THE PLACE

1. Organizing document found in Sage Library Archives (hereafter SLA). The definitive study of the Sage Library in the late nineteenth century is Christine Pawley, *Reading on the Middle Border: The Culture of Print in Late-Nineteenth-Century Osage, Iowa* (Amherst: University of Massachusetts Press, 2001). See especially chapter 3.

2. Biographical detail on officers gleaned from *Osage News* and *Mitchell County Press* (hereafter *MCP*), later *Mitchell County Press News* (hereafter *MCPN*). See also Minutes, 1/10/1871; 1/8/1872, SLA. See also *MCP*, 12/30/1897, souvenir edition.

3. Minutes, 5/27/1872, Osage Town Council, City Hall, p. 28 (hereafter cited as Council Minutes); Mitchell County Historical Society, *Mitchell County, 1851–1973* (Mason City, IA: Klipto Printing Company, 1973), 80–81. See also Charles N. Wells, comp., "History of Sage Library," n.p. (a compilation of copied newspaper articles from *MCP*, November 1935–April 1936), document in SLA.

4. *Mitchell County, 1851–1873*, 240, 262, 339; *MCP*, 2/20/1907. See also *MCP*, 6/21/1956. For background information on Iowa history, see Dorothy Schwieder, "Iowa: The Middle Land," in *Heartland: Comparative Histories of the Midwestern States*, ed. James H. Madison (Bloomington: Indiana University Press, 1988) , 276–96.

5. See Hamlin Garland, *Son of the Middle Border* (New York: Penguin Books, 1995), 91–93, 98–99, 151–52, 176–77.

6. Minutes, 1/13/1873, 1/20/1873, SLA; letter, Sage to Trustees of Town of Osage, copy found in Council Minutes, 6/10/1873, pp. 530–31.

7. Independence, Iowa, was the first. See Letha Pearl McGuire, "Public Library Movement in Iowa," *Iowa Journal of History and Politics* 35, no. 1 (1937): 28, 37. See also Minutes, 12/1/1873, SLA; Council Minutes, 1/5/1874, p. 51; 2/11/1874, p. 52; 2/28/1874, p. 55; 3/11/1874, p. 57; 3/13/1874, p. 58; 4/6/1874, p. 60. See also Wells, "History of the Sage Public Library," n.p. Letter dated December 9, 1873, from Orrin Sage in vaults, City Hall, Osage.

8. Council Minutes, 1/9/1874, p. 80; 1/11/1875, p. 85; 8/2/1875, p. 112; Board minutes, 1/10/1876, SLA; Wells, "History of the Sage Public Library," n.p. "Osage, Iowa," *Inter Ocean*, 1/27/1876. Copy of letter from Orrin Sage dated 1/2/1875 in Vaults, City Hall,

Osage. Sage died on June 23, 1875. See obituary in *New York Observer and Chronicle*, 7/15/1875.

9. *Winnebago Summit* quoted in MCP, 2/21/1884. A mass meeting organized by the WCTU on February 10, 1876, to rid Osage of its four saloons helped elect a "no license" ticket at the subsequent election. See MCPN, 6/21/1956; and Garland, *Son of the Middle Border*, 182.

10. *Inter Ocean*, 1/27/1876; MCP, 10/19/1876; 11/23/1876; 12/15/1876; 9/20/1877; 2/14/1878; 3/21/1878; 3/25/1880; 1/10/1884. See also Atherton's ad in MCP, 12/15/1877; story about YMCA reading room in 11/13/1879. See also Garland, *Son of the Middle Border*, 182. For a discussion of the role that post offices played in local communities, see David Henkin, *The Postal Age: The Emergence of Modern Communications in Nineteenth Century America* (Chicago: University of Chicago Press, 2006).

11. MCP, 5/11/1876; 5/18/1876; Council Minutes, 5/15/1876, p. 138–39; 8/7/1876, pp. 144–45.

12. Council Minutes, 12/18/1876, pp. 152–55; MCP, 12/21/1876.

13. MCP, 12/21/1876; 2/22/1877.

14. MCP, 4/5/1877; 5/24/1877; 9/20/1877. For more discussion of WCTU and ban on *Police News*, see Alison Parker, *Purifying America: Women, Cultural Reform, and Pro-Censorship Activism, 1873–1933* (Urbana, IL: University of Illinois Press, 1997), 61–62.

15. Council Minutes, 3/5/1879, p. 228; 3/24/1883, p. 364; 1/7/1884, pp. 353–54; MCP, 3/28/1878; 10/21/1880. Quotation "as will please the taste of all" in MCP, 6/10/1886. In its May 27, 1888, issue, the Congregationalist *Christian Union* also carried a notice from the Sage Library requesting back issues of the periodical "and other magazines." See also Christine Pawley, "'Not Wholly Self Culture:' The Shakespearean Women's Club, Osage Iowa, 1892–1920," *Annals of Iowa* 56 (Winter–Spring 1997): 12–45.

16. See MCP, 1/6/1887; 1/20/1887; 1/27/1887; 2/10/1887; 4/4/1887; 4/5/1887; 4/14/1887. See also Council Minutes, 6/15/1887, p. 466; 10/3/1887, p. 473.

17. MCP, 10/3/1887; 12/15/1887; 1/12/1888; 3/8/1888; 3/22/1888; 3/14/1889; Council Minutes, 3/19/1888, p. 486.

18. Council Minutes, 9/2/1889, p. 25; MCP, 10/10/1889; 3/17/1890; 4/10/1890; 9/1/1890; 10/9/1890. See also Minutes, 1/18/1890, BLA.

19. Council Minutes, 11/14/1892, pp. 190, 192, 193, 195; MCP, 5/24/1894. See also McGuire, "Public Library Movement in Iowa," 69.

20. Biographical details gleaned from pages of MCP and *Osage News*. Board members named in Council Minutes, 2/2/1895, p. 319; 2/4/1895, p. 6. For background on the 1894 law, see McGuire, "Public Library Movement in Iowa," 39–40.

21. Minutes, 2/12/1895, p. 7; 2/18/1895, pp. 8–9; 3/15/1895, p. 10, SLA.

22. Minutes, 3/25/1895, pp. 11–12; 4/8/1895, pp. 13–14; 5/20/1895, pp. 17–18, SLA. See also Council Minutes, 4/1/1895, p. 325. About the *Midland Monthly*, which endured for only four and a half years, historian Bradford Burns attributes to it an important role in encouraging the work of women's clubs, establishing public libraries, and

fostering a welcome environment for young writers, thus making the periodical "stand out as a radical innovation" that made "unique contributions to the formation of Iowa regionalism and to the growth of Iowa culture." See E. Bradford Burns, *Kinship with the Land: Regionalist Thought in Iowa* (Iowa City: University of Iowa Press, 1996), 22–27. For a discussion of periodicals in turn-of-the-century public libraries, see Charles A. Johanningsmeier, "Welcome Guests or Representatives of the 'Mal-Odorous Class'? Periodicals and Their Readers in American Public Libraries, 1876–1914," *Libraries & Culture* 39 (Summer 2004): 260–92.

23. *MCP*, 7/11/1895; 7/15/1895; 8/29/1895; 11/14/1895; Minutes, 10/21/1895, SLA.

24. *MCP*, 2/24/1898; Minutes, 6/20/1898, pp. 62–63; 1/16/1899, pp. 68–69; 9/18/1899, pp. 79–80, SLA. See also Wells, "History of the Sage Public Library," n.p.

25. *MCP*, 1/4/1900; 3/8/1900; 5/4/1900; Minutes, 2/19/1900, p. 85, SLA.

26. *Bulletin of the Iowa Library Commission* (hereafter *BILC*) 2 (April 1902): 30–31, 39. For background information on the beginnings of the Iowa Library Commission, see McGuire, "Public Library Movement in Iowa," 47–50; and Daniel Goldstein, "The Spirit of an Age: Iowa Public Libraries and Professional Librarians as Solutions to Society's Problems, 1890–1940," *Libraries & Culture* 38 (Summer 2003): 214–35.

27. See *MCP*, 1/18/1900; 3/29/1900; 7/3/1900; 12/19/1900. In 1903 the Iowa Library Commission "Traveling Library" system worked through 175 centers to circulate 227 libraries of fifty books each to nearly seven thousand rural Iowans who checked out nineteen thousand books. See McGuire, "Public Library Movement in Iowa," 62–63. In other states some public libraries used traveling libraries operated by their state library commission to supplement their collections—often with foreign-language titles. Sage board minutes reflect no interest in the traveling library system.

28. *BILC* 3 (July 1903): 45.

29. *BILC* 6 (September 1906): 97–98; Minutes, 11/13/1907, p. 212, SLA; *MCP*, 10/31/1906; 4/10/1907; 4/24/1907; 5/29/1907. See also 4/3/1907 for another Cromer's ad; and 1/8/1908 stating "Books, books, books cheap at Starr Bros. Sale." The term "official knowledge" is taken from Michael W. Apple, *Official Knowledge: Democratic Education in a Conservative Age* (New York: Routledge, 1993).

30. Minutes, 10/20/1902, p. 133; 2/16/1903, p. 135; 3/21/1903, SLA. See also Abernethy to Carnegie, 3/17/1903, Reel 23, Carnegie Corporation Papers, hereafter CCP.

31. *MCP* 4/1/1903; Bertram to Abernethy, 3/27/1903, Reel 23, CCP.

32. Minutes, 4/20/1903, p. 137, SLA; Abernethy to Carnegie, 4/24/1903, Reel 23, CCP; *MCP*, 4/29/1903. Osage's application accompanied the latter. See Reel 23, CCP.

33. Abernethy to Carnegie, 6/3/1903; 6/5/1903; 7/11/1903, Reel 23, CCP.

34. Abernethy to Carnegie, 7/11/1903; 12/18/1903, Reel 23, CCP; Minutes, 7/20/1903; 8/17/1903; 11/18/1903, p. 147; 7/11/1904, p. 155, SLA.

35. Abernethy to W. B. Allison, 12/26/1904, Reel 23, CCP; *Osage News*, 4/6/1905.

36. Minutes, 4/7/1905, p. 165; 4/15/1905, p. 166, SLA; Allison to Carnegie, 4/13/1905; G. F. Humbert to J. P. Dolliver, 4/14/1905; Allison to Carnegie, 4/17/1905; Abernethy to Carnegie, 4/21/05; Bertram to Abernethy, 4/24/1905, Reel 23, CCP; *MCP*, 5/10/1905. See also Bertram to Dolliver, 5/23/1905, Reel 23, CCP. "Although Mr. Carnegie insists that any amount he gives for a library building should be met by a guarantee of ten per cent of that amount annual for revenue," Bertram wrote, "he is not prepared to give an amount for a building equal to ten times the amount of revenue. That does not follow at all."

37. *MCP*, 5/17/1905; 7/12/1905; 7/19/1905; 7/26/1905; Minutes, 5/22/1905, p. 168, SLA; *BILC* 5 (July 1905): 43.

38. *MCP*, 3/14/1906; 4/4/1906; 6/6/1906; 7/4/1906. See also Minutes, 2/12/1906, p. 183; 3/12/1906, pp. 184–85; 7/9/1906, p. 189; 8/12/1907, p. 208, SLA.

39. *MCP*, 7/15/1908; 10/28/1908; 5/6/1909; Minutes, 7/13/1908, p. 220; 7/12/1909, pp. 237–42, SLA; *BILC* 8 (July–September 1908): 323.

40. Minutes, 9/13/1909, p. 244; 10/11/1909, p. 247, SLA. Biographical details gleaned from *MCP*. See also Wells, "History of the Sage Public Library," n.p.

41. *MCP*, 10/13/1909; *Osage News*, 10/14/1909.

42. *MCP*, 11/3/1909; *Osage News*, 11/14/1909; 11/11/1909; Minutes, 11/8/1909, p. 248, SLA.

43. Minutes, 11/16/1909, pp. 249–50; 11/29/1909, p. 251, SLA; *MCP*, 11/17/1909; *Osage News*, 11/18/1909.

44. Minutes, 12/4/1909, p. 252; 12/6/1909, p. 254, SLA; *MCP*, 1/5/1910; *Osage News*, 1/6/1910; Stacy and Cole to Carnegie, 12/6/1909, Reel 23, CCP. See also Genung to R. A. Franks (Carnegie's secretary), 1/15/1910, Reel 23, CCP; and *BILC* 6 (January–March 1910): 77. For a copy of the "Contract for Deed" dated Jan. 10, 1910, transferring the property to the library, and for a copy of the council resolution accepting it (both of which were sent to Carnegie), see SLA.

45. Minutes, 2/10/1910, p. 262, SLA; *MCP*, 3/30/1910; 4/27/1910; 6/1/1910; 7/20/1910; 7/27/1910; *Osage News*, 3/24/1910; 7/21/1910; 7/28/1910; Cole to R. A. Franks, 4/25/1910; Genung to Franks, 7/21/1910, Reel 23, CCP.

46. *Osage News*, 7/20/1911; 7/27/1911; *MCP*, 10/19/1910; 10/26/1910; 7/26/1911; 8/13/1912; Minutes, 12/14/1910, p. 284–85, SLA. When Carnegie died on August 11, 1919, the Iowa Library Commission estimated he had donated $1,709,000 for one hundred public library and seven college library buildings in the state. See *BILC* 8 (July–September, 1919): 172.

47. Minutes, 7/12/1909, pp. 237–42, SLA; *MCP*, 7/14/1909; 7/21/1909; 8/18/1909. By this time the Iowa Federation of Women's Clubs had disbanded its Library Committee, convinced that Iowa public libraries no longer needed their advocacy.

48. *MCP*, 11/3/1909; 11/10/1909; 12/1/1909.

49. Former resident B. E. Peterson recalled Main Street in 1908 in a column that the *Mitchell County Press* ran on January 23, 1933. City Clerk A. S. Wright recalled Osage in 1910 in a talk the *Press* summarized in its March 26, 1931 issue. The for-

mer editor of the *Press* recalled Main Street in 1910 in "The 'New Society,'" *MCP*, 2/15/1934; and again in 4/8/1937.

50. *MCP*, 6/23/1909; 7/28/1909; 9/8/1909; 10/11/1911; 8/7/1912; 4/21/1915; 7/8/1937; *MCPN*, 6/21/1956.

51. *MCP*, 8/9/1911; 8/23/1911; 2/21/1912; 4/8/1937; Minutes, 12/11/1911, p. 302; 2/12/1912, p. 304, SLA; *BILC* 6 (January–March 1912): 205.

52. Minutes, 4/8/1912, p. 307; 5/13/1912, p. 308; 7/1/1912, p. 322, SLA; *MCP*, 9/13/1911; 1/24/1912; 12/3/1913. Some Osage citizens also argued that the town should have a YMCA for young men, since school gymnasiums could not meet demand. See *MCP*, 10/21/1914. See also Wells, "A History of the Sage Public Library," n.p.

53. *MCP*, 10/22/1913; *BILC* 7 (January–March 1914): 65–69. See also *BILC* 7 (July–September 1915); 100–102, 170–71; 7 (October–December 1917): 256. See also *Chicago Tribune*, 3/13/1911, for report on Legler's decision to pull Alger and Optic titles from Chicago Public Library shelves.

54. Minutes, 3/9/1914, p. 332; 9/14/1914, p. 340; 5/10/1915, p. 347; 11/8/1915, pp. 355–57; 6/12/1916, p. 365; 7/1/1916, pp. 367–68, SLA; *MCP*, 12/22/1915; 1/21/1920; 3/17/1920; *Mitchell County, 1851–1973*, 213.

55. *MCP* 10/21/1921; Minutes, 6/30/1921, pp. 418–19, SLA. Comparative statistics for Iowa libraries can be found in *BILC* 9 (January–March 1922): 69–71. For evidence of the popularity of the Chautauqua programs, see *Osage News*, 3/15/1923; 8/2/1923; 10/29/1925. See also *Osage News*, 1/8/1925, for quote about Osage public library users.

56. *MCP*, 1/25/1922; *Osage News*, 10/10/1929; 11/14/1929; Minutes, 7/13/1925, p. 444, SLA.

57. *Osage News*, 9/13/1928; 11/17/1927; *MCPN*, 6/21/1956.

58. *Osage News*, 1/30/1930; 9/18/1930; 3/5/1931; 7/9/1931; 7/16/1931.

59. *MCPN*, 4/23/1936; 6/21/1938; 9/7/1933.

60. *MCPN*, 8/11/1938; 11/24/1938; "Iowa Library History," *Iowa Library Quarterly* (hereafter *ILQ*) 13 (July–September, 1938): 100–103; (October–December 1938): 127.

61. *MCPN*, 2/2/1939; 10/19/1939; 12/14/1939. See also Marjorie Hillis Roulston, *Live Alone and Like It: A Guide for the Extra Woman* (Indianapolis: Bobbs-Merrill, 1936). Roulston's book was recently issued as Marjorie Hillis, *Live Alone and Like It: The Classic Guide for the Single Woman* (New York: 5 Spot, 2008).

62. "Small Libraries," *ILQ* 13 (January–March, 1940): 196; Minutes, 7/8/1940, p. 1, SLA. On March 6, 1941, the *Press* reported that the City Federation of Women's Clubs heard the ILC's Amy Green, "rural library chairman, give a talk on the Iowa library situation." Ironically, the meeting took place in the Sage boardroom. See *MCPN*, 3/6/1941; 9/4/1941.

63. *MCPN* 3/21/1940; 5/30/1940; 7/25/1940; 12/5/1940; 2/26/1942; Wells, "A History of the Sage Public Library," n.p.

64. *MCPN*, 1/15/1942; 1/22/1942; 2/5/1942; 2/17/1942; 4/16/1942; 8/13/1942; 10/29/1942; "Libraries and the War," *ILQ* 14 (January–March 1942): 72–73; (July–September 1942):

111; Minutes, 2/5/1942, p. 7, SLA. Charles Wells estimates that the Missouri land Sage gave to the library cost it $2,900 in taxes through 1936, while revenue realized from sales totaled $1,825, thus a loss of $1,075. In 1936 the Sage Library still owned one piece of land, for which it had paid $1,325 in taxes. See Wells, "A History of the Sage Public Library," n.p.

65. *MCPN*, 2/4/1943; 4/18/1943.

66. "On Defending the Freedom to Read in Libraries," *ILQ* 14 (January 1945): 243–44. The issue of censorship in the four libraries covered in this book will be discussed in more depth in chapter 5.

67. Minutes, 1/30/1945, p. 12; 6/11/1945, p. 14; 10/10/1945, p. 15, 7/12/1946, p. 17, SLA; *MCPN* 5/30/1946; 12/19/1946.

68. Minutes, 1/17/1947, pp. 18–19; 7/8/1947, 21–22, SLA; *MCPN*, 1/30/1947; 5/1/1947; 5/8/1947.

69. Minutes, 5/15/1948, pp. 23–24, SLA; *MCPN*, 7/8/1948; 7/22/1948; *ILQ* 15 (July 1948): 238.

70. *MCPN* 8/5/1948; 8/26/1948; 10/21/1948; 11/25/1948; 12/9/1948; *ILQ* 16 (April 1949): 10.

71. Board letter to mayor and council found in SLA. See also Minutes, 12/12/1949, p. 28, SLA; *MCPN*, 1/26/1950; 2/16/1950. For other press coverage of the high school library, see *MCPN*, 11/9/1950; 11/30/1950; 5/3/1951.

72. Minutes, 5/8/1950, p. 28; 7/10/1950, p. 31, SLA. See also *ILQ* 16 (July 1950): 85; *MCPN*, 12/14/1950; 2/1/1951; 3/22/1951.

73. *ILQ* 16 (July 1951): 154; Minutes, 3/29/1951, p. 33; 4/2/1951, p. 34, SLA; *MCPN*, 4/5/1951.

74. Minutes, 7/2/1951, p. 37, SLA; *MCPN*, 11/8/1951; 6/26/1952; 11/27/1952. For American reaction to Salinger, see Pamela Hunt Steinle, *In Cold Fear: The 'Catcher in the Rye' Censorship Controversies and Postwar American Character* (Columbus: Ohio State University Press, 2000). In its review, *Booklist* described *Catcher in the Rye* as "an unusual book on a pertinent theme—the conflicts within an adolescent as he tries to adjust to the perverted values of an adult world. . . . Will not appeal to everyone but is certainly worth attention for its sensitive insight into a currently important topic, as well as for the quality of the writing." *Booklist* 47 (July 15, 1951): 401.

75. *MCPN*, 11/22/1951; 11/29/1951; 10/16/1952; 10/30/1952.

76. *MCPN*, 5/14/1953; 5/14/1953.

77. *MCPN*, 10/22/1953; 11/19/1953; 11/4/1954; 11/11/1954; 11/17/1954; 12/30/1954; *ILQ* 17 (July 1954): 60–61.

THREE. TOURIST ATTRACTION

1. For background history on Michigan, see Martha Mitchell Bigelow, "Michigan: A State in the Vanguard," in *Heartland: Comparative Histories of the Midwestern States*, ed. James H. Madison (Bloomington: Indiana University Press, 1988), 32–58. For background history of Lexington, see John Dal Bell, *An Early History of Lexington, Michigan: The Building of a Small Town* (Lansing: Michigan Dept. of State, Michigan History Division, 1968); Philomena Falls, "Moore Public Library," document dated 1976 in Moore Library Archives (hereafter cited as MLA); Florence H. Walther, *A*

History of Lexington (privately printed by Florence Walther, 1931; hereafter Walther, *History*); and Hazel Arnold Trumble, ed., *Sanilac County History, 1834–1984* (Shawnee Mission, KS: Inter-Collegiate Press, 1984).

2. Thirty years later, the county seat was moved to the more centrally located Sandusky. For years, however, Lexingtonians continued to refer to their village as the "Mother Town of Sanilac County." See *Sanilac Jeffersonian*, 10/9/1942 (hereafter *SJ*). See also Willis F. Dunbar and George May, *Michigan: A History of the Wolverine State* (Grand Rapids, MI: Eerdmans, 1980), 339, 346; Walther, *History*, 31.

3. *Portrait and Biographical Album of Sanilac County: Containing Portraits and Biographical Sketches of Citizens of the County* (Chicago: Chapman Brothers, 1884), 481; Walther, *History*, 21, 77; Dunbar and May, *Michigan*, 395; Willis F. Dunbar, "The Opera House as a Social Institution in Michigan," *Michigan History Magazine* 27 (October–December 1993): 661–72.

4. Chronology constructed from *Croswell Jeffersonian*, 1/23/1925 (hereafter cited as *CJ*); *SJ* 1/15/1953; nomination form Moore Library filled out for application to National Register of Historic Places, 1957; MLA; and Walther, *History*.

5. A dated copy of "Rules" for the Woods Library can be found in MLA.

6. *SJ*, 10/24/1902; 10/31/1902; 1/15/1953; Minutes, 11/3/1902, MLA; application for National Register of Historic Places, MLA; and copy of library's early history written into initial pages of minute books for 1953–1967, MLA.

7. Biographical details gleaned from the *Jeffersonian*.

8. Information gleaned from *SJ*, 1/16/1903; 1/15/1953; *Lexington News*, 1/17/1903; and library's early history in minutes book for 1953–1967, MLA. See also C. N. Crossman (chairman of the Finance Committee of the village of Lexington) to Mrs. Norman (president of the library board), 1/2/1936, MLA. Construction of sidewalks noted in *SJ*, 6/26/1903.

9. *SJ*, 1/15/1909; 5/19/1911.

10. See *SJ*, 3/17/1909; Minutes, 1/7/1910, MLA. See also chapter 5.

11. *Michigan Libraries* (hereafter cited as *ML*) 1 (June 1911): 5; 14–18.

12. Biographical sketch can be found in Neva DuMond, *Thumb Diggings: Adventures into Michigan's Thumb Area* (Lexington, MI: Neva DuMond, 1962), 255. See also *SJ*, 10/13/1911; and Minutes, 10/11/1911, MLA.

13. See James F. Norman, *The Episcopal Church in Lexington, Michigan: An Historical Sketch* (Lexington, MI: James F. Norman, 1975), 7; SJ, 2/2/1909; 11/15/1912; 7/24/1914; 6/26/1916.

14. Undated *Detroit Tribune* article quoted in *Michigan State Library Quarterly Bulletin* (hereafter cited as *MSLQB*) 6 (April–June 1915): 23.

15. *MSLQB* 6 (July–September 1915): 44.

16. Ibid., 41, 43.

17. *CJ*, 11/3/1916; 11/10/1916; 2/23/1917; 7/17/1917; 9/21/1917; *MLB* 8 (January–February 1917): 31.

18. Board members are listed in Minutes, 4/2/1918, MLA.

19. See Trumble, *Sanilac County History, 1834–1984*, 71; *CJ*, 7/18/1919; 11/14/1919; 2/20/1920; 3/12/1920; and Minutes, 4/1/1920, MLA.

20. Biographical details gleaned from newspaper reports of local activities. See also Minutes, 4/1/1922, MLA; *CJ*, 4/21/1922; 5/12/1922; and *MSLQB* 13 (March–June 1922): 22–23.

21. *CJ* 10/6/1922; 10/13/1922; 11/3/1922; 11/12/1923.

22. Minutes, April 1923, MLA. See also *CJ* 1/24/1924; 2/1/1924; 6/27/1924; 9/18/1925; 11/16/1925; 8/11/1926; 9/3/1926; 11/19/1926; and 8/7/1928. The October 2, 1925, edition of *CJ* reprinted a story that had appeared in the *Detroit Free Press* about Lexington as a resort community.

23. *CJ* 1/20/1928. See also 1/13/1928. Biographical details gleaned from *CJ* columns, one of which noted (3/15/1929) that in the previous election Margaret Nichols had been the only woman elected to any Sanilac County office that year. When the Port Huron Round Table met May 2, 1928, Margaret Nichols was the only member of the Moore Library community to attend (no one from the library had yet joined MLA). See "Port Huron," *MLB* 19 (June 1928): 65.

24. See Dunbar and May, *Michigan*, 498; "Port Huron," *MLB*, 20 (July 1929), 191–92; *CJ*, 10/26/1934.

25. Mrs. Albert Sleeper to "Marie," 2/5/1930, pasted into Minutes, MLA. See also Minutes, 2/14/1930, MLA.

26. Minutes, 1/18/1934, MLA.

27. Minutes, 4/26/1935; 10/29/1935; 11/26/1935, MLA; *CJ*, 7/26/1935; *SJ*, 7/5/1951. See also C. N. Crosman (chairman of the Finance Committee of the village of Lexington) to Mrs. Norman (president of the library board), 1/2/1936, MLA.

28. Minutes, 3/1/1936; 4/9/1936; 4/28/1936; 3/1/1937; 3/30/1937; 4/27/1937, MLA. See also *CJ*, 6/19/1936, for announcement of Atheneum Club gift of *National Geographic* to Moore Library. At its May 26, 1942, meeting, the board reviewed a communication from the state library that the Moore Library did not qualify for state aid. Minutes, 5/26/1942, MLA.

29. See Janice A. Radway, *A Feeling for Books: The Book-of-the-Month Club, Literary Taste, and Middle-Class Desire* (Chapel Hill: University of North Carolina Press, 1997), 288. For an extended discussion of middlebrow culture in the early twentieth century, see Joan Shelley Rubin, *The Making of Middle-Brow Culture* (Chapel Hill: University of North Carolina Press, 1992).

30. *SJ*, 5/6/1938; 1/20/1939; 2/10/1939; 3/14/1941; Minutes, 11/29/1938; 4/4/1939; 4/25/1939; 1/30/1940; 3/1/1940, MLA. The Bryant Library and the Rhinelander Public Library also purchased copies of *Christ in Concrete* for their collections; the Sage Library did not.

31. *SJ*, 1/16/1942; Minutes, 1/27/1942; 5/26/1942, MLA.

32. Minutes, 12/1/1942; 1/26/1943; 2/23/1943; 10/26/1943, MLA. See also Radway, *A Feeling for Books*, 286–87.

33. See Dorothy T. Hagerman, "A Survey of Library Legislation in Michigan—1937 to 1944," *ML* 10 (March 1944): 9–14. See also Minutes, 7/7/1944, MLA.

34. *SJ*, 1/19/1945.

35. Biographical data gleaned from the *Jeffersonian*. See also Minutes, 12/8/1948, MLA; *Michigan Library News* 7 (January 1948): 22–23; hereafter *MLN*.

36. *CJ*, 4/7/1949; 4/14/1949; 5/4/1950; 5/8/1952. Jim Sullivan to author, June 30, 2008. For a discussion of the messages Sullivan was receiving from *National Geographic*, see Catherine A. Lutz and Jane L. Collins, *Reading National Geographic* (Chicago: University of Chicago Press, 1993).

37. *CJ*, 1/22/1953.

38. See *MLN* 15 (Spring 1956): 22–23; *ML* 22 (March 1956): 22; Minutes, 3/1954; 12/1954, MLA.

FOUR. THOSE COMMISSION IDEAS

1. *Rhinelander Herald*, 11/6/1897; 11/27/1897; 12/18/1897; 2/5/1898 (hereafter cited as *RH*). For background information on Wisconsin history, see John D. Buenker, "Wisconsin as Maverick, Model and Microcosm," in *Heartland: Comparative Histories of the Midwestern States*, ed. James H. Madison (Bloomington: Indiana University Press, 1988), 59–85. See also C. B. Lester, "Wisconsin Libraries," in *Wisconsin: Its History and Its People, Vol. II* (Chicago: S. J. Clarke Publishing Company, 1924), chap. 37.

2. *RH*, 7/27/1895. See also T. V. Olsen, *Our First Hundred Years: A History of Rhinelander* (Rhinelander, WI: T. V. Olsen, 1981), 80; Robert J. Gough, *Farming the Cutover: A Social History of Northern Wisconsin, 1900–1940* (Lawrence: University of Kansas Press, 1997), 44; *Vindicator*, 11/16/1904; Rhinelander Paper Company, *Fifty Years of Papermaking, 1903–1953* (Rhinelander, WI: Rhinelander Paper Company, 1953).

3. *RH*, 10/5/1895; 2/29/1896; 3/14/1896; 2/20/1897.

4. *RH*, 1/4/1896. See also Genevieve G. McBride, *On Wisconsin Women: Working for Their Rights from Settlement to Suffrage* (Madison: University of Wisconsin Press, 1993), 160; David P. Thelen, *The New Citizenship: Origins of Progressivism in Wisconsin, 1885–1900* (Columbia, MO: University of Missouri Press, 1972), 92–93; *RH*, 11/6/1897; 11/27/1897. See also Janice Steinschneider, *An Improved Woman: The Wisconsin Federation of Women's Clubs, 1895–1920* (Brooklyn: Carson, 1994).

5. Biographical details gleaned from systematic reading of *RH*, and from obituaries that appeared therein.

6. Minutes, 4/4/1898, Rhinelander Public Library Archives (hereafter cited as RPLA).

7. Minutes, 1/4/1898; 7/5/1898, RPLA; *RH*, 2/12/1898; 2/26/1898; 2/28/1898; 2/11/1899.

8. Societies and churches listed in weekly issues of *Vindicator*. See, for example, 9/18/1901.

9. *RH*, 11/19/1898; 7/15/1899. See also John R. Barton and Franklin E. Rector, *The Public*

Library in Wisconsin: An Inquiry into Its Social and Educational Resources (Madison, WI: Department of Rural Sociology, Wisconsin Free Library Commission, 1951), 2.

10. Minutes, March 1900; 3/31/1900; 6/28/1900, RPLA. See also *RH*, 4/14/1900. For a discussion of the origins of the Wisconsin Library School, see Wayne A. Wiegand, "Formative Beginnings, 1896–1905," in Louise Robbins, Anne Lundin, and Michelle Besant, eds., *Tradition and Vision: Library and Information Studies at the University of Wisconsin: A Centennial History* (Madison: School of Library and Information Studies, University of Wisconsin, 2006), 2–13.

11. *Vindicator*, 8/29/1900; 2/20/1901; Minutes, 8/6/1901, RPLA. In its April 10, 1901, issue, the *Vindicator* reported that Shelton and Mrs. C. F. Barnes had "spent several days last week cataloging and numbering the new library books, which are now on the shelves ready for the library patrons."

12. Deyo memoir published in *Rhinelander Daily News* (hereafter cited as *RDN*), 4/28/1950. The cataloging team also cataloged the high school library collection "uniformly with the Public Library" in 1900 in hopes that in the future, Mary Shelton noted, "the libraries may be combined" in one larger library "with one arrangement." See Shelton to Carnegie, 10/1/1902, Reel 26, CCP.

13. *Vindicator*, 2/20/1901; 2/27/1901; 3/20/1901; 3/27/1901; 7/17/1901; 10/2/1901; 12/4/1901; 12/11/1901; Minutes, 8/6/1901, RPLA. For an example of a serialized fiction story, see 10/23/1901. For a brief account of the Rhinelander Book Club, see 4/23/1902. The RPL eventually acquired seven of Marie Corelli's novels, beginning with *Thelma* in 1906. So far as is known, no Rhinelander wife murdered her husband as a result of exposure to Corelli's fiction.

14. *Vindicator*, 12/11/1901; 1/15/1902; 1/29/1902; Minutes, September 1901, RPLA. Report of "Library Day" in WHS Pamphlet Collection.

15. Letter, E. O. Brown Jr. to Carnegie, 1/24/1902, Reel 26, CCP. See also *Vindicator*, 1/7/1903.

16. Minutes, 2/24/1902; 4/14/1902; *Vindicator*, 4/16/1902; 4/23/1902.

17. *Vindicator*, 5/14/1902; 6/4/1902. See also Annual Report, 9/30/1902, RPLA.

18. *Vindicator*, 5/21/1902; 6/4/1902; 7/9/1902; Minutes, 8/18/1902; Annual Report, 9/30/1902, RPLA.

19. Shelton to Carnegie, 10/1/1902, Reel 26, CCP; *Vindicator*, 10/22/1902; 10/29/1902; Minutes, 11/26/1902, RPLA. See also Shelton to Carnegie, 1/6/1903, Reel 26, CCP.

20. Shelton to Carnegie, 11/27/1902; Bertram to Shelton, 1/2/1903, Reel 26, CCP; *Vindicator*, 1/7/1909.

21. Minutes, 1/6/1903, RPLA; *Vindicator*, 1/7/1903; 1/14/1903; Shelton to Carnegie, 1/6/1903; 1/7/1903; Bertram to Shelton, 1/12/1903, Reel 26, CCP. See also E. O. Brown to Library Board, 1/6/1903, copy found in Reel 26, which confirmed the site gift, but also urged the council to increase its annual appropriation to $1,500 so Carnegie might be induced to increase his gift to $15,000.

22. Minutes, 1/30/1903, RPLA; *Vindicator*, 2/11/1903; 2/22/1903; Kurt Daniel Kortenhof, *Long Live the Hodag! The Life and Legacy of Eugene Simeon Shepard, 1854–1923* (Rhinelander, WI: Hodag Press, 1966), 62.

23. *New North* quoted in Kortenhof, *Long Live the Hodag*, 61–62. History of the origins of the Rhinelander Paper Company, which later became Ripco, in *RDN*, 6/5/1953. See also Gough, *Farming the Cutover*, 220–21.

24. *Vindicator*, 7/8/1903; 8/12/1903; 8/26/1903; 9/20/1903; *New North*, 10/1/1903; Minutes, 7/2/1903; 7/14/1903; 8/11/1903; 9/21/1903, RPLA; W. E. Brown to Bertram, 7/8/1903; Sam Miller (president of the library board) to Carnegie, 7/11/1903; 7/27/1903; Bertram to W. E. Brown, 7/23/1903, Reel 26, CCP.

25. See *RDN*, 6/5/1905, which quoted heavily from *New North* reports on the "race riot."

26. *Vindicator*, 12/2/1903; 12/16/1903; 5/18/1904; Minutes, 12/7/1903; 5/11/1904; 12/2/1904, RPLA.

27. Circulation rules found in RPLA. See also Minutes, 5/11/1904; 7/26/1904; 11/8/1904, RPLA; and *Wisconsin Library Bulletin* (hereafter *WLB*) 1 (January 1905): 8.

28. Ceremony described in *Vindicator*, 11/16/1904.

29. Minutes, 1/11/1905, RPLA; *WLB* 1 (March 1905): 23, 27; *Vindicator*, 2/15/1905; 4/26/1905.

30. Annual Report, 6/30/1905, RPLA; *WLB* 1 (July 1905): 60; *Vindicator*, 8/9/1905.

31. "These books have been selected with great care by competent people conversant with the language," the *Rhinelander News* reassured readers. See *Rhinelander News* (hereafter *RN*), 9/15/1911. Comment about the WFLC in *Vindicator*, 11/17/1911. See also "What Shall Libraries Do About Bad Books," *Library Journal*, 33 (September 1908): 352 (hereafter *LJ*).

32. *Vindicator*, 5/9/1906; 5/16/1906; 6/13/1906; Annual Report, 6/30/1906, RPLA.

33. Mrs. John Collins (RPL board secretary) to Carnegie, 2/28/1907; Bertram to Collins, 3/4/1907, Reel 26, CCP; *WLB* 3 (April 1907): 38. See also *Vindicator*, 4/3/1907; Katherine McDonald (WFLC) to Collins, 5/17/1907; Minutes, 4/30/1907, RPLA.

34. McCarthy to Collins, 5/16/1907; 5/22/1907; 6/1/1907; Annual Report, 6/30/1907, RPLA. One of McCarthy's successors, also a WLS graduate, noted that, beginning in 1907, "the quality of additions [new books] gradually improve[d]" because McCarthy's training assured that no gifts would be accepted by the library "that are not up to the Wisconsin library commission standards." See *RDN*, 3/17/1950.

35. McCarthy to Hazeltine, 11/21/1907; Hazeltine to McCarthy, 12/13/1907, Wisconsin Free Library Commission Records (hereafter WFLC Mss.), Acc. No. 1967/45, Box 9, WHS. See also WFLC Annual Report on RPL by H. P. Sawyer, September 28, 1907, WFLC Mss., 1902–1963, Community Files, "Rhinelander", WHS.

36. *Vindicator*, 2/5/1908; 4/1/1908; McCarthy to Hazeltine, 3/12/1908; 4/4/1908, WFLC Mss., Acc. No. 1967/45, Box 9, WHS. For a summary of the Hazeltine years at WLS, see Charles A. Seavey, "The Hazeltine Years: 1906–1938," in *Tradition and Vision: Library and Information Studies at the University of Wisconsin: A Centennial History*,

ed. Louise S. Robbins, Anne H. Lundin, and Michelle Besant (Madison: School of Library and Information Studies, University of Wisconsin-Madison, 2006), 14–41.

37. *WLB* 3 (October 1907): 88; *Vindicator*, 1/4/1907.

38. *Vindicator*, 1/8/1908; "Magazines for the Small Library," *WLB* 4 (February 1908): 1–9. Newspapers included: *Milwaukee Daily News, Evening Wisconsin, Minneapolis Journal, Ashland News*, and *Washington Post* (dailies); and *Antigo Republican, Waupaca Record, Wausau Central Wisconsin*, and the three Rhinelander newspapers (weeklies). Periodicals included *Nation, Colliers, Outlook, Scientific American*, and *Life* (weeklies), and *Atlantic, Bird-lore, Book Review Digest, Century, Electrician and Mechanic, Good Housekeeping, Harper's Monthly, Harper's Bazaar, Ladies Home Journal, McClure Masters in Art, North American Review, Outing, Scribner, Review of Reviews*, and *World To-day* (monthlies).

39. Annual Report, 6/30/1908, RPLA; *Vindicator*, 7/29/1908; 10/7/1908. For an explanation and justification of the practice of removing the comics section from Sunday newspapers to which public libraries subscribed, see Lutie Stearns, "The Problem of the Comic Supplement," *WLB* 4 (December 1908): 102–3.

40. "Reaching the Reading Public: The Library at Rhinelander and the Workingman," *WLB* 4 (October 1908): 88–89; Hazeltine to McCarthy, 10/3/1908, WFLC Mss., Acc. No. 1967/45, Box 9, WHS. See also Lutie Stearns to "Librarian," 1/20/1910, RPLA.

41. Anna Leadbetter (club secretary) to S. S. Miller (board president), 3/17/1909; Minutes, 4/13/1909, RPLA; *Vindicator* 4/21/1909.

42. Annual Report 6/30/1909; Minutes, 9/28/1909, RPLA; WLB, 5 (August 1909): 64; *Vindicator*, 9/15/1909; 10/13/1909; *RN*, 10/28/1910.

43. *WLB* 6 (February 1910): 18; *Vindicator*, 3/23/1910. Upon entering the WLS, Allen was evaluated as "school-marmy," with an "inability to adapt herself to different kinds of work." See Harriet Allen File, Alumni Records, University of Wisconsin–Madison Archives (hereafter cited as UWA). In a December 15, 1909, letter to Hazeltine, McCarthy said that the superintendent of schools (an ex officio member of the board) had resisted hiring Allen because he wanted to hire someone from the school system. See McCarthy to Hazeltine, 12/15/1909, CLS-Library School, Placement Work, 7/20/05, File "R," Box 5, UWA.

44. Annual Report, 6/30/1910, RPLA; *RN*, 9/23/1910.

45. Minutes, 5/18/1911, RPLA; Lutie Stearns, "The Library and the Social Center," *WLB* 6 (June 1911): 84–85.

46. Annual Report, 6/30/1911; and *RN* 11/5/1911, for comment about movies. Pressure on the Bijou was successful. The *News* later complimented the manager "on the class of pictures he is showing in his theatre." See *RN* 5/16/1913.

47. *RN*, 2/16/1912; 5/17/1912; 5/31/1912; 9/20/1912; Annual Report, 6/30/1912; Minutes, 9/9/1912, RPLA. See also McBride, *On Wisconsin Women*, 217.

48. WFLC Mss., Community Files, 1902–1963, "Rhinelander", WHS; *RN*, 12/20/1912; 1/19/1913; 3/10–11/1913.

49. Minutes, 5/19/1914; Annual Report, 6/30/1914, RPLA; *RN*, 5/22/1914; 7/17/1914; *WLB* 10 (April 1914): 83; (May 1914): 97.

50. Letter, Allen to Hazeltine, 5/21/1914, CLS-Library School, Placement Work, 7/20/1905, File "R," Box 5, UWA.

51. Rose Robert Sears to Hazeltine, 5/26/1913, Bingham File, UWA. When Hazeltine wrote a recommendation for Bingham to another potential employer a year later, she noted that "her character, personality, education and good judgment are much above average." Hazeltine to N. D. C. Hodges, 5/19/1914, Bingham File, UWA. The recommended reading list for the oral "Extra Entrance Requirement" is in this file. None of the directors at the other three libraries were asked or expected to have this command of highbrow literature.

52. *RN*, 7/31/1914; 8/14/1914; 9/18/1914; 9/25/1914; 10/16/1914; Bingham to ALA Publishing, 6/1/1915; Bingham to Mrs. A. L. Mayers of the WFLC Traveling Library Department, 11/4/1915, RPLA.

53. WFLC Annual Report, 3/16/1915, WFLC Mss., Community Files, 1902–1963, "Rhinelander," WHS; *RN*, 3/19/1915; 11/15/1915; *WLB* 11 (April 1915): 113.

54. *RN*, 6/25/1915; 10/22/1915; 2/26/1952; Annual Report, 6/30/1915, RPLA.

55. *RN*, 9/24/1915; 11/12/1915; 11/26/1915.

56. *RN*, 12/10/1915.

57. WFLC report by J. Welles, September 4–5, 1916, WFLC Mss., Community Files, 1902–1963, "Rhinelander," WHS; WFLC report by J. Welles, March 9, 1918, WFLC Mss., Community Files, 1902–1963, "Rhinelander," WHS.

58. Annual Report, 6/30/1916, RPLA; *RN*, 5/26/1916; 7/7/1916; 7/14/1916; Emilida Baensch, "An Evening's Inspection," *WLB* 13 (March 1917): 71–74.

59. Helen Turvill, "Progressive Libraries," *WLB* 13 (March 1917): 71–74; *RN* 4/6/1917.

60. Annual Report, 6/30/1918, RPLA.

61. See also Flora H. Whyte, "The Routine of Work in the Small Library," *WLB* 15 (May 1919): 126–30; *WLB* 16 (January 1920): 8; Shelton to RPL Directors, 10/27/1919, RPLA; *RDN*, 12/10/1919; 12/16/1919; 12/17/1919; 3/11/1920; 3/22/1920. See also Barton and Rector, *The Public Library in Wisconsin*, 2.

62. *RN*, 4/9/1920; 4/21/1920; 5/3/1920; 5/5/1920; 5/8/1920; 7/24/1920; *WLB* 16 (June 1920): 103. This phenomenon was certainly not unique to this time and this place. For an extended discussion of labor and its uses of popular fiction in late-nineteenth-century America, see Michael Denning, *Mechanic Accents: Dime Novels and Working Class Culture in America* (New York: Verso, 1987).

63. A *Wisconsin Library Bulletin* article entitled "We Buy More Rent Books" listed reasons for a rental plan: "Meets demand for popular books without wasting public money. Lessens demand on free copies. Brings books back sooner. Attracts a group of people who might not come otherwise." See Jessie Welles, "We Buy More Rent Books," *WLB* 16 (December 1920): 208–10.

64. Annual Statistical Report, RPLA; Merrill's reports dated January 9–10, 1922 and

February 28–March 1, 1922, both in WFLC Mss., Community Files, 1902–1963, "Rhinelander," WHS; "Circulation Statistics," *WLB* 18 (February 1922): 33.

65. *WLB*, 18 (November 1922): 227–33.

66. *RDN*, 12/6/1922; 12/23/1922; 5/17/1923; 7/14/1923; 9/26/1923; 12/12/1923; 12/15/1923; 6/22/1926; 12/14/1926; 12/23/1926; Annual Report, 12/31/1922, RPLA.

67. Edward Thierry, "Is Modern Sex Fiction Harmful?" *RDN*, 3/14/1923.

68. *RDN*, 3/24/1925.

69. *RDN*, 6/23/1926; 10/21/26. See also WFLC Annual Report, February 18–19, 1926, WFLC Mss., Community Files, 1902–1963, "Rhinelander," WHS.

70. *RDN*, 10/25/1927; 11/29/1927; 12/13/1927, and 1/10/1928; Leadbetter to Hazeltine, WFLS Mss., Acc. No. 1967/45, Box 9, WHS. Throughout the time period that the city council and city manager were discussing the library, the *RDN* offered no editorial comment on the matter, and gave it minimal coverage of council proceedings.

71. Bingham to Hazeltine, 1/24/1928, WFLC Mss., Acc. No. 1967/45, Box 9, WHS; *RDN*, 3/10/1928; 3/17/1928.

72. Hazeltine to Glenn Parker (Baker & Taylor), 4/5/1928; Hazeltine to H. R. Huntting Co. (of Springfield, Massachusetts), 4/5/1928; both found in WFLC Mss., Acc. No. 1967/45, Box 9, WHS; *RDN*, 5/16/1928; 6/9/1928; 6/14/1928; 9/13/1928.

73. *RDN*, 10/13/1928; 10/23/1928; 11/14/1928; Raymond to Wilson, 10/15/1928, RPLA, "Rhinelander," *WLB* 24 (November 1928): 297; (December 1928): 321. Neither Raymond nor the *WLB* mentioned that at the same time he authorized funds to improve the physical plant, Grau also reduced library salaries.

74. *RDN*, 1/22/1929; 2/13/1929; Harriet Long (of the WFLC Traveling Library and Study Club) to Raymond, 2/2/1929, RPLA. Part of the reason the library could purchase more titles was that the RWC trust fund yielded eight hundred dollars more than usual in early 1929. See *RDN*, 4/10/1929.

75. *RDN*, 5/6/1929; 11/12/1929; 12/12/1929; 2/19/1930. For a list of radio programs, see 6/13/1929. McRae's ad ran again on 5/17/1930 and 8/20/1930.

76. *RDN*, 2/25/1930. See also 3/4/1930; 3/11/1930; 3/19/1930; 4/8/1930; 4/16/1930; 5/7/1930.

77. *RDN*, 11/15/1930; 11/22/1930; 12/8/1930; 1/4/1931; 2/7/1931; 2/10/1931.

78. *RDN*, 11/18/1931; 12/4/1931; 4/5/1932. Grau had cancelled the old rental plan in 1928.

79. *RDN*, 4/27/1932; 1/11/1933; Raymond to Hazeltine, 4/29/1932, WFLC Mss., Acc. No. 1967/45, Box 9, WHS; *WLB* 28 (June 1932): 195.

80. Smith's report, dated 1/30/33, in WFLC Mss., Community Files, 1902–1963, "Rhinelander," WHS. See also Smith to City Manager Theodore Wardwell, February 6, 1933; and Wardwell to Smith, February 9, 1933, WFLC Mss., Acc. No. 1967/45, Box 9, WHS.

81. *RDN*, 4/3/1933; 9/22/1933; 9/23/1933.

82. Report, February 24–26, 1934, Blanche Smith to WFLC, WFLC Mss., Community File, 1902–1963, "Rhinelander," WHS; Alice Raymond to Hazeltine, January 12, 1934, RPLA; *RDN*, 3/1/1934.

83. *RDN*, 3/1/1934. Raymond later sent Smith a clipping of the story, and Smith used it to construct her own report on Rhinelander in the next issue of *WLB*. See *WLB* 30 (April 1934): 86–87. See also *RDN*, 5/23/1934; 7/13/1934.

84. Smith to WFLC, September 14–17, 1934, WFLC Mss., Community Files, 1902–1963, "Rhinelander," WHS. The city manager was true to his word. The 1935 city budget called for $4,765 for the library—a 30 percent increase from the previous year. See also *RDN*, 11/13/1934; 1/2/1935; 12/14/1971; *WLB* 31 (January 1935): 7; and Raymond to Smith, December 6, 1934, WFLC Mss., Acc. No. 1967/45, Box 9, WHS.

85. Whittaker to Hazeltine, June 10, 1935; Raymond to Smith, August 28, 1935; Smith to Raymond, September 13, 1935, WFLC Mss., Acc. No. 1967/45, Box 9, WHS; *RDN*, 9/19/1935; 11/19/1935; 12/7/1935; 4/27/1936.

86. Report by Blanche Smith, September 10–11, 1936, WFLC Mss., Community Files, 1902–1963, "Rhinelander," WHS.

87. *RDN*, 1/23/1937. See also 8/11/1936; 1/12/1938; 2/4/1938; 10/15/1946.

88. Blanche Smith Report, September 15–16, 1937, WFLC Mss., Community Files, 1902–1963, "Rhinelander," WHS; Smith to Whittaker, September 21, 1937; WFLC Mss., Acc. No. 1967/45, Box 9, WHS.

89. *RDN*, 2/15/1940. Raymond later made news by taking a sociology course at the University of Mississippi at the age of eighty-one. See *RDN*, 10/19/1954.

90. *RDN* 6/14/1940; 2/12/1941.

91. *RDN*, 5/9/1941; 7/2/1941.

92. *RDN*, 1/19/1942; 1/24/1942; 1/12/1943; 1/15/1943; 2/25/1943; 5/28/1944.

93. *RDN*, 11/26/1943. See also 2/25/1944; 7/8/1944; 8/16/1944. The "Read and See" project continued in future years. See *RDN*, 10/25/1946.

94. October 19–20, 1944, WFLC Mss., Community Files, 1902–1963, "Rhinelander," WHS. See also July 18, 1945, WFLC Mss., Community Files, 1902–1963, "Rhinelander," WHS, in which Whittaker reported "the continued falling off in the use of children's books."

95. *WLB* 43 (May 1947): 77; *WLB* 44 (April 1948): 77. A script of the program for April 29, 1948, is in RLA. See also Whittaker to Anne Farrington, November 21, 1951, WFLC, 11/6/00, "Oneida/Rhinelander," WHS; and "The Library Helps the Jack Pine Artists," *WLB* 49 (March–April 1953): 60–63. In this set of activities, Whittaker replicated most of the methods used by Wisconsin public librarians to advertise library services. See Barton and Rector, *The Public Library in Wisconsin*, 47–48.

96. *RDN*, 11/2/1949; 11/7/1949; 11/8/1949; 10/26/1950. For some negative public reaction to the Board of Supervisors vote, see Olga Dahlstrand's "Letter to the Editor," *RDN*, 11/9/1949. For a comprehensive history of the experiences of another three-year Wisconsin demonstration project approved by local officials in Door and Kewaunee Counties in November 1949, see Christine Pawley, *Reading Places: Literacy, Democracy, and the Public Library in Cold War America* (Amherst: University of Massachusetts Press, 2010).

97. *RDN*, 5/13/1952. Biographical data gleaned from *RDN*. By 1950 the Rhinelander Paper Company had grown to become the largest Wisconsin paper mill under one roof. Union members who worked there, which included 75 father-and-son sets and 120 sets of brothers (six Stefonik brothers posed for *RDN* pictures) constituted a large fraction of the voting population in Rhinelander. For history of Ripco, see *RDN*, 6/5/1953. When Manthey moved from Rhinelander two years later, the Rhinelander Central Labor Council submitted two names to fill his vacancy on the board, which then chose Robert Oelerich, whose name was sent on to the common council. See Minutes, 1/5/1954, RPLA; *RDN*, 1/13/1954.

98. Memo, Botsford to Helen Kremer and Anne Farrington, May 21, 1952, WFLC Mss. 11/6/oo, "Oneida/Rhinelander," WHS.

99. Minutes, 6/3/1952; 7/2/1952, RPLA; Memo, Anne Farrington, 6/3/1952, copy in WFLC Mss., 1902–1963, Community Files, "Rhinelander," WHS.

100. Minutes, 8/5/1952; 10/7/1952, RPLA; *RDN*, 9/10/1952; Kremer to Busse, August 11, 1952, WFLC Mss., 11/6/oo, "Oneida/Rhinelander," WHS. For a summary of the bookmobile project, see also Kremer to Walter Kruschke (superintendent of instruction), November 21, 1952, WFLC Mss., 11/6/oo, "Oneida/Rhinelander," WHS. For a summary of the American Heritage Project in Wisconsin, see *WLB* 48 (September/October 1952): 195–97. The nomenclature "People's Library Committee" probably came from a recommendation in Wisconsin Free Library Commission, *The Wisconsin-Wide Library Idea for Voluntary Education through Reading: A Detailed but Tentative Statement* (Madison: Wisconsin Free Library Commission, 1948), 9–10.

101. *RDN*, 10/8/1952; 10/14/1952; 10/16/1952; 10/17/1952; 10/23/1952; WFLC Consultant Report, Elizabeth Burr, October 19–23, 1952, WFLC Mss., Community Files, 1902–1963, "Rhinelander," WHS.

102. *RDN*, 10/24/1952; 10/28/1952; 11/1/1952. See also Botsford to Graeber, November 7, 1952; Botsford to Whittaker, November 7, 1952, both in WFLC Mss., 11/6/oo, "Rhinelander"; and "Report made by Erma Graeber to Federated Women's Club of Rhinelander," copy in WFLC Mss., 11/6/oo, "Oneida/Rhinelander," WHS. Graeber radio script in WFLC Mss., 11/6/oo, "Oneida/Rhinelander," WHS.

103. Minutes, 12/2/1952, RPLA; *RDN*, 12/10/1952; 12/16/1952. See also Kremer to Kruschke, November 21, 1952, WFLC Mss., 11/6/oo, "Oneida/Rhinelander," WHS. Graeber's speech in *WLB* 49 (January/February 1953), 24–29. See also *WLB* 49 (January/February 1953): 34, for an announcement that after her resignation Graeber would be doing silk-screening for hire. "*All of us* wish Erma well in this new venture," editors noted.

104. Kremer Report, dated November 3, 1953, in WFLC Mss., Community Files, 1902–1965, "Rhinelander," WHS. See also Minutes, 11/3/1953, RPLA. At its January meeting, the board voted to offer minimum library service to any interested towns in Oneida County at $150 per thousand population. Pelican and Pine Lake accepted

the offer. See Whittaker to Botsford, March 2, 1954, WFLC Mss., 11/6/00, "Oneida/ Rhinelander," WHS; and Minutes, 5/4/1954, RPLA. The attitude Whittaker displayed toward the Wisconsin Free Library Commission was not unique. In his essay on Wisconsin history in *Heartland: Comparative Histories of the Midwestern States*, historian John Buenker argues that residents in northern Wisconsin were generally suspicious of downstate politics, state agencies, and even downstate people in general. See Buenker, "Wisconsin as Maverick, Model and Microcosm," in *Heartland: Comparative Histories of the Midwestern States*, ed. James H. Madison (Bloomington: Indiana University Press, 1988), 69.

105. Information taken from *Rhinelander City Directory, 1956*, 11–24.

106. List taken from *Rhinelander City Directory, 1956*. Union High School library described in RDN, 7/21/1956. See also Minutes, 5/2/1956, RPLA.

107. RDN, 10/27/1956.

FIVE. LITERATURE SUITABLE FOR A SMALL PUBLIC LIBRARY

1. Monthly magazine sales rose from eighteen million in 1890 to sixty-four million in 1905. See Richard Ohmann, "Diverging Paths: Books and Magazines in the Transition to Corporate Capitalism," in *A History of the Book In America, Vol. 4: Print in Motion: The Expansion of Publishing and Reading in the United States, 1880–1940*, ed. Carl F. Kaestle and Janice A. Radway (Chapel Hill: University of North Carolina Press, 2009), 102–15. In 1902 the Bryant Library subscribed to *Poole's Guide to Periodical Literature*, which provided some index access to its periodicals collection. Before 1905, however, none of the four libraries subscribed to *Readers' Guide to Periodical Literature*, started by the H. W. Wilson Company in 1901.

2. On March 16, 1905, for example, the Bryant Library board rejected Clara Louis Burnham's *Jewel: A Chapter in Her Life* (1903), despite the fact that the library had six other titles by this popular novelist. A week later the board rejected *Pigs in Clover* (1903) by Frank Danby, pseudonym for Julia Frankau. Although none of the four libraries covered in this book acquired *Pigs in Clover*, in 1905 the Sage Library had twenty-four Burnham titles (including four copies of *Jewel*), and RPL had four (including one copy of *Jewel*). See also Minutes, 3/16/1905; 5/25/1905, BLA.

3. Christine Pawley, *Reading on the Middle Border: The Culture of Print in Late-Nineteenth-Century Osage, Iowa* (Amherst: University of Massachusetts Press, 2001), 69–77; 104–5.

4. Pawley, *Reading on the Middle Border*. Tables discussed are on pp. 92 and 96.

5. See *Washington Post*, 2/15/1901 and 2/21/1901.

6. Several of these titles entered some library collections two and three decades later (probably as gifts), when these titles were perceived to be no longer controversial.

7. Ella McLoney, "Iowa Library Association," *Public Libraries* 5 (January 1900): 25. About the Des Moines Public Library practice of sequestering *Tom Sawyer* and

Huckleberry Finn, the *Washington Post* commented: "The more one reflects, the more wonderful does it seem that boys turn out as well as they do to-day, considering the fearful handicaps they are obliged to overcome, such as now furnished by this Iowa library." See *Washington Post*, 12/22/1904.

8. *SCH*, 3/28/1907; 4/25/1907; 5/9/1907; 5/23/1907.

9. *SCH*, 6/13/1907; 6/20/1907. One wonders whether Oehler's review of *Garden of Allah* increased demand for it at the Bryant Library circulation desk, and, if so, whether the librarian gave it out without comment.

10. For lists of books recently arrived and recently replaced at the library, see *SCH* 11/28/1907; 12/26/1907; 2/26/1908; 4/23/1908; 8/27/1908; 12/17/1908; and 12/16/1909. Among the other three, the Moore Library acquired single copies of *Garden of Allah* in 1909 and *Saul of Tarsus* in 1907; the Sage Library acquired one copy of *Vesty of the Basin* and two copies of *Garden of Allah* and *Saul of Tarsus* shortly after they were published; and RPL acquired one copy of *Saul of Tarsus* in 1907. Except for the Bryant Library, none of the libraries ever acquired copies of *Self Control, The Northerner*, or *Raymond Benson at Krampton*.

11. See Paul Boyer, *Purity in Print: Book Censorship in America from the Gilded Age to the Computer Age* (Madison: University of Wisconsin Press, 2002), 31–32, 33–35.

12. Arthur E. Bostwick, "The Librarian As Censor," *LJ* 33 (July 1908): 264; "What Shall Libraries Do About Bad Books?" *LJ* 33 (September 1908): 349–54; (October 1908): 390–93.

13. Lutie Stearns, "Magazines and Morals," *WLB* 7 (December 1911): 172–73.

14. Elva Bascom, "Selection of Fiction," *WLB* 9 (April 1913): 34–40.

15. *Booklist*, 4 (March 1908): 87; 4 (December 1908): 305; 5 (June 1909): 186; 7 (November 1910) 128; 7 (May 1911): 395; 8 (January 1912): 234; 8 (May 1912): 379, 380; 8 (June 1912): 411, 412; 8 (October 1911): 77; 8 (November 1911): 116; 8 (December 1912): 171; 11 (October 1914): 78.

16. Minutes, 6/20/1912; 11/21/1912, BLA; *SCH*, 7/18/1912; 12/12/1912; 4/10/1913; *LN&N* 3 (September 1912): 180. For one reader's response to a Gene Stratton Porter novel—and her memory of that response as a ten-year-old girl—see Janet Malcolm, "Capitalist Pastorale," *New York Review of Books* (January 15, 2009): 46–49.

17. One library did want its patrons to have access to some information on sex. In 1916 RPL Director Jesse Bingham wrote to the California Social Hygiene Society: "Will you kindly send us, for use in our community, the nine circulars on sex hygiene which are published by your society? If these circulars are not available now any materials you can send or recommend that will be helpful to mothers and fathers in instructing children in sex hygiene will be very much appreciated." A month later she wrote the Better Babies Bureau of *Woman's Home Companion* for pamphlets for the local "Baby Week Campaign" to be conducted through "Mother's meetings" at the schools. She reassured the bureau that the pamphlets would be responsibly

disseminated. In mid-March 1916, the *Rhinelander News* reported that the library had "much of the best and most up to date materials on the 'Care of Infants' and 'Motherhood'" issued by the Children's Bureau in Washington, DC. See Bingham to C. N. White (California Social Hygiene Society), January 18, 1916; Bingham to Clara Meyer (*Woman's Home Companion*), February 28, 1916, RPLA; *RN*, 3/17/1916.

18. Helen M. Thomas, comp., "Selected Bibliography of Woman Suffrage," *ML* 1 (June 1912): 13–17. On December 30, 1913, Chicago Public Library Director Henry Legler told the Illinois Library Association that books on civics and social problems were taking the place of "love stories and other fiction" on Chicago clubwomen's reading lists. "It may be the passing of the suffrage law in Illinois or it may be the natural development of women and their newest interest in live present day problems," he surmised. See "Chicago Club Women Pass Up Love Books," *Salt Lake Telegram*, 12/31/1913.

19. *Vindicator*, 3/10/1909; 6/1/1910.

20. See *Duluth News-Tribune*, 11/5/1911. Less than a year later, however, the Superior (WI) Public Library director complained that no one had checked out books on labor strife during the local streetcar strike. See *Duluth News-Tribune*, 10/9/1912.

21. The most thorough analysis of the connection between labor and print is Jonathan Rose, *The Intellectual Life of the British Working Class* (New Haven: Yale University Press, 2004), but see also Larry Peterson, "The Intellectual World of the IWW: An American Worker's Library in the First Half of the 20th Century," *History Workshop* 22 (1986): 153–72, and Tobias Higbie, "Unschooled but Not Uneducated: Print, Public Speaking, and the Networks of Informal Working-Class Education, 1900–1940," in *Education and the Culture of Print in Modern America*, ed. Adam R. Nelson and John L. Rudolph (Madison: University of Wisconsin Press, 2010), 103–25. See also Joseph R. Conlin, *American Radical Press, Vol. I* (Westport, CT: Greenwood Press, 1974), 54.

22. See *RH*, 3/8/1912.

23. See Barbara Howe, "The Emergence of Scientific Philanthropy, 1900–1920: Origins, Issues and Outcomes," in *Philanthropy and Cultural Imperialism: The Foundations at Home and Abroad*, ed. Robert F. Arnove (Boston: G. K. Hall, 1980), 52.

24. The definitive work on the Kerr Company is Alan Ruff, *"We Called Each Other Comrade": Charles H. Kerr & Company, Radical Publishers* (Urbana: University of Illinois Press, 1997).

25. In a 1908 address about radical influences at Dickinson College in Carlisle, Pennsylvania, former secretary of the treasury Leslie M. Shaw argued, "Our public libraries are full of socialist literature." He then quoted an urban public librarian who observed that during a large strike the reading room "was packed day after day with all kinds of people" reading about "Socialism, every one of them." See *Morning Oregonian* (Portland), 12/23/1908. Not only were the four libraries covered

here not "full of socialist literature," patrons would have had difficulty finding any information on this major political movement.

26. For a discussion of the rich history of ethnic presses in the United States between 1880 and 1940, see Sally M. Miller, "Distinctive Media: The European Ethnic Press in the United States," in Kaestle and Radway, 299–311.

27. John Cotton Dana, *A Library Primer* (Boston: Library Bureau, 1920), 243–44.

28. See Boyer, *Purity in Print*, 74–78, 130–34; and his "Gilded Age Consensus, Repressive Campaigns, and Gradual Liberalization: The Shifting Rhythms of Book Censorship," in Kaestle and Radway, 289. Quote about *Jurgen* taken from *NYT*, 10/19/1922. See also *Chicago Daily Tribune*, 5/15/1927, for the story about Voltaire and the Chicago Public Library.

29. *BILC* 9 (April–June 1921): 28; 9 (July–August, 1921): 42. For evidence that the message was frequently repeated, see Laura Duncan, "Fiction," *BILC* 9 (April–June 1924): 212. The Iowa Library Commission routinely sent the *Bulletin* to all Iowa public librarians and the presidents of their boards.

30. *MCP* 3/22/1922.

31. See "For Boys and Girls," *WLB* 22 (April 1927): 95–96; *LN& N* 9 (March 1928): 61; *LN& N* 9 (March 1929): 102. This list was later updated and republished in numerous state library journals, including *WLB* 29 (July 1933): 175; *ML* 10 (March 1944): 17–18; *ILQ* 14 (January 1944): 178–85. See also Leonard S. Marcus, *Minders of Make Believe: Idealists, Entrepreneurs, and the Shaping of American Children's Literature* (Boston: Houghton Mifflin, 2008), 105; and Marilyn S. Greenwald, *The Secret Life of the Hardy Boys: Leslie McFarlane and the Stratemeyer Syndicate* (Athens: Ohio University Press, 2004), 39.

32. Ernest F. Ayres, "Not to Be Circulated?," *Wilson Bulletin* 3 (March 1929): 528–29.

33. For lengthier discussion of the Vatican campaign in the United States, see Boyer, *Purity in Print*, 181–89. *Elmer Gantry* was especially controversial. The U.S. Post Office defended postmasters who banned it from the mails (in 1931, the Post Office even banned any catalog that listed the book), and public libraries in Boston and Camden, New Jersey, refused to put it on their shelves. On June 28, 1927, the *Rhinelander Daily News* also carried a story on the efforts of the Boston Watch and Ward Society to censor the "dirty literature" parading itself under the term "realism," as one officer argued. He specifically mentioned *The Plastic Age*, *Elmer Gantry*, *An American Tragedy*, and Upton Sinclair's *Oil!* (1927). See *RDN* 6/28/1927.

34. *SCH*, 4/7/1927. See also *SCH*, 10/24/1946.

35. For background information on Haldeman-Julius and his printing establishment, see Dale Marvin Herder, "Education for the Masses: The Haldeman-Julius Blue Books as Popular Culture during the Nineteen-Twenties" (PhD diss., Michigan State University, 1976); and Melanie Ann Brown, "Five-Cent Culture at the 'University of Print': Radical Ideology and the Marketplace in E. Haldeman-Julius's Little Blue Books, 1919–1929" (PhD diss., University of Minnesota, 2007).

36. *Life and Letters*, January 1924, 3, quoted in Herder, "Education for the Masses," 147–49.
37. Herder, "Education for the Masses," 203.
38. Ibid., 258–68.
39. For an analysis of another world of print that escaped the attention of collection guides set up by the professional library community, see James P. Danky, "Reading, Writing, and Resisting: African American Print Culture," in Kaestle and Radway, 339–58.
40. *SCH*, 3/18/1930; 4/27/1939.
41. See Rick Wartzman, *Obscene in the Extreme: The Burning and Banning of John Steinbeck's "The Grapes of Wrath"* (New York: Public Affairs, 2008).
42. For reaction by the New York publishing industry, see *NYT*, 5/16/1944.
43. M. K. R., "Book Selection from the Negative Side: What Not to Buy," *WLB* 27 (April 1931): 87–90.
44. *Illinois Libraries* referred to series fiction as "pernicious." See "Survey of Public Libraries in Illinois," *IL* 17 (April 1935): 67. See also Margaret Davidson, "Discarding: What and How, or How to Weed a Book," *ILQ* 14 (January 1945): 178–85. Months later *ILQ* published "Most Widely Used Children's Books of 1939–1945," *ILQ* 15 (July 1945): 128. For background information on Little Golden Books, see Marcus, *Minders of Make-Believe*, 162–68.
45. See Melanie Rehak, *Girl Sleuth: Nancy Drew and the Women Who Created Her* (New York: Harcourt, 2005); and Ilana Nash, *American Sweethearts: Teenage Girls in American Popular Culture* (Bloomington: Indiana University Press, 2006). See also Carolyn Stewart Dyer and Nancy Tillman Romalov, eds., *Rediscovering Nancy Drew* (Iowa City: University of Iowa Press, 1995), quotations on 98 and 102; and *NYT*, 5/30/2009.
46. On March 20, 1947, the *Mitchell County Press News* began carrying a column entitled "Readin' Right" by Rockwell City librarian Evelyn Van Wagner: "The Executive Board of the Iowa Library Association has voted to make this column available to all libraries in the state for reprinting in their local papers." In one column the *Press News* did not carry, Van Wagner noted that her "library has none of the Bobbsey Twins or Nancy Drew series of books, although hardly a week goes by without some youngster asking for them." See *ILQ* 15 (April 1948): 205. Ironically, the article appeared in *ILQ* shortly after the Sage Library began to acquire multiple copies of Nancy Drew.
47. "My first major purchase as Rhinelander children's librarian in the mid-1970s was three complete sets of Nancy Drew, Hardy Boys, and Bobbsey Twin mysteries," Kris Wendt wrote in her June 1, 2003, *Rhinelander Daily Herald* column, "Reading Between the Lines." Wendt had read Nancy Drew books as a child. "Not everyone, however, shared my enthusiasm," she continued. "Several months after the books arrived, a rather formidable colleague . . . accosted me in the ladies room during a

regional children's services workshop [saying, among other things,] 'You have lowered the standard of children's literature for the entire Wisconsin Valley!'" Despite the attack, Wendt held her ground; the Nancy Drew books stayed in RPL stacks, to the delight of many Rhinelander children.

48. *RDN* 6/3/1940.

49. See Marcus, *Minders of Make Believe*, 96–97.

50. Ibid.

51. *RDN*, 10/9/1946.

52. Ibid., 11/19/1946.

53. Marie Kokke, "The Case of the Comic-Reading Youngsters," *WLB* 42 (November 1946): 143–44. For background information on librarians' attitudes toward comic books, see Christopher J. Steele, "'Why Don't They Read a Good Book Instead?' Librarians and Comic Books, 1949–1955," (master's thesis, University of North Carolina at Chapel Hill, 2005).

54. This article quoted in *RDN*, 6/26/1948.

55. *RDN*, 5/16/1950. Barton and Rector's research showed that in 1950 women's groups were active supporters in 50 percent of Wisconsin public libraries (63 percent in towns with populations between five thousand and forty thousand). At 11 percent, veterans constituted the second most important group of active participants. See Barton and Rector, *The Public Library in Wisconsin*, 46.

56. *RDN*, 4/11/1951.

57. See John R. Barton and Franklin E. Rector, *The Public Library in Wisconsin: An Inquiry into Its Social and Educational Resources* (Madison: Department of Rural Sociology, Wisconsin Free Library Commission, 1951), 23–24. In one study undertaken for the California Library Association's Intellectual Freedom Committee, Marjorie Fiske discovered that although librarians "expressed unequivocal freedom-to-read convictions," almost two-thirds of the book selectors she talked with "reported instances where the controversiality of a book or author resulted in a decision not to buy." Even worse, she reported, "nearly one-fifth" of the librarians she interviewed "habitually avoided buying any material which is known to be controversial or which they believe might be controversial." Evidence suggested that many librarians in other states acted no differently. See Marjorie L. Fiske, *Book Selection and Censorship: A Study of School and Public Libraries in California* (Berkeley: University of California Press, 1959).

58. Much of the background information on NODL is taken from William B. Lockhart and Robert C. McClure, "Literature, the Law of Obscenity, and the Constitution," *Minnesota Law Review* 38 (March 1954): 295–354. See also Christopher Finan, *From the Palmer Raids to the Patriot Act: A History of the Fight for Free Speech in America* (Boston: Beacon Press, 2007), 174–77; and Thomas O'Connor, "The National Organization for Decent Literature: A Phase in American Catholic Censorship," *Library Quarterly* 65 (October 1995): 386–414. "Because NODL engaged in nonlibrary censor-

ship," O'Connor notes, "the American Library Association did not actively oppose it" (p. 386).

59. On January 17, 1957, the Detroit police commissioner banned John O'Hara's *Ten North Frederick* from Detroit bookstores. See *NYT*, 1/18/1957. The Detroit Public Library refused to honor the ban, however, and successfully fought off his attempts. See *Christian Science Monitor*, 1/19/1957. At the time, the Moore Library had no O'Hara novels.

60. *SCH*, 4/24/1952; 6/5/1952; 6/19/1952; 7/10/1952. At this writing the public library acquisitions filtering system for printed materials described here remains largely in place. Ironically, the universe of print it systematically (if unobtrusively) filtered for most of the twentieth century was seldom acknowledged when professional library organizations in recent years persistently resisted demands for Internet filters to eliminate children's exposure to pornography on public library computers.

61. *RDN*, 12/11/1952; 12/13/1952; 12/27/1952. This activity preceded a notice in the *Wisconsin Library Bulletin* about the climate of censorship, referred to recent efforts to censor the Boston Public Library, and reaffirmed the Library Bill of Rights. See "The Library Bill of Rights," *WLB* 49 (January–February 1953): 3–4.

62. For *Booklist* selection criteria, see *Booklist* 47 (January 1, 1951): 164. That *Booklist* reviewers were sensitive to tensions surrounding acquisition decisions at the local level is obvious. Among the titles NODL condemned that *Booklist* did cite, the review for Fredric Brown's *Here Comes a Candle* (1950) noted that it was "eerie, powerful, and a bit tough" 46 (September 1950; p. 12). The review for Fritz Peters's *Finistere* (1951) remarked: "[S]ensitive treatment and above-average writing distinguish this novel on the sub rosa theme of homosexuality" 47 (March 15, 1951): p. 254. The review for Margaret Long's *Louisville Saturday* (1950), however, noted: "Many libraries will not be able to use this story of women in wartime because it is as uncompromisingly frank as a novel of military life" 46 (January 1, 1950): 62.

63. In 1961 the Sage Library acquired a copy of Mickey Spillane's *The Deep*, which New American Library issued as a paperback in 1951.

64. See Laura J. Miller, *Reluctant Capitalists: Bookselling and the Culture of Consumption* (Chicago: University of Chicago Press, 2006), 27–28, 34–35. Carl Kaestle and Janice Radway note that between 1880 and 1940 the hardbound book was the form of print culture "with highest authority and permanence." See Kaestle and Radway, 7–21. That the four libraries studied here considered themselves local institutions of cultural authority may explain why they retained hardbound titles of the same texts they rejected in paperback.

65. *NYT*, 6/22/1953; *SJ*, 12/12/1946.

66. *RDN*, 6/15/1953; 6/23/1953; 7/6/1953; 7/8/1953; *NYT*, 6/22/1953; *CJ*, 12/26/1946.

67. *SCH*, 8/19/1954; 9/16/1954.

68. Minutes, 1/5/1955, RPLA.

69. Howard Fast was represented there once, but the Moore Library copy of *The Amer-ican* was not acquired until 1968.

EPILOGUE

1. Letter, Calloway to Congressman H. R. Gross, January 25, 1952, copy found in SLA.
2. For an account of its origins, see Edward G. Holley and Robert Schremsher, *The Library Services and Construction Act: An Historical Overview from the Viewpoint of Major Participants* (Greenwich, CT: JAI Press, 1983).
3. Indiana refused LSA funds for fear, its governor said, that Hoosiers would be "brainwashed with books handpicked by Washington bureaucrats." See Douglas Raber, "Ideological Opposition to Federal Library Legislation: The Case of the Library Services Act of 1956," *Public Libraries* 34 (May–June, 1995): 162–69. See also James W. Fry, "LSA and LSCA, 1956–1973," *Library Trends* 24 (July 1975): 7–26.
4. See Minutes, 11/16/1956, p. 49; 11/28/1956, p. 50, SLA.
5. Minutes, 8/22/1957, p. 54; 10/11/1961, p. 107; 12/13/1961, p. 111; 1/10/1962, p. 112; 4/11/1962, p. 117; 6/13/1962, p. 121, SLA.
6. The *Rhinelander Daily News* had written an editorial supporting the legislation in June 1955, and had periodically reprinted similar supporting editorials from news-papers elsewhere in the state. See *RDN*, 6/16/1955; 8/24/1955; 4/30/1956; 11/27/1956; Nelson Report to WFLC in WFLC Mss., 11/6/00, "Oneida/Rhinelander," WHS. Copy of May, 1959, agreement in RPLA.
7. See reports dated 9/11/1961 and 4/19/962, both in WFLC Mss., Community Files, 1902–1963, "Rhinelander," WHS.
8. Rosalind Gilbert, *Our Century: Revisiting Sauk Centre in the 20th Century* (Sauk Centre, MN: Sauk Centre Herald, 2000), 247, 267, 272.
9. The richness and reach of the essays in Kaestle and Radway bear witness to the narrowed contours these Main Street libraries crafted for their collections in a much larger culture of American print.
10. These conclusions largely support the observations of Robert Williams, who argues that public library development manifests three thematic explanations: "social conditions" (numerous social forces worked in unique combinations to es-tablish a public library); "democratic tradition" (the public library was a natural outcome of the growth of democracy); and "social control" (elites imposed their will by establishing a public library to force social control). See Robert V. Wil-liams, "Theoretical Issues and Constructs Underlying the Study of Library Devel-opment," *Libri* 34 (1984): 1–16. Michael Harris first introduced the "social control" theory to librarianship, and because it directly challenged the "library faith" he initiated a debate that continues in the twenty-first century. See Michael H. Har-ris, "The Purpose of the American Public Library: A Revisionist Interpretation," *LJ* 98 (1973): 2509–14.

11. Late in life Sinclair Lewis noted in his "Chronology" that he had a "totally normal boyhood—dull school routine, skating, sliding, skiing, swimming, duck-hunting —except for inordinate (and discoordinated) [*sic*] reading." Most of that reading came from Bryant Library collections. See Folder 834, "Chronology—Sinclair Lewis," Box 58, Lewis Mss.

12. Richard Lingeman, *Sinclair Lewis: Rebel from Main Street* (New York: Random House, 2002), 295; Richard V. Francaviglia, *Main Street Revisited: Time, Space, and Image Building in Small-Town America* (Iowa City: University of Iowa Press, 1996), 167.

13. Louise Rosenblatt, *Literature as Exploration* (New York: Appleton-Century, 1938).

14. See Douglas Waples and Ralph Tyler, *What People Want to Read About: A Study of Group Interests and a Survey of Problems in Adult Reading* (Chicago: American Library Association, 1931), 82; and Pierce Butler, *An Introduction to Library Science* (Chicago: University of Chicago Press, 1933), 82. Joan Shelley Rubin explains this research in "Making Meaning: Analysis and Effect in the Study and Practice of Reading," in Kaestle and Radway, 511–27. See also Helen Damon-Moore and Carl F. Kaestle, "Surveying American Readers," in Kaestle, et al., *Literacy in the United States*, 180–203.

15. Jesse Hauk Shera, "Toward a Theory of Librarianship and Information Science," in Shera, *Knowing Books and Men: Knowing Computers, Too* (Littleton, CO: Libraries Unlimited, 1973), 94; Charles B. Osburn, *The Social Transcript: Uncovering Library Philosophy* (Westport, CT: Libraries Unlimited, 2009), 135, 208; Patrick Williams, *The Public Library and the Problem of Purpose* (Westport, CT: Greenwood Press, 1988); Michael Gorman, *The Enduring Library: Technology, Tradition, and the Quest for Balance* (Chicago: American Library Association, 2003).

16. David Welky, *Everything Was Better in America: Print Culture in the Great Depression* (Urbana: University of Illinois Press, 2008), 218.

17. Alice Payne Hackett, *60 Years of Best Sellers, 1895–1945* (New York: R. R. Bowker Company, 1956).

Bibliography

SECONDARY SOURCES

Alexander, Jeffrey C. *The Civil Sphere.* New York: Oxford University Press, 2006.

Anderson, Benedict. *Imagined Communities: Reflections on the Origin and Spread of Nationalism.* New York: Verso, 1983.

Apple, Michael W. *Official Knowledge: Democratic Education in a Conservative Age.* New York: Routledge, 1993.

Asheim, Lester. "Not Censorship, but Selection." *Wilson Library Bulletin* 28 (September 1953): 63–67.

Atherton, Lewis. *Main Street on the Middle Border.* Bloomington: Indiana University Press, 1984.

Augst, Thomas. *The Clerk's Tale: Young Men and Moral Life in Nineteenth-Century America.* Chicago: University of Chicago Press, 2003.

Augst, Thomas, and Kenneth Carpenter, eds. *Institutions of Reading: The Social Life of Libraries in the United States.* Amherst: University of Massachusetts Press, 2007.

Augst, Thomas, and Wayne A. Wiegand, eds. *Libraries as Agencies of Culture.* Madison: University of Wisconsin Press, 2001.

Avalanche. Sauk Centre, Minnesota, newspaper, 1887–1900 (archived at Bryant Library, Sauk Centre, Minnesota).

Ayres, Ernest F. "Not To Be Circulated?" *Wilson Library Bulletin* 3 (March 1929): 528–29.

Bacon-Smith, Camille. *Science Fiction Culture.* Philadelphia: University of Pennsylvania Press, 1999.

Barron, Hal S. *Mixed Harvest: The Second Great Transformation in the Rural North, 1870–1930.* Chapel Hill: University of North Carolina, 1997.

Barton, John R., and Franklin E. Rector. *The Public Library in Wisconsin: An Inquiry into Its Social and Educational Resources.* Madison: Department of Rural Sociology, Wisconsin Free Library Commission, 1951.

Becker, Patti Clayton. *Books and Libraries in American Society during World War II: Weapons in the War of Ideas.* New York: Routledge, 2005.

Bell, John Dal. *An Early History of Lexington, Michigan: The Building of a Small Town.* Lansing: Michigan Dept. of State, Michigan History Division, 1968.

Beninger, James R. *The Control Revolution: Technological and Economic Origins of the Information Society.* Cambridge: Harvard University Press, 1986.

Bergquist, Ronald E. "'It Could Have Been Bigger, but Its Residents Like It as It Is': Small Town Libraries in Moore County, North Carolina." PhD diss., University of North Carolina at Chapel Hill, 2006.

Bevans, George E. "How Workingmen Spend Their Spare Time." PhD diss., Columbia University, 1913.

Biedermann, William H. *A Brief History of Mitchell County.* 1973. (Six-page manuscript in Special Collections, University of Iowa Libraries)

Bird, Elizabeth S. *For Enquiring Minds: A Cultural Study of Supermarket Tabloids.* Knoxville: University of Tennessee Press, 1992.

Blair, Karen J. *The Clubwoman as Feminist: True Womanhood Redefined, 1868–1914.* New York: Holmes & Meier, 1980.

Blegen, Theodore. *Grass Roots History.* Minneapolis: University of Minnesota Press, 1947.

——. *Minnesota: A History of the State.* Minneapolis: University of Minnesota Press, 1975.

Bliven, Bruce. "A Stroll on Main Street." *New Republic* 37 (December 12, 1923): 63–66.

Bloomberg, Britta L., and Dennis A. Gimmestad. "Original Main Street: Sauk Centre, Minnesota." *Minnesota History* 54 (1994): 164–69.

Blumin, Stuart M. *The Emergence of the Middle Class: Social Experience in the American City, 1760–1900.* New York: Cambridge University Press, 1989.

Bobinski, George. *Carnegie Libraries: Their Histories and Impact on American Public Library Development.* Chicago: American Library Association, 1969.

Bostwick, Arthur E. *The American Public Library.* New York: D. Appleton, 1910.

Bourdieu, Pierre. *Distinction: A Social Critique of the Judgement of Taste.* London: Routledge, 1986.

Bourjaily, Vance. "'Red Lewis' Town Is Kinder to Him Than He Was to It." *Smithsonian* 16 (December 1985), 51.

Bowers, William L. *The Country Life Movement in America, 1900–1912.* Port Washington, NY: Kennikatt, 1974.

Boyarin, Jonathan, ed. *The Ethnography of Reading.* Berkeley: University of California Press, 1992.

Boyer, Paul S. *Purity in Print: Book Censorship in America from the Gilded Age to the Computer Age.* Madison: University of Wisconsin Press, 2002.

Brinkman, Marilyn. *Bringing Home the Cows: Family Dairy Farming in Stearns County, 1853–1986.* St. Cloud, MN: Stearns County Historical Society, 1988.

Brown, Melanie Ann. "Five-Cent Culture at the 'University of Print': Radical Ideology in the Marketplace in E. Haldeman-Julius's Little Blue Books." PhD diss., University of Minnesota, 2007.

Brown, Richard D. *Strength of a People: The Idea of an Informed Citizenry in America, 1650–1870.* Chapel Hill: University of North Carolina Press, 1996.

Bulletin of the Iowa Library Commission.

Burke, Peter. *A Social History of Knowledge from Gutenberg to Diderot*. London: Polity Press, 2000.

Burns, E. Bradford. *Kinship with the Land: Regionalist Thought in Iowa, 1894–1942*. Iowa City: University of Iowa Press, 1996.

Buschman, John E., and Gloria J. Leckie, eds. *The Library as Place: History, Community, and Culture*. Westport, CT: Libraries Unlimited, 2007.

Butler, Pierce. *An Introduction to Library Science*. Chicago: University of Chicago Press, 1933.

Campion, Amy, and Gary Alan Fine. "Main Street on Main Street: Community Identity and the Reputation of Sinclair Lewis." *Sociological Quarterly* 39 (1998): 79–99.

Carlson, Sharon Lee. "Ladies Library Associations of Michigan: Women, Reform, and Use of Public Space." PhD diss., Western Michigan University, 2002.

Carrier, Esther Jane. *Fiction in Public Libraries, 1876–1900*. New York: Scarecrow Press, 1965.

———. *Fiction in Public Libraries, 1900–1950*. Englewood, CO: Libraries Unlimited, 1985.

Casper, Scott E., Jeffrey D. Groves, Stephen W. Nissenbaum, and Michael Winship, eds. *A History of the Book in America, Volume 3; The Industrial Book, 1840–1880*. Chapel Hill: University of North Carolina Press, 2007.

Cawelti, John G. *The Six-Gun Mystique*. Bowling Green, OH: Bowling Green State University Press, 1984.

Cayton, Andrew R. L., and Susan E. Gray, eds. *The Identity of the American Midwest: Essays on Regional History*. Bloomington: Indiana University Press, 2001.

Chandler, Alfred D., Jr., and James W. Cortada, eds. *A Nation Transformed by Information: How Information Has Shaped the United States from Colonial Times to the Present*. New York: Oxford University Press, 2000.

Charles, Jeffrey A. *Service Clubs in American Society: Rotary, Kiwanis, and Lions*. Urbana: University of Illinois Press, 1993.

Chartier, Roger. *Forms and Meanings: Texts, Performances, and Audiences from Codex to Computer*. Philadelphia: University of Pennsylvania Press, 1995.

———. *The Order of Books: Readers, Authors, and Libraries in Europe between the Fourteenth and Eighteenth Centuries*. Stanford: Stanford University Press, 1988.

Cheap Homes in the Sauk Valley. Sauk Centre, MN: Sauk Valley Immigration Association, 1879.

Clark, Beverly Lyon. *Kiddie Lit: The Cultural Construction of Children's Literature in America*. Baltimore: Johns Hopkins University Press, 2003.

Colson, John C. "The Public Library Movement in Wisconsin, 1836–1900." PhD diss., University of Chicago, 1973.

Conklin, Groff. *How to Run a Rental Library*. New York: R. R. Bowker Company, 1934.

Conlin, Joseph R. *American Radical Press, Vol. I*. Westport, CT: Greenwood Press, 1974.

Connolly, James J., and E. Bruce Geelhood, eds. "The Small City in the Midwest." *Indiana Magazine of History* 99 (December 2003): 307–86.

Conzen, Kathleen Neils, "Mainstreams and Side Channels: The Localization of Immigrant Cultures." *Journal of American Ethnic History* 11 (1991): 5–20.

Dana. John Cotton. *A Library Primer*. Boston: Library Bureau, 1920.

Danbom, David D. *Born in the Country: A History of Rural America*. Baltimore: Johns Hopkins University Press, 1995.

Darnton, Robert. "What Is the History of Books?" *Daedalus* 111 (1982): 65–83.

———. "History of Reading." In *New Perspectives on Historical Writing*, ed. Peter Burke, 140–67. University Park: Pennsylvania State University, 1992.

Davidson, Cathy N., ed. *Reading in America: Literature and Social History*. Baltimore: Johns Hopkins University Press, 1989.

Davies, D. W. *Public Libraries as Cultural and Social Centers: The Origin of the Concept*. Metuchen, NJ: Scarecrow Press, 1974.

Davies, Richard O. *Main Street Blues: The Decline of Small-Town America*. Columbus: Ohio State University Press, 1998.

de Certeau, Michael. *The Practice of Everyday Life*. Berkeley: University of California Press, 1984.

Denning, Michael. *The Cultural Front: The Laboring of American Culture in the Twentieth Century*. New York: Verso, 1996.

———. *Mechanic Accents: Dime Novels and Working-Class Culture in America*. London: Verso, 1987.

Dilevko, Juris, and Candace F. C. Magowan. *Readers' Advisory Service in North American Public Libraries, 1870–2005: A History and Critical Analysis*. Jefferson, NC: McFarland, 2007.

Ditzion, Sydney. *Arsenals of a Democratic Culture: A Social History of the American Public Library Movement in New England and the Middle Atlantic States from 1850 to 1900*. Chicago: American Library Association, 1947.

Dumenil, Lynn. *Freemasonry and American Culture, 1880–1930*. Princeton: Princeton University Press, 1984.

DuMond, Neva. *Thumb Diggings: Adventures into Michigan's Thumb Area*. Lexington, MI: Neva Du Mond, 1962.

Dunbar, Willis F. "The Opera House as a Social Institution in Michigan." *Michigan History Magazine* 27 (October–December 1993): 661–72.

Dunbar, Willis F., and George May. *Michigan: A History of the Wolverine State*. Grand Rapids, MI: Eerdmans, 1980.

Dyer, Carolyn Stewart, and Nancy Tillman Romalov, eds. *Rediscovering Nancy Drew*. Iowa City: University of Iowa Press, 1995.

Eddy, Jacalyn. *Bookwomen: Creating an Empire in Children's Book Publishing, 1919–1939*. Madison: University of Wisconsin Press, 2006.

Ensted, Nan. *Ladies of Labor, Girls of Adventure: Working Women, Popular Culture, and Labor Politics at the Turn of the Century.* New York: Columbia University Press, 1999.

Finan, Christopher. *From the Palmer Raids to the Patriot Act: A History of the Fight for Free Speech in America.* Boston: Beacon Press, 2007.

Fink, Deborah. *Open Country Iowa: Rural Women, Tradition and Change.* Albany: State University of New York Press, 1986.

Fiske, Marjorie L. *Book Selection and Censorship: A Study of School and Public Libraries in California.* Berkeley: University of California Press, 1959.

Fish, Stanley. *Is There a Text in This Class? The Authority of Interpretive Communities.* Cambridge: Harvard University Press, 1980.

Foster, Jeannette H. "An Approach to Fiction through the Characteristics of Its Readers." *Library Quarterly* 6 (April 1936): 124–74.

Francaviglia, Richard V. *Main Street Revisited: Time, Space, and Image Building in Small-Town America.* Iowa City: University of Iowa Press, 1996.

Frankel, Oz. *States of Inquiry: Social Investigations and Print Culture in Nineteenth Century Britain and the United States.* Baltimore: Johns Hopkins University Press, 2006.

Fry, James W. "LSA and LSCA, 1956–1973." *Library Trends* 24 (July 1975): 7–26.

Furstenberg, François. *In the Name of the Father: Washington's Legacy, Slavery, and the Making of a Nation.* New York: Penguin, 2006.

Gans, Herbert. *Popular Culture and High Culture: An Analysis and Evaluation of Taste.* New York: Basic Books, 1974.

Garceau, Oliver. *The Public Library in the Political Process.* New York: Columbia University Press, 1949.

Garland, Hamlin. *Son of the Middle Border.* Edited by Joseph B. McCullough. New York: Penguin, 1995.

Garrison, Dee. *Apostles of Culture: The Public Librarian and American Society, 1876–1920.* Madison: University of Wisconsin Press, 2003.

Geller, Evelyn. *Forbidden Books in American Public Libraries, 1876–1939.* Westport, CT: Greenwood Publishing Group, 1977.

Gere, Anne Ruggles. *Intimate Practices: Literacy and Cultural Work in the U.S. Women's Clubs, 1880–1920.* Urbana: University of Illinois Press, 1997.

Gilbert, Rosalind. *Our Century: Revisiting Sauk Centre in the 20th Century.* Sauk Centre, MN: Sauk Centre Herald, 2000.

Gjerde, Jon. *The Minds of the West: The Ethnocultural Evolution in the Rural Middle-West, 1830–1917.* Chapel Hill: University of North Carolina Press, 1997.

Goldstein, Daniel. "The Spirit of an Age: Iowa Public Libraries and Professional Librarians as Solutions to Society's Problems, 1890–1940." *Libraries & Culture* 38 (Summer 2003): 215–35.

Gorman, Michael. *The Enduring Library: Technology, Tradition, and the Quest for Balance.* Chicago: American Library Association, 2003.

Gough, Robert J. *Farming the Cutover: A Social History of Northern Wisconsin, 1900–1940*. Lawrence: University of Kansas Press, 1997.

Gray, Susan E. *The Yankee West: Community Life on the Michigan Frontier*. Chapel Hill: University of North Carolina Press, 1996.

Gray, William S., and Ruth Munroe. *Reading Interests and Habits of Adults: A Preliminary Report*. New York: Macmillan, 1929.

Greenberg, Amy S. *Cause for Alarm: The Volunteer Fire Department in the Nineteenth Century City*. Princeton: Princeton University Press, 1998.

Greenblatt, Stephen. *Renaissance Self-Fashioning: From More to Shakespeare*. Chicago: University of Chicago Press, 1980.

Greenwald, Marilyn S. *The Secret Life of the Hardy Boys: Leslie McFarlane and the Stratemeyer Syndicate*. Athens: Ohio University Press, 2004.

Griffith, Sally Foreman. *Home Town News: William Allen White and the "Emporia Gazette."* New York: Oxford University Press, 1989.

Habermas, Jurgen. *The Structural Transformation of the Public Sphere: An Inquiry into a Category of Bourgeois Society*. Cambridge: MIT Press, 1989.

Hackett, Alice Payne. *60 Years of Bestsellers, 1895–1945*. New York: R. R. Bowker, 1956.

Hagerman, Dorothy T. "A Survey of Library Legislation in Michigan—1937 to 1944." *Michigan Libraries* 10 (March 1944): 9–14.

Hahn, Steven, and Jonathan Prude, eds. *The Countryside in the Age of Capitalist Transformation: Essays in the Society History of Rural America*. Chapel Hill: University of North Carolina Press, 1985.

Hall, Peter Dobkin. *The Organization of American Culture, 1700–1900: Private Institutions, Elites, and the Origins of American Nationality*. New York: New York University Press, 1982.

Hampsten, Elizabeth. *Read This Only to Yourself: The Private Writings of Midwestern Women, 1880–1910*. Bloomington: Indiana University Press, 1982.

Harris, Michael J. "The Purpose of the American Public Library: A Revisionist Interpretation." *Library Journal* 98 (September 1973): 2509–14.

Hart, James D. *The Popular Book: A History of America's Literary Taste*. New York: Oxford University Press, 1950.

Henkin, David. *City Reading: Written Words and Public Spaces in Antebellum New York*. New York: Columbia University Press, 1998.

———. *The Postal Age: The Emergence of Modern Communications in Nineteenth Century America*. Chicago: University of Chicago Press, 2006.

Herder, Dale Marvin. "Education for the Masses: The Haldeman-Julius Blue Books as Popular Culture during the Nineteen-Twenties." PhD diss., Michigan State University, 1976.

Higbie, Tobias. "Unschooled but Not Uneducated: Print, Public Speaking, and the Networks of Informal Working-Class Education, 1900–1940." In *Education and the Culture of Print in Modern America*, ed. Adam R. Nelson and John L. Rudolph, 103–25. Madison: University of Wisconsin Press, 2010.

Hildebrand, Ivy Louise. "Sauk Centre—A Study of the Growth of a Frontier Town." Master's thesis, St. Cloud State College, 1960.

———. *Sauk Centre: The Story of a Frontier Town: The First 50 Years, 1855–1905*. Sauk Centre, MN: Sauk Centre Historical Society, 1993.

Hiss, Tony. *The Experience of Place*. New York: Alfred A. Knopf, 1990.

A Historical Sketch of Sauk Centre. Sauk Centre, MN: First State Bank of Sauk Centre, 1954.

History of Mitchell and Worth Counties, Iowa. Springfield, IL: Union Publishing, 1884.

Holley, Edward G., and Robert Schremsher, eds. *The Library Services and Construction Act: An Historical Overview from the Viewpoint of Major Participants*. Greenwich, CT: JAI Press, 1983.

Howe, Barbara. "The Emergence of Scientific Philanthropy, 1900–1920: Origins, Issues and Outcomes." In *Philanthropies and Cultural Imperialism: The Foundations at Home and Abroad*, ed. Robert F. Arnove, 48–61. G. K. Hall, 1980.

Hudson, John C. *Making the Corn Belt: A Geographical History of Middle-Western Agriculture*. Bloomington: Indiana University Press, 1994.

———. *Plains Country Towns*. Minneapolis: University of Minnesota Press, 1985.

Hutner, Gordon. *What America Read: Taste, Class, and the Novel, 1920–1940*. Chapel Hill: University of North Carolina Press, 2009.

Iowa Library Quarterly.

Iser, Wolfgang. *The Act of Reading: A Theory of Aesthetic Response*. Baltimore: Johns Hopkins University Press, 1978.

Jeffersonian, 1899–1960. Sanilac County, Michigan, newspaper. Variant titles: *Croswell Jeffersonian*, *Sanilac Jeffersonian*. Archived in microfilm at Croswell Public Library.

Jenkins, Christine. "The Strength of the Inconspicuous: Youth Service Librarians, the American Library Association, and Intellectual Freedom for the Young, 1939-1955." PhD diss., University of Wisconsin-Madison, 1995.

Jenkins, Henry. *Textual Poachers: Television Fans & Participatory Culture*. New York: Routledge, 1992.

Johanningsmeier, Charles A. *Fiction and the American Literary Marketplace: The Role of Newspaper Syndicates in America, 1860–1900*. New York: Cambridge University Press, 1997.

———. "Welcome Guests or Representatives of the 'Mal-Odorous Class'? Periodicals and Their Readers in American Public Libraries, 1876–1914." *Libraries & Culture* 39 (Summer 2004): 260–92.

Johnson, Henry. *The Other Side of Main Street: A History Teacher from Sauk Centre*. New York: Columbia University Press, 1943.

Jones, Plummer Alston, Jr. *Still Struggling for Equality: American Public Library Services with Minorities*. Westport, CT: Libraries Unlimited, 2004.

Kaestle, Carl F., et al., eds. *Literacy in the United States*. New Haven: Yale University Press, 1991.

——, and Janice A. Radway, eds. *A History of the Book In America, Vol. 4: Print in Motion: The Expansion of Publishing and Reading in the United States, 1880–1940.* Chapel Hill: University of North Carolina Press, 2009.

Kellogg, Arthur P. "Small Town Rejuvenated: How a Social Center Has Succeeded New Community Spirit." *Survey* 32 (May 16, 1914): 32.

Kortenhof, Kurt Daniel. *Long Live the Hodag! The Life and Legacy of Eugene Simeon Shepard, 1854–1923.* Rhinelander, WI: Hodag Press, 1996.

Krashen, Stephen. "Anything but Reading." *Knowledge Quest* 37 (May–June, 2009): 18–25.

——. *The Power of Reading: Insights from the Research.* Portsmouth, NH: Heinemann, 2004.

Learned, William S. *The American Public Library and the Diffusion of Knowledge.* New York: Harcourt, Brace, 1924.

Lester, C. B. "Wisconsin Libraries." Chapter 37 in *Wisconsin: Its History and People, Vol. II.* Chicago: S. J. Clarke Publishing Company, 1924.

Levine, Lawrence W. *Highbrow, Lowbrow: The Emergence of Cultural Hierarchy in America.* Cambridge: Harvard University Press, 1988.

Lewis, Alison, ed. *Questioning Library Neutrality: Essays from "Progressive Librarian."* Duluth, MN: Library Juice Press, 2008.

Lewis, Sinclair. *Main Street.* New York: New American Library, 1961.

Library News & Notes, 1904–1937. Minnesota State Library Commission.

Lingeman, Richard. *Sinclair Lewis: Rebel from Main Street.* New York: Random House, 2002.

——. *Small Town America: A Narrative History, 1620 to the Present.* New York: Putnam's, 1979.

Lockhart, William B., and Robert C. McClure. "Literature, the Law of Obscenity, and the Constitution." *Minnesota Law Review* 38 (March 1954): 295–372.

Lofland, Lyn H. *The Public Realm: Exploring the City's Quintessential Social Territory.* New York: Aldine De Gruyter, 1998.

Long, Elizabeth. *Book Clubs: Women and the Uses of Reading in Everyday Life.* Chicago: University of Chicago Press, 2003.

Lutz, Catherine A., and Jane L. Collins. *Reading National Geographic.* Chicago: University of Chicago Press, 1993.

Lynd, Robert S., and Helen M. Lynd. *Middletown: A Study in Modern American Culture.* New York: Harcourt, Brace & World, 1929.

——, and Helen M. Lynd. *Middletown in Transition: A Study in Cultural Conflicts.* New York: Harcourt, Brace & World, 1937.

McBride, Genevieve G. *On Wisconsin Women: Working for Their Rights from Settlement to Suffrage.* Madison: University of Wisconsin Press, 1993.

McCloud, Scott. *Understanding Comics.* Northampton, MA: Kitchen Sink Press, 1993.

McCormick, Virginia E. *Farm Wife: A Self-Portrait, 1886–1896.* Ames: Iowa State University Press, 1990.

McGuire, Letha Pearl. "Public Library Movement in Iowa." *Iowa Journal of History and Politics* 35, no. 1 (1937): 28–37.

McHenry, Elizabeth. *Forgotten Readers: Recovering the Lost History of African American Literary Societies*. Durham: Duke University Press, 2002.

McLeod, David I. *Carnegie Libraries in Wisconsin*. Madison: Department of History, University of Wisconsin, 1968.

Madison, James H., ed. *Heartland: Comparative Histories of the Midwestern States*. Bloomington: Indiana University Press, 1988.

Marcum, Deanna. *Good Books in a Country Home: The Public Library as a Cultural Force in Hagerstown, Maryland, 1878–1920*. Westport, CT: Greenwood Press, 1994.

Marcus, Leonard S. *Minders of Make-Believe: Idealists, Entrepreneurs, and the Shaping of American Children's Literature*. Boston: Houghton Mifflin, 2008.

Martin, Robert Sidney, ed. *Carnegie Denied: Rejecting Carnegie Construction Grants, 1895–1928*. Westport, CT: Greenwood Press, 1993.

Martin, Theodora Penny. *The Sound of Our Own Voices: Women's Study Clubs, 1860–1910*. Boston: Beacon Press, 1987.

May, Elaine Tyler. *Homeward Bound: American Families in the Cold War*. New York: Basic Books, 1988.

Michigan Librarian.

Michigan Libraries.

Michigan Library Bulletin.

Michigan Library News.

Michigan State Library Quarterly Bulletin.

Mickenberg, Julia L. *Learning from the Left: Children's Literature, the Cold War, and Radical Politics in the United States*. New York: Oxford University Press, 2006.

Miller, Laura J. *Reluctant Capitalists: Bookselling and the Culture of Consumption*. Chicago: University of Chicago Press, 2006.

Mitchell County Historical Society. *The Story of Mitchell County, 1851–1973*. Mason City, IA: Klipto Printing, 1973.

Mitchell County Press. Iowa newspaper. Variant titles: *Mitchell County Press News* (1956–), *Mitchell County Press and Osage Journal* (1902–12), *Mitchell County Press and the Osage News, Consolidated* (1931–56).

Mitchell, William Bell. *A History of Stearns County, Minnesota*. 2 volumes. Chicago: H. B. Cooper Jr., 1915.

Munt, Sally. *Murder by the Book? Feminism and the Crime Novel*. New York: Routledge, 1994.

Nash, Ilana. *American Sweethearts: Teenage Girls in Popular Culture*. Bloomington: Indiana University Press, 2006.

New North, 1882–1947. Published in Rhinelander, Wisconsin. Archived at Wisconsin Historical Society, Madison, Wisconsin.

Nord, David Paul. *Communities of Journalism: A History of American Newspapers and Their Readers*. Urbana: University of Illinois Press, 2001.

Norman, James F. *The Episcopal Church in Lexington, Michigan: An Historical Sketch.* Lexington, MI: James F. Norman, 1975.

O'Connor, Thomas. "The National Organization for Decent Literature: A Phase in American Catholic Censorship." *Library Quarterly* 65 (October 1995): 386–414.

Ohmann, Richard. *Selling Culture: Magazines, Markets, and Class at the Turn of the Century.* London: Verso, 1996.

Oldenberg, Ray. *The Great Good Place: Cafes, Coffee Shops, Community Centers, Beauty Parlors, General Stores, Hangouts, and How They Get You Through the Day.* New York: Paragon House, 1997.

Olsen, T. V. *Our First Hundred Years: A History of Rhinelander.* Rhinelander, WI: T. V. Olsen, 1981.

Osage News, 1883–1931. Iowa newspaper (archived in microfilm at Sage Public Library).

Osburn, Charles B. *The Social Transcript: Uncovering Library Philosophy.* Westport, CT: Libraries Unlimited, 2009.

Parker, Alison. *Purifying America: Women, Cultural Reform, and Pro-Censorship Activism, 1873–1933.* Urbana: University of Illinois Press, 1997.

Passet, Joanne. *Cultural Crusaders: Women Librarians in the American West, 1900–1917.* Albuquerque: University of New Mexico Press, 1994.

Pawley, Christine. "Advocate for Access: Lutie Stearns and the Traveling Libraries of the Wisconsin Free Library Commission, 1895–1914." *Libraries & Culture* 35 (Summer 2000): 434–58.

———. "Better Than Billiards: Reading and the Public Library in Osage, Iowa, 1890–95." In *Print Culture in a Diverse America*, ed. James P. Danky and Wayne A. Wiegand, 173–99. Urbana: University of Illinois Press, 1998.

———. "Beyond Market Models and Resistance Organization as a Middle Layer in the History of Reading." *Library Quarterly* 79 (January 2009): 73–93.

———. "'Not Wholly Self Culture': The Shakespearean Women's Club, Osage, Iowa, 1892–1920." *Annals of Iowa* 56 (Winter–Spring 1997/1998): 12–45.

———. *Reading on the Middle Border: The Culture of Print in Late-Nineteenth-Century Osage, Iowa.* Amherst: University of Massachusetts Press, 2001.

———. *Reading Places: Literacy, Democracy, and the Public Library in Cold War America.* Amherst: University of Massachusetts Press, 2010.

Pederson, Jane Marie. *Between Memory and Reality: Family and Community in Rural Wisconsin, 1870–1970.* Madison: University of Wisconsin Press, 1992.

Peterson, Larry. "The Intellectual World of the IWW: An American Worker's Library in the First Half of the 20th Century." *History Workshop* 22 (1986): 153–72.

Portrait and Biographical Album of Sanilac County: Containing Portraits and Biographical Sketches of Citizens of the County. Chicago: Chapman Brothers, 1884.

Pustz, Matthew J. *Comic Book Culture: Fanboys and True Believers.* Jackson: University Press of Mississippi, 1999.

Putnam, Robert. *Better Together: Restoring the American Community.* New York: Simon and Schuster, 2003.

————. *Bowling Alone: The Collapse and Revival of American Community.* New York: Simon and Schuster, 2000.

Raber, Douglas. "Ideological Opposition to Federal Library Legislation: The Case of the Library Services Act of 1956." *Public Libraries* 34 (May–June 1995), 162–69.

————. *Librarianship and Legitimacy: The Ideology of the Public Library Inquiry.* Westport, CT: Greenwood Press, 1997.

Radway, Janice. *A Feeling for Books: The Book-of-the-Month Club, Literary Taste, and Middle-Class Desire.* Chapel Hill: University of North Carolina Press, 1997.

————. *Reading the Romance: Women, Patriarchy, and Popular Literature.* Chapel Hill: University of North Carolina Press, 1991.

Rehak, Melanie. *Girl Sleuth: Nancy Drew and the Women Who Created Her.* New York: Harcourt, 2005.

Rhinelander (WI) Daily News, 1882–1960. Variant title: *Rhinelander News.* Archived in microfilm at Wisconsin Historical Society, Madison, Wisconsin.

Rhinelander Paper Company. *Fifty Years of Papermaking, 1903–1953.* Rhinelander, WI: Rhinelander Paper Company, 1953.

Rifkin, Jeremy. *The Age of Access: How the Shift from Ownership to Access Is Transforming Modern Life.* New York: Penguin, 2000.

Riley, Glenda. *Frontierswomen: The Iowa Experience.* Ames: Iowa State University Press, 1975.

————, ed. *Prairie Voices: Iowa's Pioneering Women.* Ames: Iowa State University Press, 1996.

Robbins, Louise S. *Censorship and the American Library: The American Library Association's Response to Threats to Intellectual Freedom, 1939–1969.* Westport, CT: Greenwood, 1997.

————. *The Dismissal of Miss Ruth Brown: Civil Rights, Censorship, and the American Library.* Norman: University of Oklahoma Press, 2000.

Robbins, Louis S., Anne H. Lundin, and Michelle Besant, eds. *Tradition and Vision: Library and Information Studies at the University of Wisconsin: A Centennial History.* Madison: School of Library and Information Studies, University of Wisconsin-Madison, 2006.

Rose, Jonathan. *The Intellectual Life of the British Working Classes.* New Haven: Yale University Press, 2001.

Rose, Lisle Abbott. *The Cold War Comes to Main Street: America in 1950.* Lawrence: University Press of Kansas, 1999.

Rosenblatt, Louise. *Literature as Exploration.* New York: Appleton-Century, 1938.

Rubin, Joan Shelley. *The Making of Middlebrow Culture.* Chapel Hill: University of North Carolina Press, 1992.

————. *Songs of Ourselves: The Uses of Poetry in America.* Cambridge, MA: Belknap, 2007.

————. "What Is the History of the History of Books?" *Journal of American History* (2003): 555–75.

Ruff, Alan. *"We Called Each Other Comrade": Charles H. Kerr & Company, Radical Publishers*. Urbana: University of Illinois Press, 1997.

Ryan, Barbara and Amy M. Thomas, eds. *Reading Acts: U.S. Readers' Interactions with Literature, 1800–1950*. Knoxville: University of Tennessee Press, 2002.

Sage, Leland. *A History of Iowa*. Ames: Iowa State University Press, 1974.

Salamon, Sonya. *Prairie Patrimony: Family, Farming, and Community in the Midwest*. Chapel Hill: University of North Carolina Press, 1992.

Satterfield, Jay. *The World's Best Books: Taste, Culture, and the Modern Library*. Amherst: University of Massachusetts Press, 2002.

Sauk Centre Herald, 1886–1960. Minnesota newspaper (archived in microfilm at Bryant Library).

Savage, William W. *Comic Books and America, 1945–1954*. Norman: University of Oklahoma Press, 1990.

Schorer, Mark. *Sinclair Lewis: An American Life*. New York: McGraw-Hill, 1961.

Schudson, Michael. *The Good Citizen: A History of American Civic Life*. New York: Free Press, 1998.

Schwieder, Dorothy. *Patterns and Perspectives in Iowa History*. Ames: Iowa State University Press, 1973.

Scott, Anne Firor. *Natural Allies: Women's Associations in American History*. Urbana: University of Illinois Press, 1984.

Secord, James A. *Victorian Sensation: The Extraordinary Publication, Reception, and Secret Authorship of "Vestiges of the Natural History of Creation."* Chicago: University of Chicago Press, 2001.

Shera, Jesse. *Foundations of the Public Library: The Origins of the Public Library Movement in New England, 1629–1855*. Chicago: University of Chicago Press, 1949.

———. *Knowing Books and Men: Knowing Computers, Too*. Littleton, CO: Libraries Unlimited, 1973.

Simpson, Lee M. A. *Stearns County, Minnesota*. Chicago: Arcadia, 2000.

Smith, Erin. *Hard-Boiled: Working-Class Readers and Pulp Magazines*. Philadelphia: Temple University Press, 2000.

Soltow, Martha Jane. "Public Libraries' Service to Organized Labor: An Overview." *RQ* 23 (Winter 1984): 163–68.

Spencer, Brett. "Preparing for an Air Attack: Libraries and American Air Raid Defense During World War II." *Libraries & the Cultural Record* 43, no. 2 (2008): 125–49.

Steele, Christopher J. "'Why Don't They Read a Good Book Instead?' Librarians and Comic Books, 1949–1955." Master's thesis, University of North Carolina at Chapel Hill, 2005.

Steinle, Pamela Hunt. *In Cold Fear: The "Catcher in the Rye" Censorship Controversies and Postwar American Character*. Columbus: Ohio State University Press, 2000.

Steinschneider, Janice. *An Improved Woman: The Wisconsin Federation of Women's Clubs, 1895–1920*. Brooklyn: Carson, 1994.

Stock, Catherine McNicol. *Main Street in Crisis: The Great Depression and the Old Middle Class on the Northern Plains*. Chapel Hill: University of North Carolina Press, 1992.

Swain, Martha. "A New Deal in Libraries: Federal Relief Work and Library Service, 1933–43." *Libraries & Culture* 30 (Summer 1995): 265–83.

Thelen, David P. *The New Citizenship: Origins of Progressivism in Wisconsin, 1885–1900*. Columbia: University of Missouri Press, 1972.

Tompkins, Jane. *West of Everything: The Inner Life of Westerns*. New York: Oxford University Press, 1992.

Trumble, Hazel Arnold, ed. *Sanilac County History, 1834–1984*. Shawnee Mission, KS: Inter-Collegiate Press, 1984.

United States Bureau of Education. *Public Libraries in the United States of America: Their History, Condition, and Management*. Washington, DC: Department of the Interior, 1876.

Vandegrift, Kay E. "Female Advocacy and Harmonious Voices: A History of Public Library Services and Publishing for Children in the United States." *Library Trends* 44 (Spring 1996): 681–718.

Van Slyck, Abigail. *Free to All: Carnegie Libraries & American Culture, 1890–1920*. Chicago: University of Chicago Press, 1995.

Vindicator, 1890–1910. Rhinelander, Wisconsin, newspaper (archived in microfilm at Wisconsin Historical Society, Madison, Wisconsin).

Walker, Nancy A. *Shaping Our Mothers' World: American Women's Magazines*. Jackson: University Press of Mississippi, 2000.

Walther, Florence H. *A History of Lexington*. Privately printed by Florence Walther, 1931.

Waples, Douglas. *People and Print: Social Aspects of Reading in the Depression*. Chicago: University of Chicago Press, 1938.

Waples, Douglas, and Ralph Tyler. *What People Want to Read About: A Study of Group Interests and a Survey of Problems in Adult Reading*. Chicago: American Library Association and the University of Chicago Press, 1931.

Wartzman, Rick. *Obscene in the Extreme: The Burning and Banning of John Steinbeck's "The Grapes of Wrath."* New York: Public Affairs, 2008.

Watson, Paul D. "Founding Mothers: The Contribution of Women's Organizations to Public Library Development in the United States." *Library Quarterly* 64 (July 1994): 233–69.

Welky, David. *Everything Was Better in America: Print Culture in the Great Depression*. Urbana: University of Illinois Press, 2008.

Wendorf, Richard, ed. *America's Membership Libraries*. New Castle, DE: Oak Knoll Press, 2007.

Whitehill, Walter M. *Boston Public Library: A Centennial History, 1854–1954.* Cambridge: Harvard University Press, 1956.

Wiebe, Robert. *The Search for Order, 1877–1920.* New York: Hill & Wang, 1975.

Wiegand, Wayne A. *"An Active Instrument for Propaganda": The American Public Library During World War I.* Westport, CT: Greenwood Press, 1989.

———. "Catalog of 'A.L.A. Library' (1893): Origins of a Genre." In *For the Good of the Order: Essays in Honor of Edward G. Holley,* ed. Delmas E. Williams et al., 237–54. Greenwich, CT: JAI Press, 1994.

———. "Collecting Contested Titles: The Experience of Five Small Public Libraries in the Rural Midwest, 1893–1956." *Libraries & Culture* 40 (Summer 2005): 368–84.

———. *Irrepressible Reformer: A Biography of Melvil Dewey.* Chicago: American Library Association, 1996.

———. "On the Social Nature of Reading." In *Genreflecting: A Guide to Popular Reading Interests,* 6th ed., ed. Dianne Tixier Herald, 3–14. Westport, CT: Libraries Unlimited, 2006.

———. *Politics of an Emerging Profession: The American Library Association, 1876–1917.* Westport, CT: Greenwood Press, 1986.

———. "The Structure of Librarianship: Essay on an Information Profession." *Canadian Journal of Library and Information Studies* 24 (April 1999): 17–37.

Williams, Patrick. *The Public Library and the Problem of Purpose.* Westport, CT: Greenwood Press, 1988.

Williams, Robert V. "Theoretical Issues and Constructs Underlying the Study of Library Development." *Libri* 34 (1984): 1–16.

Wilson, Louis Round. *The Geography of Reading: A Study of the Distribution and Status of Libraries in the United States.* Chicago: University of Chicago Press, 1938.

Wisconsin Free Library Commission. *The Wisconsin-Wide Library Idea for Voluntary Education through Reading: A Detailed but Tentative Statement.* Madison: Wisconsin Free Library Commission, 1948.

Wisconsin Library Bulletin.

Wright, Bradford W. *Comic Book Nation: The Transformation of Youth Culture in America.* Baltimore: Johns Hopkins University Press, 2001.

Young, Arthur P. *Books for Sammies: The American Library Association and World War I.* Pittsburgh: Beta Phi Mu, 1981.

Zboray, Ronald J., and Mary Saracino Zboray. *Everyday Ideas: Socioliterary Experience among Antebellum New Englanders.* Knoxville: University of Tennessee Press, 2006.

———. *Literary Dollars and Social Sense: A People's History of the Mass Market Book.* New York: Routledge, 2005.

Zweizig, Douglas L. "Predicting Amount of Library Use: An Empirical Study of the Public Library in the Life of the Adult Public." PhD diss., Syracuse University, 1973.

ARCHIVAL SOURCES
Bryant Library Board Minutes. Bryant Library Archives. Sauk Centre, Minnesota.
Carnegie Corporation Papers. Rare Books and Manuscripts Reading Room. Columbia University, New York City.
Ladies Musical Club Minutes. Bryant Library Archives. Sauk Centre, Minnesota.
Minnesota Historical Society. Oral History Collection. Twentieth-Century Radicalism in Minnesota Oral History Project. Benjamin F. Du Bois, Sr., interview.
Moore Library Archives. Lexington, Michigan.
Osage City Hall Archives. Osage, Iowa.
Rhinelander Public Library Archives. Rhinelander, Wisconsin. Variant name: Rhinelander District Public Library Archives.
Sage Public Library Archives. Osage, Iowa.
Sinclair Lewis Papers. Beinecke Rare Books & Manuscripts Library, Yale University. New Haven, Connecticut.
University of Wisconsin–Madison Archives. Library School Records.
Wisconsin Free Library Commission Records. Wisconsin Historical Society. Madison, Wisconsin.

OTHER SOURCES
Hedin, Richard. Telephone interview with author, August 12, 2008.
Main Street Public Library Database (my database of the entire inventory of the four public libraries studied in this book, from approximately 1900—when librarians started entering data into accessions books—through 1970).

Index